AT LAST, THE KOREAN WAR ~ ~~~ *END.*
General MacArthur and memories of this "forgotten war" were
fading into history as the MASH units were folding their tents and
returning to the States. It was an innocent time—a time when
American prestige was high, and its citizens were welcome in most
countries. The year was 1954.
At this moment in history, a young American naval reserve
officer began a dangerous and fascinating world trip....

*

"What can you say about a Korean War veteran who sets sail
with a pirate around Bali, seeks out mountain gorillas in African
forests, sequesters himself in monasteries, gets high with pygmies
reliving ancient tribal lore, crosses the Sahara on a camel, dives for
shells with bare-breasted Japanese maidens, goes on patrol in
guerilla-infested jungles, hunts killer tigers and so much more...
except to say, man, I wish I'd done that....
"W. Fleming Reeder took the long way home, into the heart
and soul of the world's diverse cultural, spiritual and warrior
traditions. And he did it in the measured and deliberate pace of an
explorer seeking to know himself and his world. Fortunately for us,
he writes as well as he travels."
~ **Don Williams, columnist for 'The Knoxville News-Sentinel'**
and editor of *New Millennium Writings*

*

"From the battlefields of Korea to the waters of the Aegean
Sea, W. Fleming Reeder has lived life to the fullest. Reading this
book was an adventure."
~ **David Hunter, novelist, police writer, columnist and poet**

The Long Journey Home
A Chronicle of Travel and Adventure

W. Fleming Reeder

Warship Press Inc.

8905 Kingston Pike, #12-144
Knoxville, TN 37923

*

In association with
New Messenger Books
PO Box 2463
Knoxville, TN 37901

Photographs by W. Fleming Reeder unless otherwise credited
Photographs initially printed by David Fahey

Cover by Mark Maxwell
Typesetting by Don Williams
Computer coordination by Sidney Forbes

Published in Knoxville, Tennessee, by Warship Press, Inc., in
association with New Messenger Books. Printed by Vaughan Printing
of Nashville, TN, in the United States of America.

ISBN 1-888338-10-5
Library of Congress Catalogue Card Number: 98-60379

SUMMER 2013

FOR LISA,
MY FRIEND

For

Nancye

My Beloved Wife

I HOPE THAT YOU
ENJOY READING
ABOUT MY TRIP
AROUND THE WORLD
SOME SIXTY YEARS
AGO.

Fleming Reeder

Contents

~ Prologue ~
Racing Up Fuji

My five navy friends and I climbed the steep trail leading to the summit of Mount Fujiyama. Cinders blowing in the cold night wind stung our faces, making us squint as we followed the rays of our flashlights. My legs, which were accustomed to the decks of an aircraft carrier, felt as though they were petrifying. Gradually, we slowed our pace. Reaching the sixth rest station, we sprawled on the ground and passed our canteens and bottles.

Before we could relax, a group of some fifty high school students marched in quick time through the rest area. With the air of a drum major, the faculty leader waved a banner emblazoned with blackbirds on a yellow field. Puffing on a police whistle, he led them forward. Within a couple of minutes, the group had shuffled through the area, stirring up billows of dust. After intimidating most of us at the rest station with their dust and martial spirit, they grew quieter as they disappeared in the darkness.

"Damn, what a racket," said Charlie, an aviator from another ship in our fleet, before taking a swig from my saki bottle.

"Charlie, you've no right to complain; you made a bigger racket at that nightclub in Pearl," I said, and laughed.

"Oh, that native dance I tried to lead?"

"Native, hell, you were leading a conga line around the pool. Remember, all of us followed while you carried the American flag."

"Vaguely, I do remember; that night I was broke, and you promised to buy me all the zombies I could drink."

"Hey, now you have the picture. You drank seven; I counted."

"I do remember, sort of, but things went black at the pool."

Clasping his massive shoulder with my hand to keep his mind from wandering, I said, "Charlie, now hear this loud and clear."

"Oh, hell, here it comes," he muttered, hanging his head.

"Not only did you lead a drunken conga line, you led most of us into the pool. You were responsible for soaking every guy and girl, turning over tables and damaging a steel guitar and a ukulele."

"Yeah, but you were part of this, Reeder, ol' friend."

"Hey, not me; you've got the wrong guy...." Before I could finish my reply, dust from a new group of students covered us. Everyone in our climbing party was coughing and trying to catch his breath.

Clearing his throat, Tom Dooley said, "Reeder, I'll bet that's one bunch you'll never catch."

"No way. I'm not gonna try," I said.

"You still plan on filming the sunrise from the summit?"

"If I can get there early enough."

"Tell you what, Reeder. If you do film the sunrise from the top, I'll give you my extra bottle of saki."

"Sounds like a good deal," I said, and we shook hands on it. Soon I raced away from my climbing group. Draping my secondhand movie camera over my shoulder, I disappeared into a massive wall of fog.

Our climbing party had been assembled by my friend, Dr. Dooley. Years later, Tom was destined to become world-famous for his medical work in underdeveloped nations. But at the time, he was stationed at the U.S. Navy Hospital in Yokosuka, Japan—the port where my aircraft carrier, the *U.S.S. Point Cruz,* was temporarily docked.

With his whirlwind energy, Tom had somehow organized our climbing party in less than twenty-four hours. Deftly, he had scrounged warm aviator jackets, gloves, canteens and flashlights for our climb and then driven us in his convertible to our starting point.

After our break, I hiked briskly for about an hour, until I reached hundreds of school children who clogged the narrow trail. Impatiently,

I shuffled behind them. As they trudged into the shifting fog, I decided to pass them by leaving the trail.

Stumbling up a dark depression, I could no longer hear the echoing voices of the students. A cold mist flowed over me; the lamb's wool on my jacket collar seemed to freeze. Although there was no path, I made constant progress.

During the early morning hours, I saw the spokes of a yellow light beaming through the mist. After scrambling over a few boulders, I watched five white-robed pilgrims climbing along a sleeve of snow. At first, I could not understand what they mumbled. Swinging a paper lantern in an easy rhythm, their leader guided them slowly upward. They seemed to float in the fog like supernatural Shinto deities. Drawing closer, I could finally understand parts of their guttural chant:

> *Rokkon Shojo,*
> *Rokkon Shojo,*
> *Rokkon Shojo.*

> "Let our six senses be purified."

With every other step they wearily lifted and lowered their long wooden staffs. Lantern light wavered on the sides of their wide-brimmed straw hats; the wind carried the briny odor of their damp straw raincoats. While I attempted to race around them, a bright light blinded me.

"Yurusu," one of the pilgrims muttered. "I beg your pardon." He signaled for me to pass before clicking off his flashlight.

"Dohmoh ahreegahtoh," I said, in halting Japanese. "Many thanks."

Hours later, when gray light drained the darkness from the sky, I passed under a Shinto arch before climbing toward the rough edge of Fuji's summit. I waited patiently for a pilgrim at the offering box to finish his prayers. Then I dropped my coins in and bowed my head while several of the others smiled in appreciation.

The long climb had helped to ease the memories of my wild party nights, and I felt as though I were experiencing a fresh new outlook on Fuji's summit. With little trouble I was able to chat with many of the students in English and broken Japanese. Gradually, I was growing more acclimated to foreign culture and was comfortable away from my shipmates.

At last, I was near my goal. Surprisingly enough, I had reached the summit long before the rays of the sun. With renewed vigor, I rushed to a good vantage point, screwed my movie camera on a tripod and waited with other climbers for the sunrise.

On the edge of the summit, excited students wearing dark sweaters chattered like cormorants perched on night fishing boats. The twelve-thousand-foot altitude made our breathing labored. Behind us, the snowy crater remained frozen in the shadows. Some two hours later, the five pilgrims arrived; I watched as they squatted on a ledge and searched the clouds for the rising sun.

Orange beams glowed from the clouded ocean and soon flared over the mountain. A thrilling gust of wind swirled snow and lava dust. As the pilgrims bowed toward the sun, their shadows reached into the mist. Many of the students raised their staffs and yelled at the sun while others bowed reverently. For a moment the clouds thinned to reveal the lower mountains folding out into the wrinkled face of the Pacific. After shooting my film, I climbed on a snow-circled boulder to rest and wait for my navy friends.

My thoughts turned from Fuji to the world as I gazed at the view. In a few months the red tape of being released from active duty in Japan, rather than in the United States, would be over. Then I would be a civilian traveling with a student passport. My days as a young junior officer were coming to a pleasant end.

On my way back home, I planned to travel a westbound route to the United States. This would be the beginning of a two-year grand adventure—an adventure in understanding filled with excitement, pleasure and unexpected danger. On a meager budget, I planned to travel alone from Japan through southeast Asia, sectors of India, and parts of Africa and Europe. A journey such as this could be undertaken successfully only at that stage of my life. I was single, carefree and willing to take any calculated risks necessary to visit and live in fascinating, out-of-the-way locations.

In order to learn more about foreign people and their customs, I planned on working with them, living in their dwellings, eating their foods and, when practical, wearing their type clothes. Unlike most of my shipmates, who were very eager to return home to the relative ease of

American life, I was restless and yearned to undertake this difficult journey. No longer would I be subject to a twenty-four hour military routine; soon I would be able to make my own decisions. Strangely enough, I was uneasy with this sudden transition to the free life of a traveler. It would be hard to forget the naval regimentation: battle stations at all hours, long watches in the one-hundred-twenty degree heat of the engine room, and flight operations in Korean waters at night.

Before entering the navy, I had traveled very little outside my home state of Tennessee. But now I intended to wander throughout the world. In a few weeks I would travel to a primitive Japanese fishing village where the bare-breasted *ama girls* dived for abalone and other shellfish. The challenge of fishing with villagers such as these was intriguing.

My thoughts refocused on Fuji as Dr. Tom Dooley sat down near me.

"Wake up, Reeder. You're daydreaming again," he said.

"Oh, you're right. I'm mulling over my trip."

"Fantastic! You're still going—I'm happy. Don't forget, come by the hospital next week; I'll have your medical kit ready."

"Free of charge, I hope?"

"Free? Indeed, yes. Courtesy of the U.S. Navy."

"Great."

"Also, I want to give you one, final briefing on the fine art of traveling; you've got the enthusiasm. Full speed ahead, Reeder. You're almost ready to get under way!"

"By the way, Dooley, haven't you forgotten something? I got here long before sunrise. I won our bet; where is it? Where the hell is my bottle of saki?"

"Don't get my Irish up," he said in mock anger. "We drained all of the saki bottles at the eighth and ninth rest stations." He reached into his knapsack and held up an empty bottle of saki. "But we did save this dead soldier for you."

"*Dohmoh ahreegahtoh,*" I growled and shook my head. "Many thanks."

Dr. Tom gave a ceremonious Japanese bow to me and the other members of our climbing party, who had finally reached our resting place on the mountain.

Charlie drew in a deep breath and fell into the snow.

Without raising his head, he shouted: "This is the *last* damn mountain and the *last* damn sight I'm gonna see in the Far East."

"Pipe down," Dooley commanded; "this is child's play compared to

Monte Cervin, or, as you might know it, the Matterhorn."

"Matterhorn?" Charlie asked.

"Yes, the Matterhorn," Dooley said; "I had to use ice axes, climbing lines, crampons on my boots—the usual professional gear."

"You fools," Charlie said. "Both you and Reeder have to do everything the hard way. Next time I'm near some mountains, I'm going to stay on top of things—say, by about one thousand feet or more."

"Charlie, ol' buddy, if that's the case," I said, "could you fly me over Fuji next week? I wanna get some aerial footage."

"For you, Reeder, I'll make three passes and three passes only. Then, I don't want you to mention this God forsaken place again."

"Fair enough," I replied.

After he had rested for a few minutes, Charlie washed his unshaven face in the snow, then stood up suddenly. "That's them; the bastards," he said, waving his finger. "They're the ones who almost suffocated us with their dust last night. I know it's them; look at their stupid yellow flag."

"You're right," I said, "they...."

Before I could say more, Charlie began lobbing snowballs at the students, who were resting in the sunlight. Charlie howled as they fled his bombardment.

"I'm giving those damned gooks what they deserve," he boasted.

"You bigoted son-of-a-bitch," I yelled.

"Oh, don't you guys get me wrong," Charlie said. "It's not that I don't like those little Japs; it's just that I'm overdue for shore duty in Diego. The war's over. Why the hell are they keeping us here in Japan? I need to be home to kinda stay on top of things—the classy broads, nightlife, new wheels, good booze. You know, the easy life."

"Have it your way, to each his own."

"Thanks, Reeder, but level with me; what in God's name are you trying to prove by this big trip of yours?"

"Nothing much. I'm just trying to learn a little more about different people and places."

"Well, at least you're doing it on your own and not wasting *my* government's money."

Throwing his hands up in frustration, Dooley located a few students who had been victims of Charlie's marksmanship. His apologies were profuse. However, I think Dooley's rapid-fire combination of French,

English and Japanese thoroughly confused most of them. I played with the idea of dropping a large ball of snow on Charlie's head, but I felt it would do little to alter his intolerant mind-set.

After resting for some two hours, Dr. Dooley led our party down the mountain. This time we slid down the *sunabashiri*, black volcanic sand, on the north side of the mountain. With each step we could gleefully slide five or more feet.

"Yooooooooh!" I yelled as I almost tripped while trying to reach the others. On catching my balance, I realized that I could not keep up with them. If I were to drop my heavy movie camera, it could damage the lenses. Dooley and the others seemed to be racing down the mountain as fast as I had raced up it. Carefully, while nursing my camera, I made my way down the wide trail. I was relieved when I caught up with them at a small rest station. There the trail divided; one part continued downward while the other one seemed to wind around the mountain.

"Well, Reeder, which trail are you taking?" Dooley asked.

"The one less traveled, and that will make all the difference," I said.

"Ah, ha, Robert Frost?"

"Right, we've heard of him in Tennessee," I said and chuckled.

"I've often wondered."

"Tom, I'm gonna leave you all now."

"You mean you have extra leave time left?"

"A couple of weeks. I'll have time to take the slower, winding trail. I wanna visit the Buddha at Kamakura again, then check out some fishing villages on the coast."

"Now you're talking. You really are taking the trail less traveled," he said, and smiled.

After a few minutes, Dooley led the others down the steep mountain trail. Unfortunately, I would see these friends only a couple of more times. After that, all of my friends would be new ones. For a long time I stayed at the rest station to enjoy hot tea and the warm sunlight. Soon, I was pleased to see the five Shinto pilgrims, whom I had met the night before, come into view. We exchanged formal bows. All of them seemed exhausted as they trudged down the same pathway my navy friends had chosen. No longer did they chant or maintain their ecclesiastical bearing, yet I remembered their words:

Rokkon shojo,
Rokkon shojo,
Rokkon shojo.

"Let our six senses be purified."

Somehow I felt as though my own senses also were cleansed by this sacred mountain. As I turned down the smaller trail, the hot tea and the exhilaration of the climb left me with a feeling of fulfillment. Yet I was very eager to continue the challenging journey before me.

On top of Mount Fuji, Dr. Tom Dooley had been right in his appraisal of my enthusiasm, when he said, "Full speed ahead, Reeder. You're ready to get under way!"

~ 1 ~

Diving with the Ama Girls

During the late spring of 1954, Japan was trying to take its place in the modern world. However, some traditional occupations were very slow to change. Among one of these endeavors was diving for shell fish and abalone by the fishing women. Traveling in the status of a student, I arranged to live in a remote fishing area on the Boso Peninsula. My long journey home continued in the village of Iwada.

A warm breeze blew along the Japanese coast like an angry breath from *Kaze-no-Kami,* the Nipponese god of wind. With an increasing moan, it swirled a mass of dark clouds above our fishing boats.

A thunder clap sent whining vibrations along the wooden gunnels of our open craft, momentarily taking our breaths. Exchanging hoarse cries, the fishermen, whose tanned bodies were clad only in soaked loincloths, pulled their heavy nets from the sea into their falling and rising boats. Rain pummeled the deck. Our trip back to shore was long and dangerous. Only the previous year a boat smashed into a reef in such a thunderstorm, throwing a fisherman overboard; his body was never recovered.

With the last of our nets coiled safely on deck, the bandy-legged man at the tiller steered our prow toward land, allowing the force of the waves to thrust us forward. We clung with desperation to deck slats to avoid tumbling overboard. The other boats were swept away from us and bobbed into the gray shadows as the rain fell harder.

Suddenly, we lurched broadside into a wave; a torrent of water flushed across our boat, dislodging the dead sea bream from our baskets. They skittered with new life across the deck.

"Capture with quickness," shouted Yoshio, the young son of the man who held the tiller.

"Will do," I yelled.

We dropped our bailing buckets to throw the plump fish back into our baskets, then tied rice-straw rope over the lids and continued to bail water back into the sea.

Skimming up to the crest of each wave, our boat slammed into its trough, shuddered, rolled back, then shot forward on the following wave. A sharp pain hit my stomach. We were spinning.

An old man crouching in the bow cried to Yoshio's father to steer the boat to the port quarter. Ahead, a coral reef loomed. Spasmodically, white waves crashed against the reef and sprayed mist into the dark sky.

Minutes later our boat careened above the waves and sailed though the air, narrowly missing the reef; it almost slammed into the ocean bottom. Our feet and buttocks stung with the impact; our eyes burned with brine. Several baskets of fish twirled and blew overboard, casting away the bodies of the fish like confetti.

I was never concerned with seasickness on my smooth-riding aircraft carrier, but here in this insanely tossing boat, I fought hard to keep from vomiting. Nearly exhausted, we sighed when we rocked into the comparatively calm waters leading to the beach. On the far shore, the huddled mass of fishermen's houses was vaguely outlined. They appeared like dark houses in a faded Japanese print; only a few dwellings and a gnarled pine were visible in the fog, leaving our imagination to complete this understated scene.

Cautiously, we followed the other boats that were swaying dangerously close to us. Anxious voices of the women and children echoed from the shore. The first boat chopped through the surf and screeched onto the pebbly beach. Quickly, the villagers ran down to meet it, then turned the craft around and fastened the stern to a long rope connected to a wooden capstan. With a muffled chant, they heaved the capstan around and around as the heavy boat slid into its berth, an abacus-like wooden frame.

Yoshio and I leapt overboard into the surf. With the help of the crew and a few villagers, we turned our boat toward the beach. After fastening the stern to the capstan line, we trotted up the beach to help the women push the wooden crossbars around. Yelling above the rain, Yoshio told his sister about our bad day of fishing, as she heaved the spokes forward. She, along with the other women, was unable to continue diving for *awabi*, abalone, and seaweed when the summer storm came. Usually, the women's tanned breasts were left uncovered as they worked, but because of the cool rain they now wore jackets.

Once all of the fishing boats were safely lined up facing the sea, in their protective frames, the fishermen unloaded the baskets and carried their catch up the trail to the village. Our boat crew followed the inland path with a long net draped over our shoulders. As we trudged along, I felt as if we were carrying a forty-foot-long sea monster which had washed up on the beach during the storm.

A cool fog settled over the village of Iwada. The breeze was rich with the smells of incense, fish, and drying squid. Slowly we slushed through the muddy streets, past the tiled-roof houses toward the fishing cooperative. Each unpainted wooden house seemed to have weathered several centuries of battering wind. Long red banners in front of the general goods shop curled and uncurled with the wind, giving the street its only color.

After slinging our net into the fish cooperative's warehouse, we squatted around a charcoal brazier. The heat from the coals was not strong enough to steam the ocean's chill from us, yet it gave us a comforting illusion of warmth.

"Our catch today, not very enthusiastic—much too much storm," Yoshio, who was on vacation from his university, said as he thumbed through my Japanese-English phrase book.

"Do you think tomorrow will be better?" I asked.

"Perhaps better if *Kami* is not angry."

His father beamed a gold-toothed smile at me as he began the tale of today's fishing expedition. In guttural Japanese tones, the crew interrupted and added to his enthusiastic description. The fat clown of the group gave a surprisingly good imitation of the storm. Even though I could speak very little of the language, it was easy to follow since they were kind enough to act out each event for my benefit.

Squatting Japanese style grew more difficult for me; I was forced to stand abruptly. The story halted. Each fisherman gazed up at my towering frame. I stood a little over six feet and was dressed in a loincloth partially covered by a red, knee-length kimono; my white headband intensified my reddish hair and my sunburned face.

Yoshio smiled at me, took the Japanese-English phrase book from my hand and thumbed through it. "Red bird, red bird," he said and smiled. *"Akanee tohree-san, akanee tohree-san."* The others seemed shocked at

Yoshio. He was calling a stranger who had been in their village less than a week a nickname.

With feigned anger, I grabbed the phrase book. *"Heeyahkeh Ahmehreekahnoh tohree-san,"* I said. "Sunburned American bird." Laughter rose from the fishermen; they were relieved that I was not seriously offended.

Although I had worked with the fishermen, their wives, and children, I was still shy about my partially-clad appearance. Somehow I felt like a flamingo stumbling around a gaggle of proudly-moving dark geese.

When I had arrived in this area of the Boso Peninsula, south of Tokyo, an innkeeper from an adjoining village had introduced me to Yoshio, his parents, and sister. Initially, they were puzzled over my desire to work with them and to share part of their lives. Yet they readily agreed to let me do so. I had to live, however, at an inn because they had no extra room in their house.

Soon, the other fishermen filled the fishing cooperative, talking loudly above the tattoo of rain on the roof. Most of the men squatted beside baskets of fish, waiting for their catch to be weighed.

"Nijitsu pondo," the burly man at the scales yelled. "Twenty pounds." He presided over his scales with the solemnity of a high judge. With brisk authority he added weights to one side of the scales while the fishermen poured their meager catch into the basket at the other end. An assistant recorded the catch. Each day that the fishing was good, the cooperative sent the best of its catch to the large cities in the north. When the fish weighing ceremony ended, Yoshio turned to me.

"You come to fish tomorrow before sun is awake," he said.

"Yoroshii desu," I said as we bowed. "Very good."

My wooden clogs dug into the muddy rice field trail leading to the village where I spent the night. A couple of times I almost slipped in the mud. As I continued, I held a sunken-eyed sole, fastened to a rope that passed through its gills. Each afternoon the fisherman gave me a fish for my evening meal as payment for my clumsy but well-intentioned work on his boat.

When the maid heard me clip-clop up the stone path to the inn, she hurried to the front door. Bowing low, she handed me a towel to wipe the mud from my feet. With a dry pair of slippers, I creaked along the polished wooden hallway to the bath.

Inside the steam-filled bathroom, I flung my kimono in a basket and scrubbed and rinsed myself outside a large sunken tub while sitting on a stool. Painfully, I sidled into the near-boiling water, sighing for breath as I allowed the water to encircle my neck. Gradually, the heat took my numb feeling away, and I relaxed. The storm seemed years away. My red, floating arms and bent legs reminded me of a giant lobster cooking in a pot. Drowsily, I crawled out of the tub into the cool air and dried myself with a small bath towel.

"*Dozo*," the maid said. "Please." She served me back in my room. Deftly, she lifted the cover from a black lacquer soup bowl. Except for a single piece of dark seaweed, the soup was clear. I sipped it with the required appreciation while she arranged the other dishes on my low table.

Unobtrusively, the maid raised another cover, allowing steam to rise from my sole with its head and tail intact. By this time, I was accustomed to eating fish in this manner and did not feel squeamish. She handed me a set of wooden chopsticks, and I nibbled at the dainty saucers of pickled radishes and sliced cucumbers after eating bits of warm sole. The maid, who knelt quietly at my side, kept my thimble-sized cup filled with hot saki.

After the maid cleared the dishes, the innkeeper came in for his usual evening chat. He was a reserved man in his late thirties who peered at me over the top of his steel-rimmed glasses. Years ago he had studied English, but seldom had the opportunity to speak it.

"Was any person injured in the storm?" he asked.

"No, I don't think so, but the prow of one boat was cracked on the reef," I said.

"*Ah so desu*," he murmured. "Oh, I see." He continued in English, "That is most bad; however, it is not difficult to mend." He lit a cigarette and gazed out the window toward the sea. "Please tell me, how do you like Japanese-style fishing thus far?"

"Very much, but I got pretty cold and tired this afternoon."

"*Ah so*, but you must remember the life of a fisherman is most difficult."

After he refilled our cups with saki, I thought this was the best moment to ask him about World War II. Many of the Japanese with whom I had talked would always change the subject when the topic of war was introduced. Perhaps this was because of the shame of defeat and the Nipponese reluctance to discuss unpleasant subjects.

"Did you meet any Americans just after the war?" I asked.

"Oh, oh," he muttered, somewhat startled by the question. "Malaya, a beautiful country—that is where I met them. Only briefly with little opportunity for talk. Malaya, that is where you must go. But is difficult for me to talk more of this. I was a prisoner of the British and Americans there."

Nervously, he lit another cigarette from a *Peace*-brand package and stared out the window.

"I'm sorry," I said. "My cousin, Sergeant Word, was a prisoner of war some two hundred miles from here; he worked in a coal mine in Omni Machi village."

"War is impossible for everyone," he said; "I hope that you were too young to fight in the Great War."

"Yes, luckily I was. Korea was enough for me."

As the maid entered and served us tea, the innkeeper paused and put his head into his hands and whispered, "Hiroshima... Nagasaki... to kill so many with the bomb was so wrong."

"I agree... I wish that World War II could have ended in a different manner."

Both of us remained silent for a long time, listening to the rain falling outside.

After the innkeeper excused himself, the maid, with her bashful teenage daughter, entered, bowed, took a quilt from a cabinet, and spread it out on the floor as my bed. Near the head of my quilt they placed a pot of fresh water and a tiny cup. In her arms, the daughter held a fresh kimono for sleeping, as her mother slipped off my daytime kimono. Discreetly, I faced away from them, allowing them to dress me from behind. I never became accustomed to this much too-personal service; each time I objected, however, they sucked in their breaths, smiled, and continued with their task.

Flies buzzing around my head awakened me the next morning before daylight. For a long time I lay in the dark, brushing them away, until I heard the innkeeper yawning in his room across the small courtyard. Drowsily, I moved my *shoji,* paper screen window, back a little and heard him pour a cup of water, clear the phlegm from his throat, mutter something to his wife and open his window with a bang. He clicked on his light. Soon he was chanting a prayer to Buddha at the family shrine.

Without waiting for breakfast, I hurried through the dark rice fields to the fishing village. Only a few stars were visible in the sky. The rhythmic roar of the surf excited me. Today I would participate in an unusual method of Japanese fishing.

I arrived in time to join a large group of some eighty men and women who dragged a long net into the surf, toward a boat. With only loincloths to protect us, the water seemed frigid. Since I was taller and could wade deeper than the others, I lifted the net up to the elder in the boat.

Quickly, we splashed back to the women on the shore. Although they wore short kimono jackets, they seemed as cold as we were in our loincloths. All of us unfolded the net and fed it to the boatman, some forty yards out from shore.

Settling in the foam, the net disappeared. We waited, each holding a side of the net like a group of wading birds closing in on a school of fish. Everyone grew silent. The periodic pounding of the surf seemed to grow louder. As the sky grew lighter, it illuminated the dark sea with the pink sheen found inside a conch shell.

Gradually, the sun bulged above the horizon. Waving his arms, the elder in the boat continued to encourage us. We began pulling in the net. On the shore, muscular women chanted and occasionally laughed while they turned the net around a squeaking wooden capstan.

Gathering around the net on the beach, the villagers examined the very small catch of quivering fish. Perfunctorily, the women put them into baskets. Here as in other places in Japan, many hands combined to work long and hard for little gain. Overpopulation and a scarcity of jobs often made it necessary to employ three people to do the work of one. This economic backwardness had caused great concern in the United States and had led to a dialogue between the two nations on ways to improve the Japanese economy. The intention was to assist Japan in returning to its pre-war economy, with the exception of not having an armed force. Few people, including myself, however, expected the Japanese to become a world economic power to rival the United States.

Although Japan was modernizing with great speed, some areas remained primitive, and I hoped that the exotic quality of life on the Boso Peninsula would change very little.

"Good morning," Yoshio said as we bowed. "Please, for you, take, eat this fish... delicious indeed." He held a sardine-sized fish quaking with life.

"Thanks, but I had a very big breakfast this morning," I lied.

Sensing that I was unaccustomed to eating a living fish, he quickly chewed one, swallowed it and smiled.

"I find another one for you," he said.

I nodded reluctantly while he scooped a handful of small fish from the net. After forcing a smile, I hastily chewed and swallowed one of the fish.

"Tasty," I said, as I tried to keep from gagging. Many of the other fishermen leaned over the net to pick out more of these small, living delicacies.

Before leaving the beach, we watched several older people bowing toward the rising sun. Clapping their hands, they chanted above the hiss of the surf as they prayed. The younger people, who were much too busy, ignored their ancient Shinto form of nature worship.

Instead of fishing with the men, Yoshio and I decided to go to the women's diving beach. We followed a trail sloping down a massive limestone cliff past the nesting places of water birds. The wide beach was littered with driftwood and seaweed from yesterday's storm.

Yoshio's mother and sister were among the many ama girls milling around the small diving boats. The mood of these divers was festive, like school children preparing for a field trip. Many of them slipped off their jackets and dropped them beside a few men who were mending nets. The divers were nude except for their red and white checked shorts. With the loss of their clothes, they moved with a wholesome grace, becoming bolder and freer than they were in the village. Yoshio's eighteen-year-old sister, Masako, smiled and asked us to go with her. Her full breasts with purple nipples swayed as she helped load buckets and small nets into her boat. Yoshio and I took seats near his father, who skulled at the stern.

As we followed the other boats, we passed long-necked cormorants riding the ground swells. Occasionally, in a burst of white, one of these birds would dive below the surface. Moments later it would surface, holding a fish in its beak. With an awkward stretching motion, it would swallow its prey and continue floating over the waves to search for more food.

On arriving in the shallows around the cove, the women jumped into the water with their wooden tubs.

"These divers are named *kachido*," Yoshio said.

"*Kachido?*" I asked.

"*Hai, akanee tohree-san,*" he said. "Yes, red bird. They dive only in the shallow water for seaweed. *Kachido* means girls who walk in sea."

We watched his sister, Masako, breathe deeply before she dived toward the brown seaweed. All around us, other girls plunged into the surprisingly clear water. When each wave rippled past us, it cast a ghostly shadow on the divers at the bottom. Their brown bodies were only a little lighter than the waving seaweed. In the refracted shafts of the sun they looked like a group of large, playful frogs.

After each dive, the girls would surface with handfuls of seaweed for the floating buckets. Then they would gasp for air. After dumping their load into the boat, they rested briefly and continued diving. Some three hours later the boats and the divers worked their way to the far side of the cove. It would soon be time for lunch.

"Yoshio, do you think they would let me dive?" I asked.

"As a sunburned American red bird you should fly. You are not destined to be Japanese diving bird," he said, and laughed.

The idea of my diving was regarded with amusement, followed by a flood of advice. The ama girls fitted me with a face mask and advised me how to blow through my nose to clear the water that might seep into the mask and told me how to hold my breath, gather seaweed and rise to the surface gradually.

Thoroughly confused by so much advice, I thought it best to jump in and learn for myself. With a rock belt around my waist for weight, I dived twelve slow feet to the seaweed bed. My lungs burned; my ears ached. Frantically, I gathered handfuls of seaweed and kicked toward the bright light above.

On breaking the surface, my head hit one of the wooden buckets. Gasping for breath, I held onto the seaweed. Somehow, I slung it into the nearest bucket. Before I could collect my wits, two girls leaped into the water to help me swim to the boat. When Yoshio realized that I was not hurt, he chuckled with his hand over his mouth and joined the girls in sympathetic smiles. I was elated over my first efforts.

When we skulled into shallow water, I wanted to show the ama girls that I had potential, however remote the possibility might seem. Diving from the boat, I soon collected a fair amount of seaweed; however, my face mask fell off. Masako dived past me as I floated toward the surface. She skillfully recovered my mask from the shadowy waters and gave it to me while I was catching my breath at the side of the boat.

The sun warmed my shaking body. Even though I was diving in shallow water, I was surprised to find it so cold. Yoshio draped a jacket over me. The girls with their extra layers of subcutaneous fat were not bothered by the temperature. Actually, women gravitated toward this type of work centuries ago because of their ability to withstand the cold. Most of the girls regarded my diving efforts with amusement, yet one or two divers scowled at me. Perhaps these girls were angry at me for attempting to participate in work set aside for women.

One afternoon, a few days later, I went out with the ama girls, who dived to depths of forty or fifty feet to collect abalone and other shellfish along the ocean floor. The six motorized boats were filled with *funado*, divers who were "ship people." Most of these divers were older and more experienced than the girls who harvested seaweed.

The sky was overcast, and it seemed as though a storm was developing far out in the Pacific Ocean. Yoshio and I accompanied his mother and sister. His father steered the boat over the surprisingly smooth ocean. The breeze was fragrant and warm. As we continued, Yoshio's parents began quarreling.

"They debate the weather," Yoshio said.

"Do you think we might turn back?" I asked.

"Yes, if weather is not become better."

Some twenty minutes later the breeze vanished, yet the sky remained overcast. His father cut off the motor and heaved an anchor overboard. Evidently, conditions were now favorable for diving. Other boats stopped and surrounded us. No longer could we see the shoreline.

"Do not speak," Yoshio whispered. "This is most dangerous event. And at this deep place you must not go diving."

"Don't you worry," I said.

After dropping a safety line toward the ocean floor, his father strung a descending line through a pulley. His mother slipped into the water and placed the iron weight of the descending line in the back of her belt. Her daughter Masako remained aboard. Slowly, at first, Yoshio's mother began breathing deeply. As she expelled the air, she made a wailing noise. Glancing around, I saw many other divers. Their breathing noises came faster and merged with hers, creating a pulsating, mournful series of sounds.

Such was the music of the ama girls.

With a quick movement, Yoshio's mother disappeared into the ocean. Her family aboard the boat seemed to breathe deeply and sympathetically as if to wish her luck with her efforts. No one talked; we peered at the foamy surface and waited.

Minutes later she broke the surface like a snorting porpoise. With a triumphant smile she handed a net full of snails and red-shelled abalone to her husband in the boat. He poured them into a bucket while she caught her breath. Her firm breasts and shoulders were covered with goose pimples. Again she went through her doleful breathing exercises and dived to the bottom of the ocean.

After some fifteen similar dives, she climbed into the boat to rest. It was time for Masako to make her initial dive in the deep ocean. At first she seemed reluctant to enter the water, but with encouraging words from her family, she finally jumped overboard. Masako went through the breathing exercises with her mother, who remained in the boat. In a minute Masako bravely dived toward the cold ocean floor.

Unlike her experienced mother, Masako quickly broke the surface of the water. Holding an abalone over her head, she tried to catch her breath, choked, lost the abalone and grasped the side of the boat. Her mother held her and congratulated her for reaching the bottom on the first attempt. To lose one abalone was of little consequence.

After Masako regained a little of her composure, her parents helped her into the boat. She was trembling from the cold. Compulsively, she wrapped her arms around her mother's warm body; mother and daughter drew comfort from each other. Our boat rocked with the waves for a long time as the ama girls in the surrounding boats continued diving.

Finally, Masako was ready to make her second dive. With determination, she went through her breathing routine and dived toward the ocean floor. All of us cheered when she emerged several minutes later with a net full of *awabi*, abalone shells. On board the boat she clapped her hands and giggled like a small girl. We were overjoyed; she had proven herself.

Late in the afternoon another boat pulled up close to us. Masako received many compliments on her initial dives and bowed to the people on the other boat each time she was praised. There was good natured teasing about which boat had the biggest catch. Today's efforts were successful for everyone. Soon the flotilla of boats glided across the Pacific toward the harbor. A soft sun broke through the clouds and reflected on the divers' face masks, now worn on their foreheads. Many of the women were singing in high spirits.

After packing their catch in barrel-shaped baskets near the drying fire, the *ama* girls hoisted the containers on their backs and walked toward the village. In an hour or so they would begin cooking the evening meal for their families.

Several afternoons later, Yoshio and I walked in a light rain to the village's Shinto shrine. We passed many children who were gathering seaweed that had washed up on the beach. This seaweed would be rolled into paper-like sheets for eating or shipped away to northern chemical laboratories for making iodine.

Twisted pine trees flanked the drab Shinto shrine that faced the sea. We passed under a red *torii,* archway, and continued up the stone walkway to the offering box. Both of us tossed a few *sen* coins in the box. I stood back quietly while Yoshio worshipped. Bowing low, he clapped his hands three times as he chanted. When finished, he turned toward me.

"I ask *Kami,* the wind god, for good weather and very enthusiastic catch of fish," he said.

"I'm sure your prayer will come true," I replied.

We wandered away from the shrine into the rice fields, where farm families in straw hats and raincoats were splashing down the rows. As they were weeding the "honorable rice," laughter and conversation broke out through the drumming of the rain. The air was pungent with the smell of "night soil," human refuse, which fertilized the rice beds. It seemed that every available plot of level ground was partitioned into rice pools to help feed this overpopulated area.

At the end of one path, we stopped to examine a stone column some three-feet high. It was clearly a phallus dedicated to some deity of fertility. Blue flowers lay at its base, perhaps an offering given by some wife invoking this god to give her a child.

"This is for very enthusiastic number of children," Yoshio said.

"And fish, too?" I asked.

"Yes, this god has no prejudice. Big numbers are his only responsibility."

On my last night in the village, Yoshio's father invited me to a farewell supper. I stepped out of my wooden clogs at the doorway and put them alongside the other mud-splattered *getas.* Yoshio's father greeted me with low bows. To show his knowledge of certain Western customs, he shook my hand for well over a minute.

Since this occasion was intended to be somewhat formal, everyone was dressed in fresh kimonos. We sat erectly on the floor around low tables. I was startled to see the transformation of the diving women and fishermen. No longer were they scantily clad and boisterous in their movements; they were now restrained to the point of pomposity. Somehow I felt as though I were with a different group of people.

Yoshio's mother slid back one of the doors, and bowing apologetically, she served us small bottles of hot saki. With unusual seriousness Masako assisted her mother. Kneeling, they poured wine into our cups and quietly withdrew into the other room where most of the women had assembled.

"We take saki to wish you a very enthusiastic journey home," Yoshio said, as all the fishermen nodded and drank.

"Dohmoh ahreegahtoh," I said and bowed. "Thank you."

We exchanged gifts; I gave the men a carton of Camel cigarettes, and they gave me a long stemmed pipe with a thimble-sized bowl. Our meal was served by Masako, her mother, and several other women. When they spoke to us, they said very little. I felt uncomfortable with all of the formality; as the evening progressed and more saki was poured, however, many of the initial rules of etiquette vanished.

Yoshio's father lifted the sleeve of my kimono and pressed my sunburned arm to make a white mark on it. He clicked his tongue and moaned sympathetically. *"Heeyahkeh ahmehreekahnoh tohree-san,"* he said. "Sunburned American bird." Everyone roared as we drank more rice wine.

Gradually, the women joined us after they had removed the dishes. As an old woman tuned her *koto*, a stringed instrument, voices grew quiet, and we lapsed into a contemplative mood. With her head tilted back, she sang in a rasping voice. A seven-year old girl dressed in a butterfly-patterned kimono danced with mincing steps to a minor-keyed song. All of us were pleased. Her billowy kimono and hair, trimmed in bangs, gave her the appearance of a dancing doll.

Slowly, as if dancing in a dream, she tugged at an imaginary fish net, pulling it back and forth to the cadence of the strings. After her lengthy story was danced out, the men loudly approved her efforts with kind words and saki toasts. Now the women were relaxed and talking freely between the dances.

Saluting and counting in a military cadence, the fat clown of the group attempted to imitate a soldier from the Great War. His performance was a sad burlesque from a second-rate circus, lacking the spontaneous humor originally displayed at the fishing cooperative. Although annoyed by the subject and poor performance, I forced a smile; the others ignored him completely.

Everyone grew quiet and gazed at me. Yoshio's father asked me to sing or tell an American story. Although I tried to beg off, the party-goers were persistent. It was the custom. With courage gained from the saki, I sang a few verses of "On Top of Old Smoky." Yoshio was quick to translate after every verse and explain my quaint Appalachian courting customs, which he had studied at his provincial university.

To everyone's amazement, the old woman played her *koto* in a minor-keyed version of the same song. The melody was difficult to follow, but she captured the mood and the spirit of a man who "lost his true lover from courting too slow." Both she and I accepted the cheers and toasts from our appreciative audience.

It was near midnight and the conversation grew louder. A gust of sea air carried the cigarette smoke outside the window where the children stood. They were sleepy yet fascinated by the antics of their elders.

In a corner of the room an old woman in a dark kimono twitched her hips seductively and sang as though she were possessed by some ribald spirit. She was encouraged by hearty laughter.

"What is she singing?" I asked.

"Is best I do not translate; after sixty, old women can sing what they please," Yoshio said, and smiled.

Before I could say good night to the family, we heard a splashing sound outside. We rushed out to learn what the disturbance was. Sprawled in the mud, the fat clown moved his arms as though he were leading an orchestra. "Old Smoky-san, Old Fuji-san, Old Smoky-san," he sang while we laughed.

After bowing several times to every guest at the party, I slipped into my wooden *getas*, spread my oil paper umbrella and sloshed through the rain back to my inn.

At ten the next morning, I stood in a crowded third-class coach of a Tokyo-bound train. As I gazed out the window toward the sea, dozens of small boats plied through the craggy inlet. About this time Yoshio and his father would be netting their second catch of the day.

~ 2 ~

Erotic Merchandise

Prostitution, the world's oldest profession, was an important business in Japan in the early 1950's. It existed in many forms. From the Tokyo nightclubs to the modest brothels in remote Japanese cities, Japan was bustling with prostitution. I found an interesting form of this oldest profession in southern Japan.

Warm undercurrents of sandalwood incense drifted through the darkened streets of Yawata, Japan. Oddly enough, the blend of the incense and open sewers merged into an agreeable odor. I sauntered through the old quarter of this city, searching for a little-known area. A policeman examined both me and my map with much curiosity before directing me toward my destination.

The facades of the buildings were glowing from warm lantern light. A three-wheeled truck left a swirl of dust in the air as it groaned past me. From a nearby intersection, I heard the piping flute call of a vendor selling hot bowls of noodles from his cart. I bought two servings and ate them leisurely with chopsticks.

Shop windows, bathed in the glare of fluorescent lights, lined both sides of the street. At first, I could not recognize what merchandise was on display. Strolling closer to one of the shops, I saw prostitutes sitting in two rows facing the street. Their bodies were swathed with expensive, brocade kimonos; they seemed like dolls in a toy shop.

A wrinkled madam rested on a stool inside the partially curtained doorway. She fanned herself as she discussed her products with three window shoppers. Now and then she would artfully close her fan and point to a promising girl. Few patrons of this ancient enterprise were browsing, since it was too early in the evening. Perhaps later the dusty streets would be filled with merchant seamen and workers from the giant Yawata steel mill.

Most of the girls were far above average in appearance. A few were beautiful. Many were hired out to brothel owners by families who were too shiftless or poor to support them. Unlike some brothels in large cities, where photographs adorning a downstairs entryway advertised the girls inside, these Yawata brothels followed the traditional method—window selection.

While Japanese men usually followed the codes of family fidelity, custom did permit an occasional fling with party girls or prostitutes. Often this entertainment was written off as a business expense. Yoshio, from the fishing village, suggested that I visit this exotic district for "your educational advancement."

I lingered in the shadows near one of the opened windows. The licorice scent of the girl's hair pomade blended with the incense. A lovely girl near me had a long neck, a particularly appealing attribute by classical Japanese tastes. An old man sighed with longing, as he watched a bead of silver perspiration flow down her sensuous neck. Without moving her head, she glanced enticingly at him. Impulsively, he mumbled something to the madam about this half-hour purchase before following his selection into the rear chambers.

Later, in another brothel, a girl was chiding her drunk customer to lower his voice as she led him toward a room. He forgot to take off his dirty boots at the entryway. Smiling and bowing, the madam scurried over to him, made him sit down and pulled his boots off for him. The customer staggered away bowing and mumbling appreciation to the madam for her kindness.

After walking down the street, past restaurants and more windows full of girls, I entered a pharmacy. An old man, smoking a long-stemmed pipe, sat on a mat in the rear. He wore an ornate tobacco pouch around his kimono waistcloth. It was secured by a *netsuke*, a delicate ivory carving, of a couple merged in an erotic embrace. Flooding the entire shop, naked light bulbs revealed a variety of contraceptive and sexual devices displayed with typical oriental frankness. A banner advertising penicillin pills in both Japanese and English hung from the ceiling. Meticulously, several men in business suits ran their fingers over several items before making a purchase.

Raunchy Japanese music blared out as I walked into a nearby restaurant and sat at a low table. Several Norwegian merchant mariners danced on a tiny floor to a recording of *Tan-ko-bushi,* "The Coal Miners' Song." They shuffled around with Japanese hostesses dressed in summer kimonos, while their shipmates drank at the tables. One seaman, holding his girl's waist, joined me.

"How did you find this area?" I asked.

"With little trouble. We seamen from Norway have an eye for the unusual—anywhere, everywhere in this world," he boasted.

We watched one of his shipmates surround himself with a cluster of girls while directing a photographer on how to shoot his harem from the most flattering angle. We shared a few beers and sea stories before I walked next door to another old-style brothel.

The madam invited me in to examine her girls more closely. As I stepped over the threshold, they stopped whispering and assumed their rigid poses and bowed slightly to me. Each of them was in competition to be selected. Twenty pairs of promise-filled eyes gazed seductively toward me. After stepping down the long row, the madam stopped in front of her youngest and prettiest girl.

"*It-desu,*" she murmured. "This is pretty good."

"*It-desu,*" I said enthusiastically, as I continued to examine each girl one by one. Movements were under way to abolish open prostitution in Japan, and for an instant, I wondered what would happen to these girls. Perhaps token attempts would be made to rehabilitate them, however a government with limited funds could do little to retrain them. Many of them might find new jobs, but perhaps others would continue their trade in a more clandestine manner.

"*Ohahyoh yoh gohzaheemahs,*" the madam said as she tugged on my sleeve. "Good morning."

"*Gomen nasai,*" I said, apologizing for my wandering attention. "I'm sorry."

Since I was not a patron of this ancient art, I asked the madam if I could inspect the rooms where the girls worked. She was puzzled yet kept her composure.

Impulsively, I took off my shoes and hurried past an expensive pine tree-painted screen and entered the hallway. The interior was furnished with the same good taste found in most first-class Japanese inns. I pulled back the sliding door to one small bedroom which overlooked a garden illuminated by paper lanterns.

A maid, who was cleaning up after the last customer, dropped her feather duster, bowed to me and trotted down the hallway. Although the room was small, it was comfortable and immaculate. A rice paper floor lamp glowed on the Chinese scroll in the *tokonoma,* alcove. There was no table, since none was needed. Amusing groans of passion came through the thin paper wall of the next room.

The madam prattled away in Japanese, as she followed me into a master bedroom reserved for long-established or wealthy patrons. By this time, she realized that I was only a sightseer; her solicitude turned to anger. With her fan she shoved me toward the front door, as I tried to explain that I thought her girls were beautiful and her house was very fine, but I was not interested in her merchandise. Also, it was impossible to convince her that I might return.

From the street I could see the madam who was probably explaining to the girls that I was a very uncivilized person who did not understand the precepts of good *Shinjuku*, house of pleasures, etiquette. After dismissing this fascinating scene with a ceremonial bow, I turned and strolled back toward the modern section of Yawata.

Yoshio, the university student, was right. My "educational advancement" increased by visiting this squalid area. Soon, I would leave Yawata's sexual commercialism and travel high into the clean mountains where Buddhist monks pursued Japanese spirituality.

~ 3 ~

Pilgrimage to
A Mountain Monastery

Mount Koyasan, a mountain monastery, was my next destination. Although this monastery had been isolated for years, the monks greeted me with warmth. I could once again continue my search to understand many of the world's great religions.

A cool, pine-scented breeze swept past the old Buddhist monk and me, as we hiked through a forest on top of Mount Koyasan—far above the hot plains of Nara, the ancient Japanese capital.

Filtering through the tree branches, sunlight beamed on stone grave markers flanking both sides of the walkway. Thousands of these monuments, marking the ashes of countless souls, seemed to have grown from the moss like giant mushrooms.

At last, we came to a clearing in the forest where stood the tomb of Kobo Daishi, founder of the Koyasan Shingon sect of Buddhism. Pilgrims crowded around a few statues of Buddha near this tomb. With a carefree air, they poured water over the statues and chatted with each other. The monk and I sidled through the pilgrims and filled long-stemmed wooden ladles with water. I followed his actions as he poured water over the heads of the statues of Buddha.

"This way we do honor to Lord Buddha and to the most holy man, Kobo Daishi," he said in the English he had learned in a provincial university.

"I'm glad to honor them," I said.

"Because you are foreign man, your respect for Buddha will be filled with great importance."

After the monk greeted many of the pilgrims, we walked through the shadowed forest toward the monastery. Both of us were clad in kimonos. He strode along with the pace of a woodsman, as I stumbled behind him holding my kimono up with one hand. In a high clearing near a stand of ancient *suji*, cedars, he stopped and wiped his glasses on his handkerchief.

"I select this path to give you special view," he said and smiled with pride.

The roofs of three separate monasteries, not yet covered by the gathering fog, resembled ships anchored in a green sea. Trails leading to these religious communities disappeared into the dark forest. Blue smoke from each cooking fire spiraled into the cool mists.

Although pilgrims came to Mount Koya for worship, the only inhabitants here were monks, novices and a few families of woodcutters. I was pleased that one large group of pilgrims had postponed their visit to the monastery during my stay. Their absence gave me more time with the holy men.

When I followed the monk through the gates of the Great Koyasan Monastery, he left me and attended to his duties. I lingered for a while to enjoy the formal garden before walking toward my room.

The interior of the monastery was golden; the afternoon sun seemed to ignite the paper windows lining the long corridor leading to the stairway. Dust particles glistened in the incense. Sunlight gilded the bronze Buddha statues and rows of landscape scrolls. It appeared as though everything in the monastery was designed for this late summer afternoon.

After climbing the polished wooden stairs, I slid back the door to my room, which joined the monks' quarters. This guest room was spacious and understated in its elegance. Hanging in the alcove, an ancient scroll displayed bold Chinese calligraphy; a vase holding a single yellow chrysanthemum rested on a low table. The sun polished the *tatami*, straw floor mats. I sat near the open window and contemplated the miniature garden and the forest beyond.

It was both comforting and stimulating to be a pilgrim at this venerable monastery. It was much like living in a grand art museum without guards, crowds or glass-enclosed areas. All things were well ordered; I began to make a partial adjustment to this century-old religious existence.

My reverie was interrupted when the monk and a novice, who was about my age but with a shaved head, slid the door open and bowed to me.

"Excuse us, please," the monk said. "We wish to join you, to take pleasure in the moment."

"Please, I'd like you to," I said, as the novice put a tray of hot tea on the table. Somehow I was unsettled by the strange, withdrawn manner of this novice. He gazed at me as though he wanted to speak, yet he abruptly turned away as the old monk scowled.

"You must understand that we have become blind to much of the beauty you admire," the monk said.

"Blind?"

"We are blind to the surface beauty. Yes, blind. Buddha has permitted us to see far beyond. The beauty of this garden and this most holy of monasteries is the beginning of many, many journeys. With each reincarnation we gain merit and see and understand more—much more."

"And your eventual goal is to reach Nirvana?"

"Yes, it is the state of being where we lose all worldly desire and become one with Buddha. Yet it requires much discipline."

"I grew accustomed to discipline in the navy."

"Oh, yes, you must have. Discipline is the required element on the long journey to enlightenment."

We sipped our tea as we savored, in silence, the golden afternoon merging into twilight. A breeze wafted across the garden and cooled us; the bamboos shuddered. Crickets and other insects chirred louder. Soon, the filament in an unshaded light bulb grew white hot, flickered, and became bright again. This intrusion of modern electricity disrupted the peaceful mood. I sighed in disappointment.

"It is difficult to escape the twentieth century," the monk said. "Today, the manager of our monastery starts the generator on time. Yesterday, it was necessary to remind him."

Early the next morning I joined the monk and five novices in their hall of worship. These were the only men needed to conduct the ceremonies of this large monastery. Rich silks, characteristic of the Shingon sect, adorned the walls. At the far end of the floor the monk and novices were seated formally on an elevated platform leading to an ornate altar. An oil ceiling lamp cast a wavering light on a statue of Buddha. Bowls of rice rested on each side of the statue as offerings. Rosewood incense swirled around us.

Momentarily, a gong reverberated. The monk chanted a Chinese sutra from a worn manuscript. Periodically, he halted to allow the novices to reply in unison. Finally, the novices lighted their incense sticks and stuck them in the ashes of a large bowl as an offering to the Lord Buddha.

After everyone bowed low to the altar, the lengthy service came to an end. We left the hall of worship in silence. Outside, almost everyone seemed to be brimming with good humor and ready for the chores of the day. However, the novice who wanted to speak to me the day before appeared sullen. Often, I felt that he was studying my every move.

Several mornings later, when I was working with the novices in the vegetable garden, the old monk called me aside to join him in the shade. "I am obliged to improve your religious understanding. Initially, I must ask a personal question."

"That's all right with me," I said.

"Did you kill any Korean person in the war?" he asked.

"No, I didn't have to," I said, stunned by his candor.

"You are most fortunate. Killing is against the teaching of Christ, Buddha and many other holy men."

"That's true," I said. "In this present life, if one avoids killing, can he gain merit?"

"Yes, merit is gained with kindness, good deeds and suffering," he added, before leaving me to dig up long white radishes with the novices.

After working in the garden, I returned to my room and read books on Buddhism and other religions. The old monk also advised me to spend time clearing my mind of worldly thoughts and to meditate on Buddha. This was my sixth day in the monastery, and I was growing tired of trying to assimilate so much religion in such a short time.

Often, during my meditation, I lapsed into daydreams of worldly things. Had many of my friends at home married? Where was my aircraft carrier? Probably my shipmates were on maneuvers or in Pearl Harbor enjoying liberty. I owed my parents and brother several letters. Were my friends in the Japanese fishing village continuing to have a successful summer? The brothel area in Yawata seemed light years away. Would I ever adjust to the monastery's vegetarian diet? Oh, how I craved fish, chicken and beef. Perhaps I would always be doomed to be a carnivore.

A couple of afternoons later, the same novice who seemed unusually interested in me slid back the door softly and entered my room. After mumbling something, he placed a book beside me. He seemed to have difficulty speaking clearly.

So I consulted my phrase book. *"Koh-koh oh, toht-teh-moh tah-noh-*

sheen-deh ee-mahs," I pronounced carefully. "I've really been enjoying it here."

After an inordinately long pause, he whispered: "Sir, I've got a big problem."

"Hey, you speak English," I said in surprise.

"Please, whisper. I'm not supposed to be here."

"But where did you learn your English?"

"Hawaii. I lived with relatives there. Look, I'll level with you. I've watched you carefully, very carefully."

"I know."

"You've got to do me a favor. I feel that I can trust you. You see, I'm here in hiding. The monks have given me protection. I'm from Sapporo, on the north island. A marriage broker there had me matched to a girl of a rich family. But she is ugly, ugly, ugly."

I chuckled and asked, "Ugly enough to run away from?"

"Have you got the picture! By now things have cooled off. Finally, I worked up the nerve to contact my parents again. They have lost face, but they may bring me enough money to go back to Honolulu in the good ol' Territory of Hawaii."

Both of us froze when we heard a noise. Sweat beaded on his face. Someone was coming.

"Could I help?" I whispered.

"Just mail this letter to my parents when you leave. I'm forbidden to write anyone. The monks want me to stay here a year or longer. I took a vow. But six months is all I can stomach. I'm Buddhist but not good enough to be a monk."

Brusquely, the old monk slid the door back with a bang as we lapsed into silence.

"The novice was kind enough to bring me a book," I mumbled. With quick bows the novice smiled and hurried out of the room.

The monk snatched up the book and thumbed through it. "I was unaware you could read Japanese," he said suspiciously.

"No, no, I don't. The drawings seemed interesting."

"That one is not to be here. He is forbidden to be alone with pilgrims. Not even to speak to them."

"Oh, I didn't understand. He just came...."

"I see. No explanation is required. He is burdened with many problems. May I ask, did he give you any messages for the outside world?"

Hanging my head in embarrassment, I remained silent.

"Never mind," the monk said with a painful look on his face. "He is much like many of the young people in Japan today. He is too much divided between Eastern and Western customs. May the Lord Buddha bestow mercy."

Having left the strict discipline of the navy, I was not willing to spend a long period of time adjusting to this rigid monastic life. Obviously, it was too soon to settle down with any one group of people. To absorb the ambience and learn even a part of this religion's meaning would take years. I was restless, churning with energy and ready to explore other exciting facets of life. Eagerly, I wanted to visit the floating markets, temples and opium dens of Bangkok.

After wandering from one shrine to another on Mount Koyasan, I decided it was time to leave. Soon I folded my kimono and put on my traveling suit. As I said goodbye to the monk, I reached inside my coat pocket for my wallet. I felt a tinge of guilt as I touched the hidden letter of the novice.

According to the custom, I placed several yen notes inside an envelope, gave it to the monk as my contribution and traveled from the tranquility of the holy mountain down to the commotion of the secular world.

~ 4 ~

New Dreams
From An Old Opiate

Various segments of life in Thailand interested me. Among the most fascinating and forbidden activities in Bangkok was life in the opium den. I intended to find the appeal of this ancient and dangerous art.

Dawn washed the darkness from the Bangkok sky; sculptured spires of numerous Buddhist temples ripened to their natural gold in the lifting sun. Sleepily, the driver of my rented motor boat maneuvered through the brown waters of the wide *klongs*, canals, leading to the downtown area.

We passed endless rows of palm-thatched houses lining each canal. Women, wearing huge straw hats resembling scalloped lampshades, glanced up as we droned forward. My driver turned off the motor as we bobbed across an enormous intersection where many boats were crossing like skittering water bugs in all directions.

A cacophony of puttering motors, throbbing diesels and crying vendors engulfed us. One gray-haired woman in a boat skimmed alongside of us; her full lips parted into a betel nut-stained grin as she held up a basket of golden mangoes.

They were inviting, so I haggled with her for a few of them. This sweet fruit made a tasty breakfast for my driver and me.

One large sampan drifted across our bow. Under the canvas roof a baby swung in a muslin hammock. The father squatted at the tiller while his wife and young daughters cleaned fish on the deck. Several Buddhist monks glided along in a water taxi; their begging bowls were empty but would soon be filled with brown rice. I was surprised to see a modern motor launch of the Royal Thailand Navy invade the century-old flotilla.

As it roared by, it nearly capsized a skiff filled with caged chickens.

Finally, we twisted out of the floating market district and motored to another part of the city. The driver opened up the throttle to pass a water bus crowded with school children before pulling into a landing near the inexpensive Chinese hotel where I stayed.

In the shabby hotel bar I found my young German friend whom I had met the week before. Several months earlier, he had deserted from the French Foreign Legion in Vietnam. His former comrades-in-arms, from many different nations, were fighting for continued French dominance in Indochina. Now he was doing odd jobs as a civilian until his sister in Frankfurt could send him enough money for his return trip home.

"I am just now very sorry," he said. "Today I vork in der restaurant. Is impossible to be vatching after you in der opium den."

"That's OK," I said, "but if I don't show up in a day or so, will you check on me?"

"Ja, ja, but there will be no trouble. Pay attention, ist verbotten to smoke too much," he said, and laughed.

"Don't worry. I'll be careful."

My driver pumped the pedals of his *samlor*, a tricycle taxi, as we raced through the back streets of Bangkok. He skidded to a stop in a narrow alley leading to a drab two-story frame building. There was no sign at the front door, and the alley was deserted.

After climbing the stairs, I entered the dark and perfumed world of an opium den. The bespectacled Chinese manager smiled as he greeted me.

"American man, are you still sickee?"

"Oh, no, I feel much better. Last time I tried to smoke too much."

"Today, I myself fix pipes for you with my own hands. You must take it easy—very easy, and you fly away into the dream of the poppy."

The manager led me through the opium *diva*, den, to a stall in the rear. After bowing, he vanished into the haze. As my eyes adjusted to the darkness, I gazed at the familiar wooden platforms around me in one huge room. Each platform was divided by low partitions into alcoves for the customers. The yellow flames of the opium lamps played on the reclining patrons who were almost uniformly dressed in black trousers with white undershirts. Initially, these smokers gave the impression of corpses lined up in a morgue.

Several days earlier I was in this den and smoked a few pipes of opium without experiencing any pleasing effects. My stomach knotted. I became very dizzy and was nauseated for several hours. Perhaps these ill effects came more from the excitement of my first trips to the den than the assault of the drug on my system.

The manager returned with a teakwood tray and sat down beside me. With a flourish, he trimmed the wick on a small hurricane lamp and lit it.

"This day, you will have dreams worthy of old Chinese emperors," he said with pride.

"I hope so."

He placed a hollow two-foot bamboo pipe near me. Deftly, he draped a cloth over a hole in the side of the pipe and screwed the doorknob-shaped bowl into it. From a tiny aluminum tube he squeezed a brown dab of opium onto his finger.

"Ahaaaa," he cooed, tasting it. "This will tame the tiger inside you."

After squeezing the paste around the head of a large needle, he worked it into the shape of a tiny ball as he allowed it to seethe and steam over the lamp.

As I rested my head on the porcelain pillow, he handed me the pipe. After placing one end of the pipe to my lips and the bowl over the lamp, I inhaled several deep breaths. My mouth tasted like caramel. Coughing, I returned the pipe. My eyes and nose smarted. After resting for a few minutes, the manager prepared another pipe for me. He bowed and left me to my dreams.

Some thirty minutes later, a warm, comforting feeling came over me. Time was suspended and of little consequence. No longer was I in a room full of strangers; now I felt like everyone was an old friend. After sipping hot tea, I seemed to be floating.

The manager prepared another pipe for me. Every detail of his pockmarked face shifted into sharp focus. The straw mat under me and the spider webs on the ceiling seemed wondrous and worthy of long contemplation. Holding up my hands, I slowly examined them as though they were great works of art.

Drifting, drifting, higher and higher, I felt as though I were leaving my body. Gazing down, I could see the entire den from somewhere in the ceiling. I chortled in amazement—I could even see myself!

Delightful music grew louder and filled the dark chamber. It was a symphony, yes, a symphony of Sibelius, the Finnish composer. By breathing at different speeds, I could direct the orchestra to play in a slower or faster tempo. No longer did such things startle me. This opium dream had enveloped me completely.

Slowly, very slowly and blissfully, I drifted above the canals of

Bangkok. Naturally, with little effort, I merged into a piece of driftwood in the Gulf of Siam. Floating along, I could see the Chinese junks and the cargo ships pass me. Soon everything merged into blackness.

Gradually the world grew light again. Was it an hour later or months before? It made little difference. My aircraft carrier appeared before me. The sky was bright red, and the planes were black. To the music of Sibelius, the aircraft circled the ship while waiting their turn to land. One by one they descended to the flight deck as I led the symphony to a climax.

Damn, this was really happening! I saw myself as an ancient king drifting down the giant Chao Phya River in my royal barge, surrounded by my queen and many shy, young concubines. This barge was escorted by other boats filled with servants and soldiers. Other grandiose images flowed through my mind and disappeared forever into sweet opium smoke.

Finally, when the drug wore off, I returned to the dark reality of the opium den. I was very thirsty. While sipping tea, I came to the realization of why the opium smokers of ancient China had enjoyed this diversion for many centuries. It gave them a feeling of euphoria and an inexpensive escape from reality. At last I felt a comfortable kinship with the smokers, both past and present. Now I understood why they enjoyed "taming the tiger."

Later I became restless and wandered down the dirty aisles.

"Do you feel sickee?" the manager asked as he stopped me.

"No, I feel great—I had great dreams," I said. As I surveyed the rows of frail addicts, I was surprised to see a muscular young man. "Could you tell me about that guy?" I asked the manager. "He seems healthy; has he been a customer long?"

"Very, very long time. He must smoke three times a week, or he cannot do his job."

"It's a shame."

"Never mind, never mind; it is the good business for me," he said and jingled his coin pouch.

In a dim corner, the only woman in the den flipped her long black hair over her face, blew an opening in it and squealed with delight. Showing only casual interest, a few men glanced at her.

"Ohhh, you excuse. This woman always cause much trouble. She is prostitute. She does not bring honor to my house," he said as he scurried away to calm her down.

She smacked a man in an adjoining alcove and then screamed. The man, in another world, did not react. Quickly, the manager prepared another pipe for the woman, and, after smoking it, she grinned and put her head down peacefully.

After passing several emaciated men who showed the effects of years of smoking, I retreated to my alcove. The manager returned and prepared another diminutive ball of opium for me. I smoked it and eased back onto my headrest. Hours passed and wondrous dreams drifted through my mind. At times I lapsed into a rational frame of mind which was perhaps worthy of the control occasionally possessed by the English opium-eater, Thomas De Quincey.

My repose was shattered by a loud voice. "Vat has happened?" my German friend commanded. "You are staying here too long. Come now, and I help you back to der hotel."

"Hey, where did you come from?" I mumbled in drugged confusion.

"You stay here two days and nights. Have you given up der custom of eating?"

"Not yet, but I haven't been hungry."

The German helped me down the aisle toward the staircase, where racks of bamboo pipes hung. I tipped the smiling manager. *"Wung cha dai pob tarn ik,"* he said. "Hope to see you again."

"Wung cha dai..." I mumbled as my friend guided me down the stairway.

Several days later I overcame my pulsating headache and stomach pain. Perhaps I was suffering from both the after-effects of opium smoking and lack of eating. Clearly, I could now understand the appeal of this powerful drug to people throughout the centuries. However, it was not until I visited a modern hospital in Bangkok that I saw its harmful effect on the many addicts.

Following a doctor through several wards, I saw many addicts dying from their habit. Since they had learned the amount of opium they could tolerate, it was not the drug itself that was killing them; they were dying from malnutrition and starvation. With limited funds, the addicts would rather smoke than eat.

The doctor told me that these patients were the lucky ones. Most addicts eventually died alone, without any medical comfort. Seeing these men was shocking. With the fluid from I.V. bottles flowing into their veins, they lay gazing into space. Their strength had evaporated.

I was finished in my experimentation with such drugs. An overdose could make me comatose, and prolonged smoking could addict me. I was somewhat remorseful, yet this drug still held its magic allure; its derivatives, morphine and heroin, undoubtedly had similar power over addicts in America.

Although steps had been taken to prevent the illegal flow of drugs from this area to other parts of the world, I felt successful control of opium would be impossible. Obviously, this trade ran into millions of dollars for the drug lords and their armies of smugglers.

The words of the manager of the opium den haunted me: "Never mind, never mind; it is the good business...."

~ 5 ~

Fighting Communist Bandits in Malaya

After the end of the Korean War, Chinese Communists from Southeast Asia filtered down the Malaya Peninsula in an attempt to overthrow the British and Malay governments. A state of emergency had been declared.

O ur army truck roared dangerously fast along a road winding through the shadowy Malayan jungle. As we emerged from a canopy of trees, we entered a large cultivated field. Drawing much comfort from the sunlight, all of us breathed a little easier.

We raced along the skirts of a large rubber plantation where the red sarongs of the tappers blurred with the endless rows of gray trees. Soon we dipped into a tropical valley that was cleared in spots to make way for thatched huts and rice paddies.

Some forty yards behind us, our heavy armored car escort kept pace with us like a giant turtle on wheels. The gunner in the thick-plated turret swung his weapon defensively from one side to the other. At every turn, our tires squealed.

"Now, you see, the faster we travel, the less chance the communist bandits have to ambush us," Lieutenant Ahmad said to me inside the truck's cab.

"But you have more wrecks this way, don't you?" I asked.

"Indeed, yes. Better to have a few extra wrecks than to give them a slow-moving target."

Later, we scattered a large cloud of yellow butterflies that hovered over a hot depression in the road. They seemed much too peaceful to come in contact with our menacing vehicles of war.

After reaching the summit of a hilly road, we slowed to a stop. We jumped out of the cab and watched the men in their olive drab fatigues tumble out of our truck bed and climb the sloping bank into the jungle. After the lieutenant waved the truck and its escort on, we scampered into the shadows to join the patrol.

"Quite often we send the armored car and lorry forward for several miles. Throws the terrorists off if they think we haven't stopped," he said softly.

Leading us in single file were two primitive Dayak trackers from Borneo. I bounded on the rubber soles of my boots down a ravine and followed the twelve-man ambush patrol. Fortunately, the inner sole of each boot was lined with a steel plate. This protected us should we fall into a camouflaged "tiger pit" brimming with wooden spikes. We unbuttoned our shirts and opened our plackets for better ventilation.

The cool, exhilarating speed of the road was over. Slowly, we continued in the sluggish Malayan afternoon heat; our moist hands curled around our weapons. Tall vine-covered trees grew together overhead, closing out the sun except for an occasional shaft of light. From the jungle floor came the stench of rotting vegetation, reminding me of nursery hothouse odors. The only sounds we heard besides the swish of our bodies through the waist-high *lallang,* elephant grass, were birds screaming.

An hour's march later we came to a drowsy stream gurgling through the underbrush. The Borneo trackers, who moved with the skill and grace of men born in the jungle, crouched down by the water and studied it for tracks of the terrorists. They seemed to find something. Moving nimbly, they took care not to destroy what they examined or to make new tracks. We waited on the bank above until one of the trackers stretched his tattooed neck upward and hissed to Lt. Ahmad. Spreading his arms out horizontally, the lieutenant gave us the signal to stand alert.

After this young officer inspected the smeared footprints and broken branches, he whispered, "The enemy." In the Malay language he told his men to divide into pairs and take cover every five paces. Ahmad and I flattened our ponchos out on the rough ground next to each other, took off our packs and lashed several bushes together to hide our daylight position. Within fifteen minutes everyone blended so well in the heavy cover that the jungle appeared void of any human encroachment.

"We have an excellent setup here," the lieutenant whispered. "That track is about four days old. I feel the bandits will return quite soon."

"How did you know to look in this area?" I asked.

"An informer told us the bandits pass this way every five days or so. They're fetching supplies at a nearby rubber plantation."

"Do they have many contacts?"

"Fewer and fewer as the days pass," he whispered, and grinned.

Lieutenant Ahmad's whispers blended into silence as I pondered the trap he had designed.

"Where's your Bren gun now?" I asked.

"It always stays in the center—it's our most deadly weapon. Remember, that pistol we issued you is for self-protection only. This is definitely not your show. You're here only as a war correspondent," the lieutenant cautioned.

We took our rations from our packs and quietly ate several biscuits and shared a tin of beef. After we finished our chocolate bars and put our trash back into our packs, the lieutenant left to check on his men. When he returned, both of us remained silent for a long time, listening intently for any unusual sound in the dimly-lighted mass of green.

The jungle night came with sinister swiftness. We could no longer see the stream that flowed in front of us. Darkness blotted out the tanned, boyish features of the lieutenant. The comparative silence of the day gave way to the shrill drone of crickets, beetles and hundreds of unidentifiable insects. Now we were lying on our bellies like predatory animals waiting for their prey to pass downstream.

A trembling feeling of apprehension swept over me, with the absence of the day's comforting colors. Unable to see the lieutenant, who lay only two feet away, I was reassured by his regular breathing and the pungent odor of his perspiration. I felt an unusual dependence on my comrades, who were almost strangers. My respect deepened for the nerve-shattering war they fought.

Hours later, a plaintive wail filled the jungle. It came faintly at first and mounted in intensity for a moment before fading back into the darkness.

"What's that?" I asked nervously.

He chuckled and whispered, "Devil bats."

"Devil bats?"

"Actually, they're harmless fruit bats that live in the treetops. Don't give a damn for the bloody racket they make, though."

"Me neither."

"Your bloody imagination plays hell with you out here. Takes a long while to get used to it. Often I wonder if you ever do."

"Do you ever have any trouble with tigers?" I whispered, to prolong the nerve-soothing conversation.

"I've lived in Malaya all my life, except when I went to Sandhurst in England, and the only tiger I've seen has been in the circus."

"What about snakes?"

"Very seldom do you see a snake. The main bothers are the bloody mosquitoes, bees and leeches. It's the sensational newspapers that make it sound like we fight more snakes and tigers than bandits."

"Do you think..."

"Please—keep quiet now. You can't tell when the commies might show."

We grew silent again and listened for the steps of the bandits, yet the only sound we heard was the persistent din of the insects.

As we lay on the rough jungle floor, my thoughts wandered back to my train trip from Bangkok down the Malay Peninsula. It was in the antique dining car after an evening meal that I met a very affable British colonel, who invited me over to his table for a Scotch and soda. He was a heavy-set man who was saved from being considered fat and clumsy by the dignified manner in which he wore his freshly-starched khaki uniform.

"Tell me did you have a good holiday in Bangkok?" he asked in his rapid manner.

"Oh, yes, it's a fascinating place."

"Did you happen to run across any blue films there?"

"No, sir. I must have missed them."

"Well, quite by chance, I stumbled onto one. Rather artistic and amusing. Don't know when I've seen so much queer sex thrown in. Strange blokes, those Siamese."

"They are very interesting—hope you had a good rest there away from your jungle warfare."

"Thank you, yes. It was the first proper holiday I've had in over two years. Now, with the terrorists under fair control, I can go back soon."

"How long do you think it will be before the 'Emergency' is over, Colonel?"

"That's a hard one to answer," he said thoughtfully, stroking his black mustache. "These bandits have been trying to seize the government for years. And I feel that there will always be somewhat of an emergency, but most areas are now controlled. Since Sir Gerald, or General Templer as you might know him, has been in command, the people have come to respect the government more. Now, we don't have so much trouble with the farmers giving food and information to the bandits. This whole bloody thing is a matter of food. Cut the supply line from the frightened farmers to the terrorists; then as they starve, we hunt them down."

As our train steamed through the dark Malayan jungle, the colonel and I became better acquainted and more congenial, with the aid of the bottled spirits from Scotland. I felt that now the time was right to ask a favor of him.

"I wonder, sir, if it wouldn't be too much trouble, could I visit your regiment? I'd like to see jungle warfare in operation."

"Harumph—uh—," he cleared his throat in surprise. "I could do it, of course; but allowing visitors about is a bit against regulations. You *do* realize it could be most dangerous."

"I do."

"However, I'll tell you what; since you are an ex-naval officer and look fit enough, I'll see if I can arrange for you to visit one of my battalions composed of Malay troops. Around my headquarters at Alor Star there's a bit of action now, so it's best if you continue on the train three stops more to Prai. Let's see—then, I'll have an escort meet you tomorrow about half-past eleven at the railway station and take you back to their headquarters. How's that?"

"Excellent. I appreciate it, sir."

"Come now, before I get off, let's have another peg of whiskey," he said, as he poured the amber liquid into the glasses trembling from the vibrations of the dining car.

The next day, across the bay from the mountainous west-coast island of Penang, I waited at the Prai station for my military escort. Punctually at eleven-thirty a land rover with three Malayan soldiers screeched to a stop in front of me.

"Pardon me," a young Malay lieutenant said, "are you Mr. Reeder?"

"That's right."

"I am Lieutenant Ahmad. If you are ready, we'll be off."

We purred along a tarmacadam road out of the city and soon passed a small billboard written in English, Arabic, Chinese and Siamese that read:

YOU ARE NOW LEAVING A WHITE AREA

"This means we are leaving an area that's been cleared of bandits. At present we're in an uncleared, or dangerous area," the lieutenant said.

"In a few minutes we'll have a look around a New Village."

"New Village?"

"That's where all the farmers are housed together behind a high wire fence. They must be kept in one place for their own protection, so they cannot take food to the bandits. Of course, in the day they work out in the fields."

"What happens if they slip out at night?"

"We have no choice; we must shoot them."

We drove past the cinder block guardhouse of the New Village and continued down the dirt road shaded by the twisted coconut palms. In the center of the area was a long recreation hall with a corrugated metal roof where motion pictures were screened three times a week. Near this building, a well-equipped clinic faced orderly rows of thatch-roofed houses.

"We consider villages like this one very important," the lieutenant said. "Here people vote on their village leaders who represent them. Before, most of the people lived in isolated spots and had no interest in government. Now that they know their vote counts, it is difficult to keep them away from the ballot box. Someday, when Malaya has complete home rule, they should be very valuable citizens."

We swung onto the main road and raced toward the army camp, leaving the unpaved village roads in warm swirls of dust. An hour later, after passing numerous rubber plantations and small rice fields interspersed with enormous stretches of heavy jungle, we came to an abrupt downhill hook in the road.

"See that high bluff there? Well, a planter was 'bushed in his motor-car there a fortnight ago."

"Did the commies kill him?"

"Fortunately, no. He was able to drive on. One of our patrols got to him in time and rushed him back to a doctor."

Hurtling down another hill onto a level strip of the road, the driver honked his horn three times and braked down to a slower speed, pausing for an armored car to burst from its shaded hiding place under a clump of *Nipha* palms. Soon this battle wagon roared up behind us. The brown-skinned gunner popped out of the turret, smiling with embarrassment as the wind almost scooped the green beret from his head.

Battalion headquarters stood in a clearing on the jungle hillside. Radiating from the combination mess hall and ammunition storehouse in the middle of the compound were many comfortable, green tents for the soldiers. Captain Salleh, a short Malay with alert brown eyes, led me to the elongated officers' bungalow that was divided into offices and sleeping quarters.

"Delighted to have you here," he said in a high-pitched voice. "You're the first visitor we have had in over two years. Your room will be the one used by a young English lieutenant who was assigned to me."

"Was he transferred?"

"No," he replied, as he searched the sky for a long time. "The commies blasted him on patrol—didn't have a chance. Bloody bandits fired on him from close range and fled before we could return fire. Was an outstanding chap."

Inside the officers' lounge, an austere room with a large table and several canvas-backed chairs, the captain and I relaxed for afternoon tea. A color lithograph of Queen Elizabeth II on one wall faced a map of the battalion's operational area on another. Stacked in one corner were many outdated issues of the *Illustrated London News*, limp from high humidity and tattered by frequent usage.

"I didn't realize you Malays have tea every day like Englishmen," I said.

"Many of us do. Actually, most of our officers have studied at Sandhurst, where we became accustomed to taking afternoon tea. In fact, some of our chaps have come back from England acting more like Englishmen than Englishmen themselves," he said, and laughed.

"Could I ask what sort of area you patrol?"

"Certainly. In your terms, we cover ten to twelve square-miles of hilly jungle. You can see it there on the map. It's marked out in red. Last year there were around one-hundred bandits. Now that we have killed some of them, and others have moved away, we need to track down twenty-eight more. It's surprising, but about one third of them are women. Only last week we killed two men and a Chinese woman."

"Do you still have many extremely dangerous areas in Malaya?"

"Only about six or so. We have succeeded in cutting off most of the food supply to these areas, yet many Chinese and a few Malays continue to aid areas partly through sympathy and partly through fear. Many commies continue to infiltrate our country by passing through Cambodia and Vietnam.

"Do you still set ambushes for them?"

"Indeed, yes. But only if we have information on which trail they might use; otherwise, we could wait for months on the wrong trail. If things are right, we just may send out a patrol tomorrow."

"Would it be possible for me to go along, say, as a war corespondent, a journalist or something? I do have these letters."

After carefully reading my letters of introduction from the editors of both my hometown newspapers, he shook his head. "These letters do not say you are a certified journalist—they describe you only as a student."

"I know that, but..."

"It is unlawful for you to go to war. What if you were killed?"

"I'm willing to take that risk," I said, trying to conceal the tremor in my voice.

"The colonel might grant—no, I do not think he would. I must approach this matter with utmost care," he said, as he started pouring more tea.

The following day, as I walked around the area, I saw several soldiers throwing knives at the trunk of a mango tree. Laughter rebounded through the camp when one burly corporal heaved his knife deep into the grass instead of an "X" mark on the trunk. The night before, the American movie *Mississippi Gambler* with Tyrone Power was shown in the mess hall. The soldiers' imaginations were stirred. Even though these men were exposed daily to real life danger, they still enjoyed pretending they were reckless knife throwers from the romantic riverboat days in America.

While I examined the camp's black wooden mosque, I learned from the captain that I could go on the ambush patrol with Lt. Ahmad. After issuing me a pistol for "self-defense only," Ahmad outfitted me in jungle fatigues and briefed me with the other soldiers. After a few hours our personnel carrier whirled over the road toward the operational area with the armored car escort following in our shadow.

Now my thoughts drowsily returned to our ambush. The lieutenant and I continued to lie silently, hour after painful hour, in the jungle night. Whining above our heads were invisible masses of mosquitoes. To slap them might give our position away. I followed Ahmad's directions and learned how to press them to death with my hands. When turning from our bellies to rest on our sides, we were careful not to stir the branches in our blind. The unaccustomed strain of keeping alert in total darkness made me tremble. Each new sound projected images of oversized Chinese bandits surrounding us. Perhaps we would be the victims of our own ambush.

Gradually, the black jungle merged into gray, and the strident din of insects became less annoying in the cooler morning air. Drops of water continued to dribble down through the pallid foliage. Now I was able to see the lieutenant's hazy form by my side; he wiped the moisture from his gun sight. I was lightheaded from the long night; however, I felt unusually alert. From my small plastic medical pouch, I took a couple of white *Paludrine,* anti-malaria pills, and swallowed them with my canteen water. I was reminded of Dr. Tom Dooley, who had given me a medical kit back in Japan for my long journey home.

On hearing a distant noise, Ahmad and I became tense. The lieutenant squirmed forward and peered apprehensively through his gun sight toward the partially-hidden trail. Both of us breathed rapidly. From somewhere behind us came a distorted cry. Bewildered, the lieutenant flicked his head to the rear like a frightened forest deer.

Some fifteen minutes later we heard a commotion in the underbrush. Upstream, someone splashed. Voices murmured. Something cracked. Strange sounds boomed and echoed.

Ahmad trained his rifle in the direction of the noises and waited. I gasped. Rifle parts shuffled. Then there was silence.

In a few moments, a chattering cry drifted from the jungle floor and lifted high into the trees. A few of our soldiers groaned.

"Monkeys—damn, bloody monkeys!" Ahmad muttered.

We chuckled in relief and blew our breaths out, making the leaves shiver.

"I have orders for you to leave," he said an hour later. "You are to rendezvous with your escort on the road in a couple of hours. Captain Salleh does not want you to stay any longer. Not worth the risk."

"Well, OK," I said, trying to disguise the pleasure in my voice.

Crouching, Ahmad moved up the line of his hidden men and returned with one of the flat-featured Borneo trackers and a slender Malay soldier.

"These men will see you safely back to the armored car. We perhaps will stick it out here for another day or two. Best of luck on your journey in Java and Bali. When this bloody 'Emergency' is over, I might just take a holiday there."

"Good, I'll write and tell you about the Balinese girls."

The two soldiers and I trudged along the dim trail back to the road where we rested until two army vehicles creaked up the hill to us. After finishing a conversation in Malay with the sergeant who was driving the land rover, the two men disappeared into the overwhelming jungle to rejoin the ambush patrol.

We drove into an afternoon shower washing the vast jungle, with its shaggy palms, and making the road to Prai shine like a black viper's back. The warm rain was refreshing; it soothed my mosquito-nettled hands and face. After discharging me at the railroad station, the sergeant wheeled around and returned to headquarters.

As I waited on the train bound for Singapore, I once again became appreciative of the safety found in a civilized area where there was little danger in becoming a target for a bandit's bullet. Yet, for some reason, an apprehensive sensation still lingered with me. I thought of the lieutenant and his men who were still in ambush, quietly and courageously doing their jobs to help restore order to a troubled Malaya.

~ 6 ~

Buddhist Shrine of Borobudur

Although the dominant religion in Java was Moslem, traces of other religions had been discovered in this densely populated island.

It was a warm, unhurried night in central Java. Atmo drove his Plymouth taxicab down the twisting jungle road toward the Buddhist shrine of Borobudur. In some unrecorded age, the Buddhists had carved this place of worship from gray volcanic rock.

I was anxious to see this gigantic monument in all its moods. A few days before, I had strolled from noon to sunset over the ancient walkways, marveling at Borobudur's harmonious form. Now I was returning with extra *rupiahs* in the hope of persuading the caretaker to let me stay on the grounds throughout the night. Javanese law had long forbidden nocturnal visits.

Our car climbed up a rising bluff, stopping in a dark grove of trees. A man in a purple sarong appeared from the shadows and greeted us with a deep yawn.

"Ini sudah tjukup," he said, examining the *rupiahs* I had given him. "This will do."

The caretaker, after mumbling a few words with Atmo, gave me a knowing smile and meandered back into the trees.

"Maybe I bring some Dutch tourists tomorrow. Then you go back with them and pay less," Atmo said, and his heavy body quaked with laughter.

"Good deal; I'll split the fare with them," I said before he drove away, back toward the city of Jogjakarta.

I walked through the trees into a broad clearing where, in the moonlight, I saw the shrine of Borobudur. It towered imposingly before me in the vague form of a black, truncated pyramid. Rising from an enormous base, the five terraces, each smaller than the one before, led toward the apex. Clustered around a huge center dome were three circular tiers of smaller bell-shaped domes; the spires of these *stupas* reached elegantly toward the night sky.

Borobudur was built centuries ago, when Java was under a strong Buddhist influence. As other religions came into dominance, this shrine was neglected and allowed to molder under jungle vines, until it was rediscovered in the eighteenth century by the Englishman, Sir Stamford Raffles. Many historians have ranked Borobudur as an equal with the Parthenon, both in its cultural significance and splendor of design. Perhaps someday it will draw the same attention from people around the world as the temple on the Acropolis in Athens.

It was fortunate that the partially blind guide, who had shown me part of the monument before, was asleep. I wanted to savor the spirit of Borobudur alone without his incessant chatter.

Leisurely, I climbed the lower platforms and rested on a terrace near the top where I gazed at the volcanic mountains jutting up into the gray sky. The night hid most of the overturned stones and earthquake-warped walkways; now Borobudur seemed restored to its former glory. For a long time I sat on the upper level, enjoying the experience of being alone on this great shrine. It was soothing and dreamlike.

Wind wafted the smells of freshly plowed land from the farms below and carried with it the scent of flowering trees. My mind wandered from thoughts of early Javanese animism, nature worship, to their era of Buddhist influence and then to Java's present-day Islamic persuasion.

Buddhism was for the most part lost in their history, and the only traces of its influence could be found in such mysterious shrines as Borobudur. I found it intriguing to muse about the effects of different religions on the Javanese people. On board my aircraft carrier I had been able to browse through several books on different religions, yet my understanding of them was indeed shallow and based chiefly on romanticism. However, with continued reading and travel in Japan, I had begun the long journey toward a little better understanding into some of the world's great religions. Gradually, I was raising my spiritual consciousness.

Perhaps, centuries ago, this temple was crowded with monks in saffron-colored robes and pilgrims bearing offerings of fruit and flowers. Thousands could have worshiped here at one time. My sweet-scented cigar reminded me of the countless sticks of incense that had been burned to Lord Buddha.

When I lit a candle to browse through my literature on Java and Borobudur, I heard a low, strange cry from one of the terraces below. I listened for another sound but there was none. With an attitude of complacency I forgot the noise as I sipped my bottle of Dutch gin and rested.

The wind whistled through the holes of the bell-like *stupas* housing the enormous Buddha statues and made my candle tremble. An unexpected gust snuffed the flame out. After gathering my papers, I leaned back and closed my eyes. Dogs barking from a nearby village mingled with the sound of a voice.

"*Tuan, Tuan,*" someone yelled. "Mister, Mister."

I remained silent until the reedy voice grew louder and closer.

"*Tuan, Tuan, Tuan,*" someone continued calling.

Finally, I recognized the voice of my old guide; I chortled, lit my candle, and shouted, "Come on up."

"*Dimanakah Tuan?*" my guide asked. "Where are you, Mister?"

"Here I am," I said. "*Saja disini.*"

"*Salam Tuan.* Peace to you, Sir. Another cigar," he pleaded. "*Berilah saja. Setutu iagi.*"

After I lighted a mild Javanese panatela for him, he hunkered down beside me. To keep him from prattling away in a language I could barely understand, I gave him my bottle of gin and a handful of cigars. Although his sight was dimmed by cataracts on both eyes, he could see me press my lips together and hold up my hand in a Buddha-like gesture. He quickly understood that I wanted no conversation.

Pensively, he blew his smoke upward. As he did, the moonlight made his clouded eyes shimmer. We enjoyed the companionship of silence as we smoked and relaxed in the peaceful evening.

Adhering to my desire for quietness, he stood and motioned with his bamboo staff for me to follow. He walked up the steps to the highest *stupa* on the temple of Borobudur. We stood reverently at the base where a spray of tropical white orchids had been placed as an offering to Buddha. The interior of this dome was void of any bronze figure symbolizing Buddha's progress upward from the physical world into the invisible realm of the spirit. Each level of this enormous temple represented a level of progressive enlightenment. Here we stood at the supreme level.

"Nirvana?" I asked, breaking the silence.

"Nirvana," he affirmed softly.

Some time later we returned to the lower worldly level from which we had come.

"Buddha dapat kembalikan matamu?" I finally asked in my awkward Javanese. "Do you believe Buddha can give you better sight?"

"Tidak, saja Islam," he said with hesitation. "No, I don't believe this. I am Muslim."

"Dokter bisa tulung?" I asked. "Can a doctor help you?"

"Tak ada wang; tak ada dokter," he said wistfully. "No money; no doctor."

Hours later, when he had smoked the rest of the cigars and finished my bottle of gin, he held out both hands to me and knelt. His obsequious manner embarrassed me. However, I was unable to refuse a donation for his cataract operation fund, yet I felt that he had no intention of visiting a clinic. He seemed content living in the half-light of his mystical Buddhist and Muslim world.

"Selamat malam," he murmured and smiled. "Good night."

He knew instinctively how to find his way through the shadows to the first level of the shrine below. As he descended, I could hear the scraping sounds of his bamboo staff.

The growing light turned the dark-grays of the jungle to a pale green. Gradually, the sun drifted high over a distant mountain range, its sphere constantly dwindling in size. The wet rice fields near a village glowed in amber. Tan-skinned farmers wearing conical straw hats walked through the bamboo trees into their rice paddies to weed and plow before the sun floated overhead. Perched on the backs of buffaloes, small boys followed their elders at the languid pace of a daydream. Soon these black beasts would pull wooden plows through the rich Javanese soil.

Sunlight filtered through the holes in the sides of the large domes and brightened the contemplative Buddha statues within. The nighttime illusion of Borobudur in its original state quickly vanished. Unfortunately, this monument was disappearing. Colored lichens seemed to be devouring the artful stone carvings of Buddha's life. Eruptions from the nearby Meperai volcano had tilted the balustrades and adjoining steps; earth tremors had beheaded many of the Buddha figures and wrinkled the walkways.

I descended from the top clusters of domes to the open sculptured terraces below, where scenes from Buddhist texts were carved in bas-relief. One gray panel stained with yellow moss depicted the bath of Buddha with his worshipers surrounding him. He stood with lightness and grace on the bank of a river. His rounded face was modeled in an expression of spiritual contentment as though his thoughts were in a passionless world.

I was overcome by the high quality and artful consistency of the many carvings in the sculptured galleries. Undoubtedly, the placid reliefs took hundreds of artists many years to complete under the close direction of some master. Somehow I felt it would be decades before archaeologists and other scholars unraveled the mystery of Borobudur. Perhaps its history might always be hidden in legend.

While I wandered around the grounds, my guide yelled to me from the shadows of a grove of trees. At first, I thought he was worshiping some animistic god beside a fire; however, as I drew closer, I saw that he was cooking a midday meal.

"Sate, sate, Tuan," he said beaming. Eagerly, he turned two skewers of meat around in the smoke. He invited me to join him. I found *sate,* an Indonesian form of shish-kebab, delicious. When we finished, I offered him a couple of *rupiahs.* He was insulted. Pouting in a childlike manner, he stood and paced around the trees. Discreetly, I slipped my money back into my wallet. With the same speed, his pleasant mood returned. Apparently, I was now his honored guest.

We spent a long time strolling around the lower sections of Borobudur. I sensed that his nonstop lecture was also free. When I heard the taxi from Jogjakarta in the distance, we said our goodbyes. He gave me a small bamboo basket covered by a colorful *batik* cloth. He asked me to open this gift away from the temple grounds. I was overcome by his generosity and felt ashamed that I had misjudged this guide.

Atmo's taxi rattled up to the shrine grounds and parked under the yellow flowering trees where it steamed in the shade.

"Oh, *Tuan,* I sorry but no tourists come today," Atmo said and chuckled. "I think you must pay full price return trip." Again, his laughter was uncontrollable.

"Did you try hard to find any tourists?" I asked.

"Tuan, you know I have a family of twelve and have little time...."

I laughed. "Well, OK, Atmo, you win. My trip has been a great one."

"Yes, *Tuan,* Borobudur is a great trip no matter what the price."

As we drove past the rice fields, I carefully unwrapped the gift from my guide. Initially, it seemed like a small rock coated with dirt. As I carefully brushed it off, I happily discovered the face of the Lord

Buddha. Probably some earthquake had sheared it from a bas-relief on Borobudur. When I rubbed my thumb across the carving, I noticed something unusual—both eyes were vacant, serene, yet all-seeing.

~ 7 ~

Java: Communists, Capitalists And The Crown Prince

In 1954, the Joseph McCarthy hearings on communist influence were under way; the world was absorbed with the increasing intensity of the Cold War. Most foreigners in Java avoided all communists. However, I was eager to learn more about them.

Later in the day, Atmo drove into downtown Jogjakarta and parked near an elegant hotel that had been built by the Dutch in their colonial era. Now it was run by Indonesians. My inexpensive room was on the second floor above an aromatic kitchen.

I invited Atmo to join me for coffee in the terraced outdoor dining area. Initially, he declined my offer since he was not in proper attire. Nevertheless, with a little persuading, he agreed to accompany me if we sat in the shadows.

Both of us tried to avoid the contemptuous stares of the Javanese businessmen while we chatted.

"Oh, oh, *Tuan*, I am surprised you want to meet communists," Atmo whispered. "They are nothing but marching parades and trouble."

"Maybe so, but I would like to see what makes them tick."

"They tick like time bombs," he said, and we both laughed boisterously. As we did, he turned over his coffee cup. I called for the waiter who seemed reluctant to serve a taxi driver and an unconventional American. After glowering, the reserved Javanese ignored us.

"I think I find the solution," Atmo whispered, while thoughtfully puffing on his cigarette. "You are crazy for the art. I know where a communist man lives who is also crazy for the art."

"Great."

"I take you there now. Politics, art, and two crazy ones. What could be better?" he said, before we again treated everyone to our laughter.

After racing through heavy traffic to the outskirts of Jogjakarta, Atmo stopped in front of a white bungalow.

"I leave you here. In one, maybe two hours, after I visit my children, I will come for you. I have no wish to visit marching communists."

Carefully, I examined the sign in the front yard. Written below a black hammer and sickle were the letters "P.K.I.," which stood for the Communist Party of Indonesia.

"Saja bole masuk?" I called at his open door. "May I come in, please?"

In a moment a young woman appeared and stretched her hands out to me in greeting. She smiled and delicately touched her sarong before leading me to a courtyard in the rear. Under a bamboo canopy a wiry man in short trousers worked on an oil painting.

After wiping his paint-smeared hands on his once white shirt, he gave me a large folder of sketches to glance through. Most of them were drawings of everyday Javanese life; a few depicted Indonesian revolutionaries fighting the Dutch for independence.

"This one," he said, pointing to a drawing of a tailor at a sewing machine, "is my own picture."

"That's a good self-portrait."

"Thank you. In the morning I work in a tailor shop in order to feed my family; in the afternoon I paint."

I thumbed through several more sketches until I came to a drawing of farmers crowded around a communist official who was giving them bags of rice. In the background hung an enormous banner depicting a hammer and sickle.

"Here is a picture of our party leader," he said, holding up a parade scene.

"Do you have a large Communist Party here?"

"It is growing each day."

"Aren't you afraid that your party will be controlled by Russia or China? Won't you lose your freedom?" I asked boldly.

He frowned disdainfully. "You Americans misunderstand. We are, of course, connected with world communism, but the leaders in old China have promised us a free hand."

"They have been known to break their promises."

"Capitalist propaganda! Because your country is capitalist, you think all should be the same. I have studied all governments in the university here and have decided Indonesia needs the communist system," he said with a sneer.

"Not exactly. I think that you should have a free government. Well, one like you have now. But under communism a small minority rules, not for the people, but more in their own self-interest. You'll have no freedom."

"Ah-ha, let me draw attention to the capitalist corruption in our capital. We communists could crush it out like this," he said, crumpling a scrap of drawing paper.

"Indonesia is the world's largest nation of Muslims, isn't it?" I asked.

"True."

"Well, in a religion that believes there is only one God and he is Allah, how can you accept the doctrine of the communists, who deny God?"

"We can educate the people to our thinking. For me, I am no longer a Muslim. Since studying at the university, I have become a free-thinker."

Later, his wife interrupted our increasingly truculent discussion by serving us hot tea brewed with the fragrant *melati* flower.

"Come now, it is much too hot to continue this politics. I want to see what you think of the rest of my drawings."

"You're right," I replied; "it is hot."

After enjoying tea, we lapsed into a spirited discussion of current art trends in America, Europe and Asia. For the moment, aesthetics transcended politics.

A shrill taxi horn interrupted our conversation. The artist presented me with a small water color of a market scene in the neighboring island of Bali. Quickly, I took a few snap shots of him and his studio and promised to send prints.

"Oh, *Tuan*, are you ready to become a marching communist?" the driver said, and laughed while we drove downtown.

"No," I said and chuckled. "I'm a capitalist. We march to a different drummer."

An east Javanese businessman gave me a ride in his black antique Ford from Jogjakarta to Solo, also known as Surakata. When we reached the farms outside the city, I suddenly remembered that the skull of the "Solo Man," a genus of an extinct primate, somewhere between man and ape on the evolutionary scale, was discovered in this general area.

"Do you happen to know where the famous 'Solo Man' was buried? I believe some Dutch archaeologist dug him up."

"I do not know this," he said, shoving back his *pitchi*, black velvet cap. "It could be that the farmer ahead might know."

We stopped by a lean farmer, who carried two baskets of red chili peppers balanced on a bamboo pole over his shoulder. He heaved his load to the ground and listened to the businessman's question. Finally, a surge of enlightenment swept across the farmer's face. Gesturing carefully, he described the best route for us to take.

After driving through Solo, we parked off the road in the rolling countryside and walked up to the hilltop. There, beneath an Indonesian flag, stood hundreds of small white grave markers.

"This must be it."

"You mean this is the location of the 'Solo Man'?" I asked in disbelief.

"Yes. Not one but many Solo men are buried here. But it is forbidden to dig them up in a military cemetery. Not even scientists can do this."

"But I wanted..."

"Excuse me. Is this not what you wanted?"

"Yes, this is fine," I acquiesced.

Since he was so generous as to drive me several miles out of his way, I dutifully took a photograph and feigned satisfaction. Later the businessman drove me to a comfortable hotel where I settled down for several days.

Late one evening, before going to bed in the hotel, I strolled through Solo's dark streets. At one corner a girl's falsetto voice accompanied by a flute pervaded the air. I followed this music to an enormous house with a large porch. Over one-hundred men sat comfortably on floor mats inside listening to a pale-faced teenage girl sing without the aid of a microphone. Her song was a sentimental tune, a *krontsong*—a form of music introduced by the Portuguese traders centuries ago.

Festooned with strings of red and green lights, the trees outside glowed. For a long time I lingered in the shadows and listened to her. As I started to walk away, two men wearing formal European coats over their sarongs, called out in Dutch.

"I am sorry. I don't speak Dutch—I'm an American."

"Then, do not go," one man beckoned. "I speak some English. We are having a circumcision celebration for my young nephew. Please to join us; it would honor the occasion."

"Thank you, I also would be honored."

They escorted me to an alcove in the rear of the house; a girl dressed in a florid sarong met me with tea and cake.

"You have arrived for the beginning of the *Wajang Kulit*. It is a shadow play," my host said.

The bare electric lights dimmed while a coconut oil lamp burned before a thirteen-foot-long canvas screen. Near the oil lamp the *dalang*, storyteller, sorted grotesque leather puppets of gods and mortals from a box. Beside him the *gamelan* player struck his mallet on the keys of his xylophonic instrument. A young man tapped both heads of a drum cradled in his lap. With anticipation, the men's deep voices chimed against the women's voices that lifted from the other side of the *Wajang Kulit* screen. As the *gamelan* and drum began to play, the voices subsided, and the narrator leaned the flat figure of a golden prince against the screen. The four-hour drama drifted forward.

"This first story he tells is of an old country. It was conquered by the enemy, and this crown prince will lead his people to win it back. See, he now puts the enemy on the far side of the screen."

"That must be a European enemy with the pink face?" I whispered.

"Yes. The bad men are on the left; the good men are on the right."

"Do any of your stories deal with present day events?"

"All things past have a bearing on the present. Even the old Hindu tales of the *Ramayana* have delicate, secret messages about the good and evil of politics today."

"When the Dutch and Japanese governed you, did they allow the storyteller any freedom?"

"Indeed not—but by secret methods the *dalang* criticized the government and gave the people hope. At this time we are independent. It is plays such as these that make us proud to be Indonesians."

With the introduction of each new figure, the mercurial voice of the storyteller ranged from an ill-controlled soprano to a growling bass that conformed with each character.

After watching the figures move before the screen for several hours, I wandered over to the women's side. Most of them talked softly, while only a few actually followed the dreamlike shadows across the screen. One old woman with a *batik* draped over her head yawned while staring vacantly at the ceiling. In her lap, a baby girl slept.

Behind the women stood large wreaths of white and yellow coconut flowers donated by the guests for the circumcision ceremony. *Selamat Datang*, Welcome and Congratulations, were written across a streamer draped over one large circle of flowers.

Around three in the morning one of the stories came to a noisy climax. With stiff arm movements, the crown prince and his army moved across center screen to subdue the evil forces beyond. As the battle raged on, the drum and *gamelan* increased their volume, stunning the drowsy celebrants to focus their complete attention on the drama.

After a shorter drama was presented, a slim boy of fourteen, dressed in a sarong and tailored coat, appeared before an elder seated in a bamboo chair, partially veiled by curtains. A faint oil lamp hid most of the boy's apprehension as he sat on the old man's lap and leaned back. Before the elder held his hands over the boy's eyes, other men spoke words of encouragement. Kneeling beside them, a white haired man with a velvet skull cap lifted the boy's sarong.

"La illa ha Illallah, Muhamad Rasul Allah," the youth prayed with a tremulous voice. "There is but one God and Mohammed is His Prophet." With the adroitness gained from many such circumcisions, the man pulled the foreskin of the boy's penis in a bamboo clamp and performed the operation. Holding his breath, the boy expressed no pain. After he was bandaged and his sarong pulled down, the boy stood up with moist eyes to receive the good wishes of his guests.

Outside, the street was touched with the hazy light of dawn. The storyteller stacked his leather figures back into his box. Many people began to move out into the cool morning air. Before leaving, I congratulated the boy and found my host once again.

"I trust you found the shadow play interesting?" he asked.

"Everything was fascinating."

"Do not worry about my nephew. A drug killed most of his pain. We are proud of this occasion, for at this time he is a man."

We nodded and shook hands lightly in the Javanese fashion before I walked toward my hotel. I was very pleased to be a part of this rite-of-passage ceremony. A young boy had entered into the realm of manhood with the loving support of his community. All of us were tired, yet warmly uplifted by the long night's celebration.

*

One morning a *betjak* driver pedaled me in his three-wheeled rickshaw to the palace gates of one of Solo's rulers. Flanking the entrance arch of the palace were two Roman style statues of the goddess Ceres. Shafts of wheat were in the hands of each statue. They seemed oddly out of place in front of a Javanese palace.

After an elderly guard checked the address on my letter of introduction to the crown prince, he escorted me through the large courtyard to a white bungalow. Near the bungalow stood the *Pendopo*, the ancient reception hall. I relaxed in a comfortable rattan chair while a barefooted servant delivered my letter.

Minutes later, the crown prince, a burly young man in a long-sleeved white shirt, greeted me with a dignity far greater than his years. His good-natured brown eyes sparkled as he examined the letter.

"I am rather pleased that my friend in Jogjakarta gave you this introduction. It's seldom I converse with Americans. He mentions you are on an extensive tour of our country."

"Yes, I'm trying to see and learn as much as possible."

"Well, then, is there any information on this area that I might help you with?" he asked as we settled in our chairs.

"I am, of course, very interested in your brother."

"I see. Well, at one time he was very powerful, but since we won our independence from the Dutch, my brother has been reduced to a figurehead. Also much of his land was taken by the present government. He now looks out over his land holdings—with the aid of his staff—and naturally he helps with charities."

"Did your father live in this palace before he became the Sultan?"

"Yes, for a while; it is traditional."

"By the way, I've read about your grandfather—he was very powerful."

"Ah, yes, he was an exemplary ruler."

A servant interrupted us with glasses of orange punch. As the prince held his glass, I noticed the nail on his left little finger was over an inch long. Previously, I had learned this was a sign of royalty. It showed they were above the realm of manual labor.

"Yes, in his reign my grandfather held the power of life and death. But he had many disputes with a neighboring ruler, which took much of his time and energy. He had four wives and many, many concubines— as a consequence he, of course, had many, many children," he said and chuckled.

"What do you think about Indonesia's future?"

"Our future will be very difficult. It will be fifty years until we reach a satisfactory level of development. You must understand that the Dutch left my people with empty heads and empty pocketbooks. When people become better off, a father can give his son a high school education, and in time this son can afford to give his son a college education."

"I imagine you went to college in Jogjakarta?"

"No, I did most of my work in Japan before the war. Here is my girl," he said as he pulled a photograph out of his wallet.

"She's very beautiful."

"Thank you. We were very close, but it would be out of the question to bring her back, since there is so much hatred of the Japanese here—after their occupation." He tilted his head back pensively while sipping the last bit of his orange drink. "My brother is not in residence at the palace now," he said, "but perhaps he might be here tomorrow night. If so, could you join us for dinner?"

"Yes. It's very kind of you."

"I shall have my chauffeur call for you at your hotel around seven," he said, as we walked through the trees in the vast courtyard.

The prospect of dining with royalty in the splendor of an ancient Javanese palace was very exciting. My only suit was inside a bag, which I checked at the air terminal in Djakarta after flying there from Singapore; I decided to wear the shirt and tie packed inside my handbag, trusting it would not be too informal.

The crown prince's chauffeur came for me the next evening and drove me through the dimly-lighted streets into the dark palace courtyard. As I waited near the car, trying to stretch out the remaining wrinkles in my tie, four young men walked from the living quarters in the rear, toward me.

"Good evening," the prince called cheerfully.

"Good evening," I said.

"My friends and I have a special surprise for you. My brother did not return, so this gives us the opportunity to show you how the progressive young Javanese dine."

"That's good," I said, somewhat baffled.

The prince mumbled an order to his driver, before we rambled through a maze of dark streets to a trim house in the suburbs.

"This is my girl's house—not the one I am betrothed to—but this one is most charming," he said, his eyes twinkling. After the prince opened the door, we stepped into a room filled with screeching music and cinnamon-scented cigarette smoke. In the center of the living room, several couples in western dress twirled to a scratchy recording of Glenn Miller's "In the Mood."

"See, we have planned an American-style party for you."

"Wonderful," I said, with false enthusiasm.

The prince's girlfriend, whose black hair was in a bun behind her pretty face, swirled around near several color posters on the wall.

"You like my American movie stars' pictures?" she asked. "There is Betty Grable, Van Heflin and Robert Taylor-man."

"They're very nice."

After we finished our meal of *nasi goreng*, a delicious fried rice dish, the prince's courtly Javanese restraint completely disappeared and never returned. He danced first with his coquettish girl and managed, throughout the evening, to jitterbug and fox-trot with all the other appreciative young ladies. A good deal of my time was spent in one corner teaching my eager students the progressive South American tango.

At three in the morning, the prince and I were the last ones to leave. He beat his hands rhythmically on the hood of his car to awaken his napping chauffeur.

"I think you were surprised we knew so many American dances," he said.

"Yes, I was. I really enjoyed the party, but I'm sorry I didn't meet your brother."

He yawned, then said, "A formal dinner in the palace is very boring—too old fashioned. It is not at all progressive, like our party tonight."

"Before your chauffeur drives me back, could you straighten me out on the 'Solo Man'—the skull?"

He laughed heartily. "It is too early in the morning to talk of skulls."

"I mean the link between man and ape that the scientists found."

"Ah, yes. But understand, I have only a passing interest in archaeology. I was away from the country when the skull was discovered. Just ask at your hotel."

Although I asked at the hotel the next day, no one knew the location where the skull of the "Solo Man" was discovered, and the only information I could find in town confused me. My time in Solo was running out. After hurriedly packing and paying my hotel bill, I scurried out to the street to hire a *betja* to drive me to the bus stop. "Mr. Reeder, Mr. Reeder," someone yelled. In the shade of the trees I saw the Crown Prince of Solo in his chauffeured car.

"I didn't expect to see you," I blurted out.

"Never you mind." We raced over here to give you a lift to the station. An hour ago, my secretary found information on the 'Solo Man.' You can read it on your way to Surabaya."

"I'm grateful...."

On board the crowded bus, I eagerly opened the envelope of papers and spread them out on my lap. I hung my head in frustration when I saw that they were all written in Dutch and Javanese.

*

In the northern seacoast city of Surabaya, Java, the heat of the morning was swelling through the windless streets into the stifling heat of noon. The streets were almost deserted. Everyone in the commercial district was indoors or resting in the shade. Even the flies and mosquitoes were in hiding.

I had arrived by bus from Solo the day before and was exploring sections of the city. In front of one modern store I stopped in amazement. Long show windows radiated with expensive luxury items: gold watches from Switzerland, small radio sets from the Netherlands, and bottles of cologne packaged in silver foil from France. As I examined the goods, a Chinese boy in his teens came out to me with a patronizing smile.

"Please, you must come in. I show everything," he said.

"Fine. But I have no money."

"No matter—I show anyway."

After a leisurely tour past the counters of musty-smelling cloth from Japan to the gleaming jewelry cases in the rear, the boy realized I was not a good prospect.

"Now you have seen everything. If possible, would you be kind enough to meet my father—he is in need of 'American know-how'."

"I'd like to."

We passed through a dim back room where two scrawny bookkeepers methodically clicked the beads of their abacuses while adding stacks of invoices. The boy hesitated a moment before disturbing the pudgy, middle-aged Chinese who gazed from his seat out of the barred window. On the windowsill a half-filled glass of steaming tea held down several papers. Slowly, in tempo with the torpid movement of the city outside, he waved a sweat-stained ivory fan slowly across his face.

After the boy spoke to him in Chinese, the heavy merchant sighed and rose from his cushioned rattan-chair with the labored air of a somnolent buffalo.

"How do you do," he said. "Forgive us for bothering you, but we are in need of some information on universities in your country. In a few years this son and my other one will be ready for university study. I want them to study in America where commerce is number one."

"Well, fine. I'll be glad to give you any information I can."

"That is generous. Then let us discuss it at my home for dinner tonight, if you can. I have several catalogs there from California and New York."

"Good, I'm very fond of Chinese food."

"Excellent. I shall have my cooks prepare—shall we say—a small banquet for you. My son will collect you in the autocar at your hotel around six."

That night the Chinese family and I gathered for supper around the traditional round table in their very comfortable home. Among the many dishes in the center of the table were ginger-steamed carp dressed in parsley, chicken lightly fried with mushrooms and bamboo shoots, and numerous bowls of aromatic Javanese rice. During the meal, the plump mother scolded her daughters, ages six and eight, for giggling. Her sons, who were on either side of the businessman, asked me intelligent questions about life in the United States.

As the servants cleared the table, we settled in the living room for after-dinner coffee. The merchant, who sagged into his chair under an ebony-framed painting of a Chinese elder, snapped his fingers authoritatively and, with a controlled smile, asked his daughters to sing.

Coyly, with almond eyes squinted, the two pony-tailed girls sang a Chinese song about a duck. With each new verse they flapped their arms before stooping down to waddle past their pleased father. After singing another song about a stork, they were dismissed by their father, with a bow; they skipped, giggling, out of the room. Their mother served us an imported creme de menthe and quietly withdrew.

"I wonder if you could tell me the least expensive way to travel to Bali?" I asked the businessman.

"Very simple—do not fly or go by ship. You must take the train to Banjoewangi in south Java, and from there you hire a sailboat."

"Good. Tell me, is that your father in the picture above you?"

"Ahhhh—that is my grandfather," he said with pride. "He came here from China with almost nothing. By hard work and clever trading, he built a modest fortune."

"I understand that the Dutch have treated the Chinese here fairly well."

"For the most part, yes. We Chinese have been accused of being parasites by coming to a country and taking what we can put our hands on. But we fill an important need. We handle the merchandising, which neither the European nor the Javanese is willing to handle."

"If you don't mind my saying it, the main complaint I've heard about the overseas Chinese is that they are loyal to China and not to Indonesia."

"That is not necessarily so. Most of us are loyal to Indonesia. If the Chinese communists come to power here, that is the way it must be. Meanwhile, most of my money is locked away in Geneva," he said with worldly satisfaction.

My evening with the Chinese and his family ended around twelve, after we had discussed American business methods and universities. The merchant's son drove me back to my small hotel in the center of town, where I shared a room with a Dutchman.

"Vat has happened with you?" he asked in bewilderment as I walked into the room. "These roses come for you," he said, pointing to a large vase of four dozen red and white flowers, sitting on the floor. "Has someone died?"

"No, I hope not."

Quickly, I bent down to read the card. "Oh, these are from the Chinese who gave me a magnificent feast tonight," I said.

He laughed and shook his head. "These Chinese are one moment being very ruthless in trading—the next they are very generous. Who can be understanding them?"

~ 8 ~

Bali: This Dream Is Real

Bali, the lush island east of Java, was slowly changing. Yet, in the 1950s, it retained its magic for the few visitors who sailed there. The main religion was a form of Hinduism which was both reverential and joyous.

L ate one night, near the Balinese village of Ubud, I sauntered down a dark lane. After tightening a sarong around my chest, I heard the tinkling strains of a xylophonic *gamelan* orchestra billow into a wave of frenzied sound. A bass gong reverberated. Then the music fell back into a softer, yet more complex, sing-song cadence.

At the entrance to the crowded temple grounds, I leaned over to a girl seated on the ground. Coyly, she pretended not to notice me and continued adjusting a red *frangipani* blossom in her black hair. Light from an oil lamp illuminated her full breasts and golden ear plugs.

"Titiang, djaga numbas sedah," I said, pointing to a tray of shredded tobacco and green pepper leaves. "Please, I'd like to buy some betel-nut." Deftly, she prepared it: sprinkled lime over fragments of broken nuts, folded them into a pepper leaf and offered it to me. An amused crone in the next vendor's stall cackled when I stuffed the mixture into my mouth with the clumsiness of a child. Her teeth and inner lips were darkly stained from many years' use of betel nut. I smiled at her and strode toward a busy area outside the walls of the open-air temple.

With carnival-like exuberance, the sarong-clad Balinese milled about while waiting for the *gamelan* orchestra to resume playing for the nocturnal drama. Under a coconut palm, I sat down next to a middle-aged woman. Her eyes were open, yet she seemed completely unaware of the activity around her. Even the tiny boy squirming on her lap did not arouse her from some unexplained stupor. Several girls sat in front of me. The scent of the coconut oil on their skin was bland compared to the sweet incense filling the air.

Soon, fifteen bare-chested men wearing blue headbands leisurely returned to seats behind their low musical instruments. With wooden mallets these *gamelan* players struck metal keys that were cradled in ornately-carved, wooden frames. In the orchestra's center, an old man tested his set of polished brass bowls by thumping them with padded sticks.

As several boys pumped up the air-pressure lanterns, circling a dirt stage, the drummers finally joined the other players. Mercurially, almost magically, the casual mood vanished. Now the players assumed elegant postures and seemed to be possessed by some unearthly spirit. Everyone grew silent.

Softly, from somewhere in the rear of the orchestra, a delicate introductory melody was tapped out and followed by the twittering of mallets on the other instruments. The sparkling counterpoint proceeded rapidly in the rhythm set by the drummers, whose hands moved like the wings of madly fluttering birds. Within minutes the high-pitched cymbals resound. A deep gong then resolved the first section, giving way to a softer interlude. The music was somewhat like a Bach fugue, with oriental modifications, played by several pipe organs.

At the far end of the stage two clowns appeared from a small curtain. Both of them wore bulging-eyed masks and colorful sarongs. During each pause in their dialogue, the audience trembled with laughter.

For a long time, I listened to the clown's chatter, until the orchestra played an imperious melody for the entrance of the prince. The clowns knelt with their hands clasped in an attitude of prayer as the prince, who wore a white mask with painted red lips, approached. Cymbals rattled and whispered; a gong moaned. After taking mincing steps around the stage, he lifted his right knee and twisted his arms into a stylized pose. As the clowns gave loud words of praise to him, the prince stepped haughtily away.

One comic slapped his own backside and whispered an obscene joke about the ruler, who had danced out of hearing range. The women and children laughed uproariously, but many men seemed bored, as though the humor was much too adolescent. After the laughter subsided, the prince returned to the clowns, who still posed in mock worship.

This long drama of Balinese history continued into the cooler hours of early morning. Frequently, one of the three actors changed behind the curtain, to reappear later as a completely transformed character, both in costume and manner. The children, who drowsed against their parents, awoke each time the music reached a crescendo. During the performance, many people ambled around or clustered near the vendors' tables to nibble peanuts and engage in easy conversation.

As I leaned against the coconut tree to rest my back, I thought about my previous conceptions of Bali. I had expected everyone to move in a highly serious manner. However, unlike Hollywood films, these people were very informal. Only priests and actors assumed airs of solemnity, in contrast to the naturally refined and relaxed ways of the other Balinese. These rituals were far more enjoyable and spontaneous than the highly-structured ceremonies of my Episcopal church at home.

Around three in the morning, I was saturated with the religious drama. I walked barefooted across the rice fields toward my bungalow in the prince's palace. A deep gong echoed. The *gamelan* orchestra continued to play. Glancing back, I saw spokes of light radiate from the trees near the old Hindu temple.

The *puri,* palace, with its maze of brick-walled courtyards, was quiet. I made my way past three thatch-roofed sleeping houses and entered one of the inside courtyards. In this area, near one of the royal dining pavilions, stood my bungalow.

The next morning, after a couple of hours sleep, I awakened to the shrill crowing of fighting cocks. For some time I rested on the hard bamboo bed, stretching my tired legs. The odor of moist thatch drifted through my mosquito netting. Birds fussed in the rafters. A tinkling bell and muffled recitation of Hindu prayers came from the royal temple.

After I tied a working sarong around my waist, one of the prince's retainers served me coffee on the front porch. Early sunlight filtered through the high palms that enclosed the palace and illuminated the tooth-filing pavilion in the center of the courtyard. This small thatch-roofed structure was used for filing front teeth to a pleasing smoothness. In Bali only dogs and demons should have pointed teeth.

Soon I heard the warm laughter of the *Chokorda,* prince, from the whitewashed royal palace. He wound his wristwatch as he strolled along the walkway cutting through the red-flowered canna plants. He was a jolly, middle-aged man with a green-checkered sports shirt over his sarong. According to Balinese standards, his face was handsome, with a blunt nose and broad cheekbones.

"Good morning to you," he said in the English he had learned from his many foreign guests.

"Good morning, *Chokorda.*"

"How did you enjoy the festival last night?"

"Very much, but I got tired and left early," I said, as we relaxed in bamboo chairs.

"Ah, you must be trying to see too much if you became tired."

"Well, maybe so," I said.

"Do you realize that I had the same difficulty when I traveled? It was when I visited my brother in Java. I was kept busy all day and night by the fast and formal pace of things there. Do you realize that I had to change shirts three times each day? Think of it—three times!"

"That does seem too much."

"Even my taxi driver went too fast. In fact, his face was made sad by the speed. Ah, yes, but here the pace is relaxed. That will be my last trip away from here for some time. Why should I go when everything is here?"

"I don't imagine you would like the whirlwind pace of life in my country. We rush continually."

"What a pity, what a pity. Other Americans have told me this, too. When do you relax with nature?"

"Well, most of us take weekend trips or vacations."

"But these trips are too short," he said with a wrinkled forehead. "You must excuse me now; I must dress for a visit to a prince near here. Notify my servants if you need anything."

"Thanks, but I'll be around the temples and rice fields today."

"Good, but do not rush—this is not America," he said laughing, and then, humming with contentment, returned to his bungalow.

Later, I strolled to the courtyard of the farm family with whom I had been working. The muscular young father, Karma, leaned over a dome-shaped basket containing his black and yellow fighting cock.

"Good morning," he said.

"Hello," I said, "are we still going to the fights?"

"Yes, yes, and you will bring me the luck to win."

After working in wet rice fields with Karma and his son, I ate and napped in the shade of his compound. In the afternoon, Karma and I set out for a cockfight in a distant village. As we hurried along the trail, two roosters swung in cages at opposite ends of a bamboo pole, which rested over Karma's shoulder. In an isolated spot he lowered the fowls to the ground; from his headband he pulled out a red pepper and forced bits of the hot pod into his rooster's beaks.

"This gives magic power," he confided in a whisper.

"But isn't this against the rules?" I asked.

"Against them?—there are no rules outside the fighting place."

At last we walked by the straw-topped walls of several living compounds and onto the far side of the village, where the men were gathered around the fighting pavilion. Karma took the black cock out of his front basket and stroked it solicitously as he crouched down. Several men approached him with their roosters, to learn if the birds had a natural antagonism for each other. But it was not until a young man placed a white cock before Karma's that a good match was found. The two birds flicked their heads to the side to appraise each other. Suddenly both roosters attacked. Everyone smiled and murmured with delight—this was a worthy match.

After the bets were placed with the timekeeper, the judge lashed a five-inch steel blade on the right leg of each bird. Karma squatted in the center of the pavilion's dirt floor, with his rooster facing its opponent. He nimbly ruffled the hackle feathers on his cock's neck and pinched its comb. The opposing white bird lunged forward and withdrew. From the corner the old timekeeper struck a high-pitched gong as he dropped half of a coconut's inner shell into a water pot. Both men eased back from their birds, and all was silent.

The roosters were motionless for some time. With flapping wings and bent heads, they loped towards each other. In a gray blur, they clashed. Broken feathers swirled in the air as they parted. A few men began jeering. Karma's bird backed away a few steps before turning and forcing the other fowl back into the air. Cautiously, the roosters circled each other, feinting and striking with their steel spurs. When the coconut shell with a tiny hole in its center sank in the waterpot, the timekeeper sounded his gong. The first round of the fight ended.

Karma tightened the thread on his bird's gaff and fondled its blood-dampened feathers. In a moment, the gong silenced the men while the two gamecocks were again paired off. With sudden anger, the white rooster forced Karma's fowl into the men who hunkered down on the front row. The judge prodded the cocks back into the ring with a bamboo stick. The white bird limped. Blood trickled down the legs of Karma's bird. Again, both roosters flashed out against each other. They circled and attacked again and again. Feathers and dust filled the air. Voices of the men clashed. My breathing was shallow. Karma moaned.

In an unexpected frenzy, the opposing fowl soared into the air and slashed its blade down through the breast of Karma's bird. The audience cried out. Karma's eyes closed, as his bird reeled and fell—a tattered mess of feathers and blood. The crippled winner lashed out at the defeated bird several more times. Satisfied that he was the victor, the other bird seemed to prance around the dying fowl with an intoxicated arrogance.

After Karma removed the blade from his fowl, he put the body near his basket and returned to watch several more fights without betting. Gradually his anger and disgust over losing his bird subsided. Near the end of the afternoon he saw a rooster that pleased him. The owner allowed Karma to toy with it to test the rooster's weight and strength. Convinced this was a good bet, Karma handed the timekeeper several *rupiah* notes and squatted down on the front row. His arms dangled over his knees in the customary Balinese manner for watching such events.

The birds fought well in the first period, but when the gong sounded for the second period, the cock on which Karma bet proved to be cowardly. Each time the other bird charged, Karma's favorite retreated. With one hand an old farmer waved at the timid rooster to charge; with the other, he motioned for the aggressive rooster to retreat. Voices fell in disgust. Someone handed the judge a bell-shaped basket. He slapped it over the retreating rooster and with a stick pushed the other one inside. Both birds were forced to fight. Wings scraped against the basket while the judge held it down. Steel blades caught the sunlight. When the judge lifted the basket, the cock Karma had bet on was on the ground breathing rapidly.

With an expressionless face, Karma left the cockpit and hoisted the baskets over his shoulder. The spare rooster that did not fight was in the rear basket, while the front one was embarrassingly empty. I carried the dead bird, which would be in tomorrow's cooking pot, as we strode toward his village.

My feelings toward the cockfight were mixed. I enjoyed the color and the excitement, yet I was somewhat disgusted and unsettled by the suffering of the birds. Karma, like many other Balinese men, was addicted to this sport. His wife's bad-tempered outbursts rankled him a bit, but they did little to prevent his attending the cockfights.

After hanging the dead fowl in the family's cookshed, I left Karma, as he sulked in a far corner of his compound. Walking toward the palace, I heard the nagging voice of Meta, his wife, rise above the crickets that had come to life in the late afternoon.

The brief tropical twilight reduced the high, brick walls of the royal *puri* to shadows. I sprawled in a chair on the front porch of my sleeping house. My feet ached from walking barefooted. A nephew of the *Chokorda* moved slowly through the courtyards to kindle the coconut oil lamps. As he ignited those around my pavilion, the dark stone gods and demons on the walls were reborn in a wavering, yellow light. On top of one inner gate the statue of *Barong*, the powerful yet good-natured lion, glowered with bulging eyes over the compound.

Voices and laughter from an adjoining enclosure mingled with the sobs of caged doves; soon, a servant brought my meal. After eating a mound of spiced rice with chunks of pork, I tossed a few scraps from my banana-leaf plate to the dog that usually browsed around our *puri*.

"Ah, I see you like dogs," the prince called, as he emerged from the shadows.

"Yes, I do. Is he yours?" I asked.

"He belongs to no person, but he likes it here so I allow him to stay," the *Chokorda* said, as he settled into a chair. "I trust the dogs do not keep you awake."

"Oh, no. I'm too tired."

"Good, but some of my visitors in the past have complained. I think we have ten times more dogs in Bali than people. They make much noise but serve a valuable function to frighten the evil spirits."

A warm breeze swept across the palace and made the oil lamps flicker. Enjoying the Balinese twilight, we remained silent for several minutes.

"Next week we must go to the fair in a neighboring village. Oh, I am sure you will like it. Then, in three months, there will be several cremations near *Ubud*. Cremations are happy occasions—they must be, since the soul must leave the body amid the joy of the living. Then, of course, the soul returns into another body later."

"I've read about them in the book, *Island of Bali*. Are they really so expensive?"

"Indeed, yes. Many people must spend all their savings for them. Yet it must be done. In fact, I am still indebted for the cremation of one of my relatives."

"I wish I could stay for the cremations, but I have to leave in a few weeks."

The *Chokorda* laughed deeply. "Just as I have said; you Americans cannot stop rushing."

As the *Chokorda* left, some time later, he stopped near my bungalow and tilted his head, close to a flowering plant.

"Listen," he whispered.

"What is it?"

"This cricket—it has a very delicate note. One of the best I have heard in a long time."

"It does?"

"That should be good music for you to sleep by," he said, as he continued down the path.

Gradually, I lapsed into a peaceful state of semi-consciousness while resting in my bamboo bed. Before sleeping, I heard the whine of mosquitoes circling my net, and the distant reverberation of a temple gong.

Several nights later, when returning from a festival in a neighboring village, I heard a sudden stir in the underbrush. An immense, swaybacked pig slid down the bank onto the moonlit road. I chortled in astonishment. The pig snorted and continued to follow closely behind me. Even though I shouted in its face many times, the pig refused to be frightened away.

I followed my shadow, flowing smoothly in front of me, thinking of the rare pleasure of experiencing the daily life of Balinese royalty and also of the farmers. The rice wine I drank at the festival gave my head a dreamlike lightness. If their belief in reincarnation were true, I should like to be included in the wheel of rebirth as a farmer. After a few hours in the rice fields, each day, I could be a sculptor or dancer and attend the exciting village festivals every night. I might even take up cockfighting and hopefully have more luck than my friend Karma had. My life would be relaxed and full of creative contentment.

Night birds skimmed and wheeled across the treetops of the royal compound as I walked through the arched entrance. From somewhere in the *puri,* a dog was barking. Once again I tried to scare the pig away, but it trotted along behind me into the outer courtyard. Finally it disappeared in the dark, leaving behind a pungent odor.

The next morning, as we walked through the compound, I told the prince about the pig.

"It is very rare for a pig to follow a person," he said gravely.

"The one last night followed me for—I guess—over five miles."

"It must be black magic, yes—black magic. You were followed by a reincarnated woman."

"A reincarnated woman?" I asked, and tried to subdue a cynical smile.

"Yes, this is unfortunate."

"Is anything supposed to happen to me?"

"It is a very bad sign, but since you are not Balinese, *perhaps* no harm will come to you."

Several evenings later, the *Chokorda* dispatched his chief servant to help me dress in a formal sarong. In a few hours, a fair in the neighboring village of Gianjar would begin. Soon the prince, his two wives, and I were pressed inside his antique Chevrolet with two of his waiting relatives. As the chauffeur drove us slowly along the road cutting through the trees, everyone chatted happily, except the prince's two reserved wives, who stared impassively out of the windows. I was so accustomed to seeing them bare-breasted that I felt strangely embarrassed by their ornate, full-bodied sarongs.

At a downhill curve in the road, a few puffs of steam escaped from under the hood. The chauffeur put the car into neutral, and we continued to roll forward. At the bottom we skidded to a stop. White clouds of steam billowed from the hood. The *Chokorda* snickered as if accustomed to the shortcomings of modern machinery.

"Aha," he said, "I had a feeling this was to be. It often happens. We can walk about while my nephew goes for water."

"Do you think we'll be late for the fair?" I asked.

"Yes, but it makes no difference; it continues all night."

After the radiator was cooled with fresh water, we chugged along to the huge, thatched arch marking the entrance to the fairground. Inside, the sarong-clad Balinese eddied about the many rows of thatch-roofed shops and eating sheds with the ease of people moving in a dream. One loud-speaker belched out sentimental Javanese recordings while another speaker announced the raffle of a bicycle propped high on a bamboo platform. The metallic clattering of a *gamelan* orchestra in a far pavilion was barely audible.

The *Chokorda* and I stopped in one shed to examine an exhibit of sculpture carved for the tourist market.

"What a pity, what a pity," he said, as he ran his fingers over a fragrant sandalwood carving of a rooster. "This was worked on with too much speed. Look at the feathers—the detail is not good."

"Is this fish any better?" I asked.

"Yes, it has elegance and style—just like the carvings of old Bali. You know, the best things are not made for selling; they are made as a tribute to the gods."

Later, the prince and I rested in an elevated pavilion where we surveyed the fairground. We sipped a warm fruit drink and nibbled on dragonflies fried in coconut oil. Although the *Chokorda* greeted and talked affably with those who passed, he was always careful to keep his princely head elevated above his subjects. While I strolled around the fairgrounds, he engaged in light-hearted conversation with a neighboring prince.

I passed by a group of men, seated on the ground, who were playing a variation of mah-jongg by the light of an air-pressure lantern. Then I entered a pavilion containing a health display. A government nurse from Java was talking to a few people about the fundamentals of sanitation. Behind her were posters showing how flies and mosquitoes spread disease. In another tent an agricultural expert was lecturing to a large number of farmers on modern methods of soil conservation. Proudly, this official leaned against a gleaming red tractor given to the Indonesians by the Russian government.

As I walked by one gaming booth, I saw Karma, who was trying to pitch a ring over a post.

"Are you winning?" I asked.

"No, no, I have no luck. But this afternoon my rooster won me much. Why you not come to watch?" he asked.

"I was in the *puri* reading. By the way, Karma, do you mind if I take your son on the Ferris wheel?"

"The big wheel—no, if you can find him," he said, continuing to fling one ring after another toward the post.

Much later, in a far corner of the grounds, I found his son, Lintar, sleeping with his head on his knees. He came to life quickly when I nudged him and pointed to the forty-foot-high wheel. We whirled around many times on the wooden contraption, while two men turned us by shifting their weight inside the spokes like hamsters in a treadmill. Lintar seemed to enjoy the rotating thrill of this foreign innovation with so much exuberance that I paid the Chinese manager to keep him spinning for thirty minutes. Dizzily, I stumbled away and regained my balance.

Some time after midnight, a slender young man wearing an ill-fitting Western suit gave me an inquisitive smile. I was garbed in a traditional Balinese sarong and wore no shoes. As we smiled at each other, a small crowd collected.

"I am a chauffeur in the city of Den Pasar," he said proudly.

"I am, er- well, a farmer from near here," I said with mock-seriousness.

When he explained this in Balinese to the amused people, their laughter soared above the volume of music from the loud-speakers.

Before leaving the fair, the *Chokorda* decided it was time to ride the Ferris wheel. Slowly he was whirled around by the two men inside the spokes. Throughout the trip he waved and smiled at those of us on the ground. As the wheel came to a stop, his laughter subsided.

"I am very happy," he said as he emerged from his seat.

"I am, too," I said.

Around three in the morning, the prince, his retinue and I climbed sleepily into the royal car which rattled back to the palace. After our car passed through the entrance gate of the outer courtyard, a puff of steam sprayed up from the overheated radiator.

"Ah, this time we just arrived. I think I will let the motorcar rest quietly for a day or so," the prince said, as we walked toward our sleeping houses.

On the morning that I boarded a bus destined for the south seacoast of Bali, the *Chokorda* came over to my front porch.

"This is not worthy," he said, giving me a finely carved wooden bird. "But it is, at least, a small departure gift."

"I like it very much."

Hurriedly, I excused myself and returned with the stone head of the Lord Buddha that the guide in Java had given me. "I want you to have this. It comes from Borobudur."

"Ah, what a rare gift indeed. Buddha was a remarkable man. Perhaps he was even divine. But who am I to question? I prefer not to dwell on foreign deities; I am kept quite busy with the gods of Bali," he said, and smiled.

When the crowded bus stopped in front of the palace gate, we shook hands in the light Balinese fashion.

"*Chokorda*, I'm really going to miss Ubud. It was like living in a dream."

He chuckled and said, "But *this* dream is real."

~ 9 ~

Sailing In Balinese Waters

After the Korean War, there were only a few government gunboats to patrol the waters around the numerous islands. Smugglers and other criminals could do as they pleased.

Walking along the black sands of a west Balinese fishing village, I saw a group of men wading out to meet a sailboat. Their cries mingled with screeching sea gulls. In anticipation, many children ran through the surf with the speed of sandpipers, while their elders kept dry on the beach. Booming waves crashed and sprayed everyone with a briny mist. The arrival of an inbound *prahu*, outrigger boat, from Java gave the villagers a pleasant break in their routine.

Without warning, the wind soared away from the sail and pelted the Balinese with sand. The sail flapped hungrily for air, then fell limp. On the next wave the white boat with its two outriggers bobbed closer to shore. As it drifted to the waiting men, the captain and his two mates unfastened the sail and lowered the mast into its "V"-shaped bamboo supports. The captain barked orders to the men in the water.

Boldly, he stood in the bow while directing their efforts to pull the boat onto the beach. Initially, I thought he was wearing a patch over one eye, but as he came closer I noticed that he was wearing sunglasses with one lens missing. A blue turban and ragged sarong tied around his waist gave him the appearance of a pirate in a comic opera.

An incoming wave helped the men beach the heavy cargo boat. Everyone crowded around the boat while the crew, and several villagers discussed which goods should be off-loaded. There was no hurry, since news from Javanese and other Balinese ports came first. After some twenty minutes, the captain ordered his mates to lower two bicycles to a Chinese merchant and his sons. Later, the captain and crew loaded boxes on the heads of several women who carried them gracefully in single file toward the village.

With the flourish of a snake oil salesman, the captain riveted the attention of the remaining villagers, while his crew held up various items that were for sale or barter. An old fisherman traded a basket of dried fish and carefully counted out many *rupiahs* for an air-pressure lantern. Eagerly, the women spread out bolts of cheap foreign cloth and discussed possible uses for it. It seemed that the Balinese were ingenious at incorporating foreign items and making them uniquely their own. After some two hours the interest of the Balinese waned, and they strolled back to the village.

Finally, I ambled over to the captain, who was sewing a patch on his sail.

"May I be a passenger on your boat?" I boldly asked, in Indonesian. *"Boleh saja numpang perahumu?"*

He seemed startled, and pondered my question for a long time. *"Tak bisa,"* he said. "That's impossible."

Then, to my surprise, he smiled cunningly and yelled at his mates to open several cargo boxes. They paraded a bewildering array of trade goods before me. It became apparent that if I were to make a purchase, he might consider my travel request. I bargained with him for a sports shirt and several tins of Dutch beef. While paying him, I asked about the missing lens in his dark glasses. He laughed raucously and snapped the remaining lens out of the frame. Before replacing it, he enjoyed seeing me cringe, as I gazed at his diseased eye. Rudely, the captain then turned his back and continued stitching his sail. Angrily I left, since I knew that any further discussion would be useless. As I walked toward the village, I could hear him laughing with his mates over the fun he had with the red-faced foreigner.

After buying some rice cakes, papayas and mangoes from a vendor, I settled down on a deserted part of the beach. This was my third attempt to find a village with a long-distance sailing boat in port. It had been my dream, while on my enormous aircraft carrier, to find such a craft. Maybe tomorrow I would hitchhike to another village. Unable to sleep, I waded through the shallow water along the beach. Finally, I rested against a palm tree and grew drowsy. The gray night passed slowly and disgustingly, measured only by the slow strokes of the surf.

The next morning I awoke to find the brazen captain standing over me. Before I could explain what was in my tattered bag, he opened it and spread a few of the contents on the sand. In a gruff manner, completely unlike that of the refined farmers of south Bali, he fingered my khaki shirts and leafed through my paperback books. To keep him from finding the valuable telescope hidden in my bag, I tried to amuse him by squirting spray deodorant in the air. Appreciatively, he sniffed the fragrance and marveled at the green plastic bottle. I ceremoniously screwed the top on and held it away from him, pretending that it was a very costly object.

Impulsively, he grabbed the bottle from me. In sign language and soft-lipped Indonesian, he told me I could sail on his boat if I gave him a pair of trousers, a belt, a flashlight and the deodorant. After several very necessary denials, I finally consented to part with these "valuable" possessions. Soon we were walking side by side down to his outrigger.

With the help of several fishermen, we pushed the boat into the surf and hoisted the sail into the south wind. Throughout the day the captain enthusiastically squirted the prized deodorant on his hair and neck. During each application the boys scampered across the cargo boxes to smell the exotic American deodorant.

The wind billowed our sail as we tacked into a quiet cove. Beneath the palms lining its beach were seven outrigger fishing boats. With large eyes painted on their bows, these *prahus* looked like mythological sea monsters luxuriating in their seaside lair. We passed several men who cast small nets while they waded in the turquoise water. Bare-breasted women gazed at us from the shore. Eventually, we dragged our craft onto the beach.

After the captain put out the display of his goods, including my former trousers, belt and flashlight, the young sailing mates and I strolled down the beach for a swim. Quickly, they stepped out of their sarongs and ran into the surf. Their buttocks were surprisingly light while the rest of their bodies were baked dark brown by the sun. On drifting out shoulder-deep in the green froth, the mates grew apprehensive and dog-paddled toward the shore. Although they were good sailors, they were poor swimmers. Perhaps the strong Indonesian fear of water demons made them feel uneasy when they were away from the relative safety of their boat.

That night a rapid thumping came from a hollow log drum in the village to announce the performance of the *gamelan* orchestra. My shipmates and I joined the others in the shadows outside the temple where the orchestra played for several hours. It was unrefined and much louder than the elegant music near the *Chokorda's* palace. Yet this music had a fresh and appealing primitive charm.

At the fringes of the crowd, the captain and I saw a boy dozing with two small monkeys beside him. I was eager to buy one for a pet. The seaman agreed to handle the entire transaction for me. In a loud voice, he awakened the youth and badgered him into selling a monkey for the equivalent of three American dollars.

The next morning we cast off into a smooth sea with the frightened monkey tethered to the mast. When our mascot relaxed a little in his new environment, we released him, so that he could climb about freely. Because he continually chattered, I nicknamed him "Windy," after a loudmouthed boatswain's mate on my aircraft carrier.

As we sailed along, I stood my watch at the tiller, under the guidance of the captain. The telescope that I had hidden in the bottom of my bag enabled me to see ships on the horizon clearly. It also intrigued the captain, who commandeered it for his own use. He cussed at his mates when they wanted to borrow it. As he was in command, I let him have his way. He was pleased that it fit perfectly through the opening of his empty sunglass frame.

Occasionally, I would lie in the shade of the sail and read or daydream. Rising from the clouds in the distance was a massive volcanic mountain that seemed to sway as our boat rocked across the waves. To our south, a cruise ship lounged on the horizon. Here, as in all Bali, I came to know and finally appreciate the relaxing experience of living almost entirely in the open. I had a contented feeling of being close to the elements. Now and then, however, I longed to escape into the darkness of some air-conditioned room.

When the bottle of spray deodorant no longer gave up its sweet juices, the captain grew irritated. In sign language, I explained that the fragrance would not renew itself. Once he understood the concept, he searched around the deck for materials to solve his problem. With typical Indonesian ingenuity, he crushed some flowers into a bowl filled with coconut oil. After mixing spices with this, he poured the concoction into the plastic bottle. Now he could mirthfully squirt us with the new ingredients.

Chanting a song of contentment, he disappeared to the bow of the ship and returned with a dagger. Its silver blade sparkled in the light, as he slipped it out of the scabbard. While I examined the jeweled handle, I wondered if this dagger were intended for barter or even battle. Before

I could fully appreciate this artifact, he grabbed it and hid it somewhere in the stern of the boat.

One afternoon, dark clouds pressed down on us, carrying with them the stench of decaying tropical foliage. Warm rain stung us while the sea began to wobble like an unending mass of green gelatin. A sudden stab of lightning took our breaths as thunder crashed through our bamboo mast and outriggers, sending Windy screeching to the bow. Immediately, we lashed down the cargo. I felt apprehensive. Windy trembled.

Impulsively, we hauled down the sail. The storm was taking us away from the coast like a piece of driftwood. We tied ourselves to the deck. To stand would be foolhardy. As I carefully crawled to the bow to retrieve our mascot, a heavy breaker splashed across us and rumbled toward the distant shore. Windy toppled overboard.

The storm quickly vanished, and we began searching for Windy. After sailing in circles for over an hour, we had little hope of finding Windy. Suddenly, we saw him on our port side, bobbing along on top of the waves. Our expectations soared. We quickly paddled toward our mascot. Another wave slung our boat across the gray-foamed water and into a trough where Windy floated. I held a bamboo pole out and called to him. Rescue seemed eminent.

Rocking closer, we could see that the object we thought was Windy was nothing more than a split coconut husk. The captain and crew seemed disheartened. I was crestfallen and seasick.

When the storm swept over the mainland, we hoisted our sail and tacked closer to the shore. The captain tore a small square from a banana leaf, sprinkled it with rice and dropped it overboard, then chanted an Islamic prayer for our mascot's spirit.

For several days we sailed from one port to another, trading with different people and transporting their wares to various markets. After rounding the southern tip of Bali, we skimmed with the breezes toward the northeast.

Shortly before sunset we put ashore in the quiet village of Kusamba on the east coast. After eating fish and rice, we spread our mats on the warm sands and went to sleep early. During the night I was awakened by something. At first, I listened, but could locate nothing dangerous. Peering through the starlight, I saw the two mates sleeping near the outrigger. Slowly, I turned to search for the captain, who slept at the stern of the boat. His mat was vacant.

When my eyes grew more adjusted to the dim light, I saw a dark figure glide along the far side of the boat. The figure seemed to drift aboard and vanish. Breathing heavily, I waited for several minutes. Soon this figure stood erect. It was the captain.

After peering at me, he seemed to conclude that I was fast asleep. Soon he bent over to open my bag. With the skill of a cat-burglar, he rummaged through my belongings. Stealthily, he took out my telescope. After peering at the stars, he took the telescope and secured it in a box near the mast.

Like a serpent, he slithered over the gunnels of the boat, crawled through the bamboo outriggers and curled up on his sleeping mat. Satisfied that I was still asleep, he lit a clove cigarette and hummed a minor-keyed melody to the slow beat of the surf. Finally, he drifted into sleep.

My mounting rage kept me awake. I walked down the beach and quietly returned to the far side of the craft. Without hesitation, I slipped aboard to look for my telescope. Now and then I glanced at the captain and the mates to see if they were still asleep. I did not find my telescope, but I found other things of interest. My search continued until the gray light of the approaching day glimmered over the ocean.

After sunrise, the captain was frantic to get under way. Wildly, he shouted orders. I attempted to talk to him. No matter how hard I tried, he pretended not to understand me. Additionally, he demanded that I give him more *rupiahs* for my passage on his boat. He made it apparent that he would not give my bag to me unless I paid him.

Begrudgingly, I handed him a few *rupiahs* and grumbled several choice naval phrases at him. He seemed to understand the harsh tone of my English expletives.

"Selamat tinggal," he yelled defiantly as the outrigger floated out with the tide. "Good-bye."

"Good-bye," I yelled in English, "you pirate bastard."

As the outrigger continued to drift out, he threw my bag to me while I sloshed through the surf. A few minutes later, the captain hoisted his inverted triangular sail, and it ballooned in the wind. With a gleeful look, he put my telescope to his good eye and focused on me.

From my bag, I slowly and proudly withdrew the captain's best ceremonial sarong and his jewel-encrusted dagger. In a triumphant farewell gesture, I held them high in the early morning sunlight.

~ 10 ~

Pain In Paradise

During the reign of the Dutch, Japanese and, later, free-Indonesian government, inadequate health care was provided for the Balinese people. Many decades would pass before conditions improved.

After waving defiantly to the captain, I boarded a bus that trundled down a forest road leading to a coastal village. Outside a primary school, I called through the open windows to the teacher. He invited me inside and read the letter of introduction that the *Chokorda* had given me. The teacher's bright disposition changed when he finally understood my destination. He mumbled something to the students, whose excitement on seeing a foreigner quickly disappeared. Whispers filled the room. The students' faces registered shock and disbelief.

With a grave expression the teacher dispatched a boy to escort me toward my destination. As we strolled through the schoolyard, a noisy soccer game came to a halt when my guide explained who I was and where I was going. The dark eyes of the players widened with curiosity. Usually, the children in Bali eagerly returned my smiles and waves, but not at this remote playground.

Soon the student led me to the entrance of an isolated dirt road leading to the coast. He stopped suddenly. In a voice cracked by fear, he muttered "Boegboeg—Boegboeg." I had the impression that swarms of insects were lying in wait for me. After pointing down the road, he turned and ran toward the village. In a minute, he returned to retrieve the gratuity that he had dropped. Flashing an embarrassed smile, he again sprinted off.

Although apprehensive over the reactions of the teacher and students, I was comforted by the peaceful scenery. Before me was a view worthy of a two-page spread in an expensive travel book. A meadow, dotted by tan cattle, dipped into the sea. As the cows munched on the grass near the red flowering trees, their wooden bells merged with the murmuring surf. At the end of the meadow, a coconut grove curved around a serene inlet.

The road led me to a dismal barbed wire compound that reminded me of a prison camp; I breathed a little faster. Now I could fully understand why the villagers stayed away. A sign in English warned me:

LEPROSARIUM OF BOEGBOEG

Sakit Gede or the "Great Sickness" could take an unfortunate Balinese from his well-adjusted village life and isolate him until death in a lonely colony. Being exiled from the village is a punishment reserved only for criminals and lepers.

After a moment's hesitation at the gate of the compound, I decided to enter, remembering that the disease is rarely contagious. Three old women who were chatting in the shade of the wooden clinic glanced at me with startled expressions. One of them cried out angrily. Her tan legs were puffed with pink and black sores; her fingertips had been destroyed by the disease.

Beyond the clinic, in the center of the compound, stood a large cooking pavilion flanked by two rows of tile-roofed huts for the patients. Sitting down on his front porch, an old man stared with despair into space. He ignored my greeting. With her only pliable hand, a pug-nosed girl of about sixteen was scattering peanuts along the ground to dry in the sun. Her other hand was useless since the fingers curled into her palm. She offered a smile. Able to work, she appeared less depressed than the other patients.

Some time later the young caretaker strode into the compound from the beach with a fishing net over his shoulders. After reading my letter of introduction, he welcomed me warmly and led me outside the compound where several lepers were thatching a roof on one of the cattle sheds. Nearby, a rice paddy was partially filled with squawking ducks. For the most part the colony was self-sufficient, and those who could work were encouraged to do so.

"Berapa sering dokter datang?" I asked, while thumbing through my phrase book. "How often does the doctor come?"

"Ekali sepuluh nari," the caretaker replied. "Every ten days."

"Apakah dia bisa mengobat itu penjakit?" I asked. "Does he stop the disease from spreading?"

"Sekali—sekali dapat," he said, and frowned. "Sometimes yes; sometimes, no."

The petite wife of the caretaker served me *arrack*, rice wine, in their comfortable hut. After expressing my interest in the welfare of the patients, I guiltily gave him the dagger and sarong which I had "borrowed" from the sea captain. Perhaps he could trade these items for extra medicine which the lepers could use. Although he seemed highly pleased with the gifts, he was confounded that I owned such valuable articles.

Before sunset, the caretaker and I returned to the compound. I found an old lady and asked her to pose for a photograph. With the help of the caretaker, I finally persuaded the shrunken-breasted woman to stand alone and gaze at a distant bluff. I wanted to emphasize the pain and loneliness of a Balinese leper who must suffer amid such harmonious scenery.

As directed, she tilted her head back and looked mournfully at the bluff. While I stooped down to focus my camera, several of her old friends hobbled on their leprous feet to join her. I chuckled at my vain attempt to editorialize, and snapped the picture. Even though the lepers are outcasts of their old communities, the members of the colony seemed to have developed a warm camaraderie in suffering.

After sleeping in a vacant hut in the barbed wire compound, I arose early and strolled along the seashore. In an hour or two, the morning bus would stop in the village. As I left the compound, I saw a young man resting on the front porch of his hut. His head seemed to be bent with sorrow. His hand rested lovingly on a fighting rooster cage. This bell-shaped enclosure was in shambles and depressingly empty.

Later in the day, I caught a bus to Bali's largest city, Den Pasar. It took me little time to find and check in at an inexpensive, back-street Chinese hotel. Den Pasar was very disappointing. Movie houses and blocks of colorless shops that displayed tacky European goods and Balinese tourist figurines cheapened the scene. Tomorrow I planned on traveling by bus to the north, where the countryside was unspoiled.

Before settling into my small, windowless room for the night, I ate bowls of steamed vegetables in a Chinese restaurant. That night I fell asleep listening to the shrieks of children running in the halls and the laughter of four old men in the next cubicle playing Mah-Jongg.

During the night, I was startled into consciousness by someone knocking at my door. As I opened the door, a beam of light struck my face and a dark hand yanked me into the hallway. Completely blinded, and in a whirlwind of confusion, I stumbled into a fleshy object.

"Please pardon, but—" a voice whispered from the dark.

"Who are you?" I demanded.

"I am innkeeper. Two police have come for you," he said.

"Me! Why?"

"A story in the newspaper tells you are United States Naval Officer. You signed register as student. This is illegal."

"But I am no longer a naval officer. I'm a civilian—traveling as a student," I explained.

"We will just see. Give them your passport. This they will read at headquarters."

Slowly, the police turned the flashlight down from my face onto the passport and took it with them as they marched out of the dark hotel. Agitated, I returned to bed.

The next morning, around ten o'clock, an official jeep stopped outside the small hotel lobby. Four policemen in khaki uniforms marched inside and sat down around me. The innkeeper served everyone small cups of bitter coffee.

"We do not have the understanding why you stay this place instead of the number-one tourist hotel," a young police officer finally said.

"I can't afford it; I'm on a *very low* budget."

"We must apologize then; we thought you were hiding here. Do you remember the government official you met in Singaradja, Bali?"

"Oh, yes—he gave me a letter of introduction to a prince near here."

"The official thought you remained in the navy—all foreign military personnel must be registered. You see, he checked with the Chief of Army Staff and found you were not registered. Also, your embassy did not know of you. It was then an order was issued for your arrest. That is why newspapers all over Indonesia and even in far away Singapore have had stories asking people to search for you."

"Oh—and they couldn't find me because I was living in a small village," I said.

"That is so. It was a national and international manhunt. But since your passport says you are a student, you are free to go."

When the police roared down the street in their jeep, the innkeeper, in his black pajamas, shuffled over to me and grinned.

"I am sorry you miss bus," he said, "but there will be one in a few days. Meanwhile, I am pleased to have you remain as my customer."

"I'll bet you are," I said. Both of us laughed.

A couple of days later I stuffed myself into an overcrowded bus, which hummed along with surprising speed over the unpaved roads to the north. The passengers gazed with boredom at the rice fields and the shadowy forests. Only when the bus killed a dog did they show any interest. Then a series of embarrassed snickers rippled through the bus. Perhaps they laughed with amusement or because of their belief that one must be happy when a soul leaves the body.

After a good night's rest at a small inn in the village of Negara, I awoke at daybreak, lathered my face with a bar of soap and shaved in a cool pan of water. As I buttoned my khaki trousers and sports shirt, I heard a loud knock on my door.

"Yes?" I said.

"We are police," someone said.

"Are what?" I asked.

"We are police."

After I finished shaving, two policemen escorted me down the palm-lined street to their headquarters, a white building with a red tile roof.

Inside, I was seated in a large room where I waited for over an hour. At last, several military policemen wandered in and pulled up chairs in a circle around me. In an arrogant manner one officer examined my passport.

"We have standing orders to take you to Den Pasar," he said.

"But your police there looked at my passport and let me go."

"This can be so, but we cannot believe you. I think you can be a Russian spy in disguise of an American officer."

"That's absurd—I am an American student."

"We shall see," he said, as he walked toward a map of the world on the wall. "Now tell me, what is the precise distance from Boston to San Diego?"

"I guess it's around two thousand miles."

"Wrong," he said with delight.

"You must tell me the capital city of Delaware," another officer demanded.

"Is it Wilmington?"

"It is Dover," he said disdainfully.

"Without looking at the map, I wonder if you can tell me how far it is from Medan, Sumatra, to your village?" I brazenly asked.

On leave, the author climbed Mount Fuji at night with a group of young naval officers. Near exhaustion after racing to the summit to film the sunrise, he was the last of this group to descend the mountain.

Shortly after climbing
Mount Fuji, the author visited the Buddha of Kamakura
to continue his inquiry into
different religions

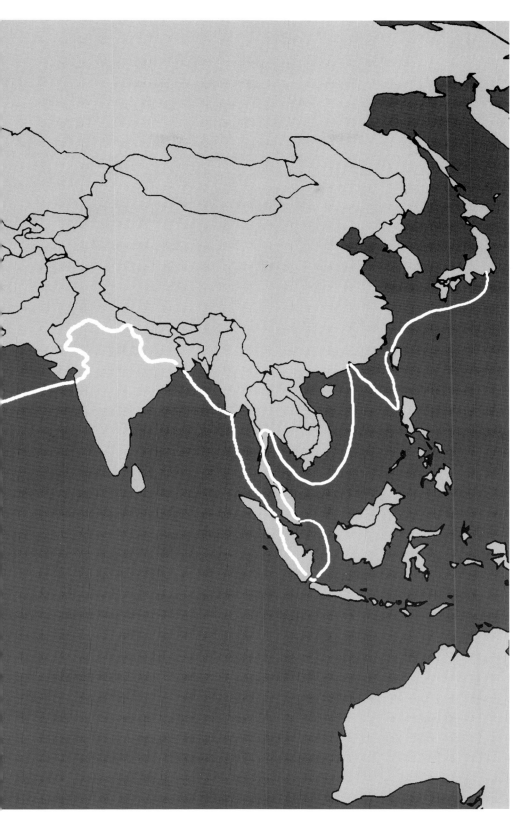

During the latter part of the Korean War, the *U.S.S Point Cruz* (CVE 119) an escort carrier, w
on anti-submarine patrol in Korean waters.

Aboard the *U.S.S. Point Cruz*, the author served in the communications, engineering and gunnery div
sions

After being released from active duty, the author travled on a student passport and smoked the pipe of exotic dreams in this Bangkok opium den.

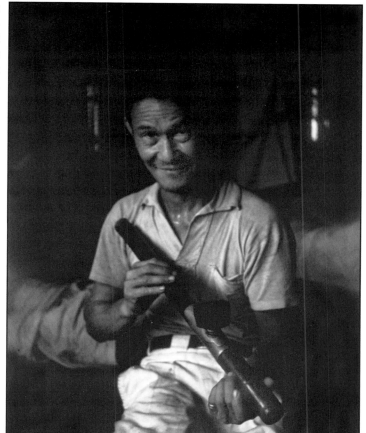

day before going on an ush patrol with these ish-trained Maylay troops, author posed with the pla-

A rice farmer stands by one of the bell-shaped stupas near the top of the Buddhist temple of Borobudur in Java.

A young dancer who was married to a European artist performs an ancient temple dance.

Woman and girls, bearing fruit offerings to the gods, enter a Balinese temple.

Middlemen who have bartered with the primitive Kubus for logs and rattan float on them some fift miles downriver toward a sawmil

The author tried to coax one woman at a leper colony to stand alone to emphasize her solitude; however, she was quickly joined by her friends.

The author and his government guide paddled to this isolated village of primitive Kubus. These same Kubus were said to have killed two Dutch missionaries ten years before.

The shy Kubus often avoided eye contact with the author and his guide. the Kubus' custom was to don their best clothing before meeting people from the outside world.

Prior to leading the author on a hunt for wild boar, this Kubu inspects his spear.

The Kubu hunter, posing here in an attack stance, shows off his primary weapon. Although the Kubus hunted boars in the wild, they wisely avoided tigers.

Weighing strips of rattan is one of the official duties of the old Kubu chief with mustache, on the right.

The Indonesian government has encouraged many Kubus to leave their jungle huts and transmigrate to other areas. After spending most of his long life in the jungle, this Kubu chief now lives in a new, progressive village supervised by the government.

Isolated in mountainous India, the Untouchables concoct many primative remedies. Here, Harsha's mother treats his injured knee with a poultice made from cow manure.

Harsha's mother adjusts a water pot on her head prior to the three mile hike down the mountain to the nearest well.

Harsha, the young Untouchable boy, looks out over a barren valley and his bleak future.

Unaware of his poverty and isolatio[n] Harsha always seemed cheerful and content.

The author worked with the people in many countries. However he was unqualified to give them advice; Eisenhower was still president and Kennedy's Peace Corps would not be organized until many years later.

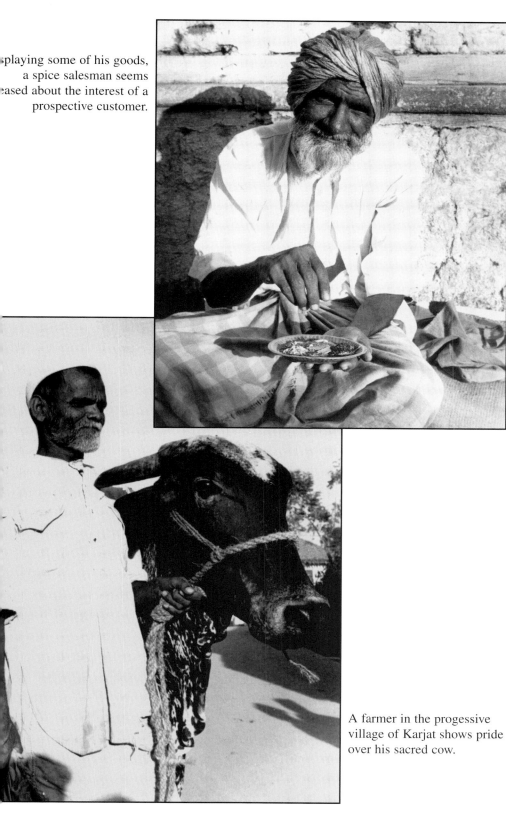

splaying some of his goods, a spice salesman seems eased about the interest of a prospective customer.

A farmer in the progessive village of Karjat shows pride over his sacred cow.

Free spirited women and a boy gather around one of the many wells in Karjat to gossip and bask in the winter sun.

Fortunately, Vasant, a twelve-year old boy who lived in Karjat, faced a fairly prosperous life because his village was under the guidance of the government-sponsored Community Development Project.

Both of their faces wrinkled in thought, but they could not answer. After that, they asked me no more questions about distances.

Later, an officer, two guards and I climbed into a jeep and whirred along the dusty road back to Den Pasar. Although I was under arrest, they allowed me to stop at several temples en route. Yet they could not understand what appeal Hindu art had for a foreigner, as they were Muslims from Java and seemed to appreciate only Islamic art.

After my guards led me to a room within the large brick building of the military police, they left to confer with their commanding officer. Four hours evaporated in the heat of the small cubicle with its barred window. My door was ajar, but it would have been foolish to attempt an escape with so many armed policemen around. I puffed nervously on my pipe. My amusement over the ridiculous nature of events merged into anxiety. Dejectedly, I walked around my cell. Perhaps this was the prince's prediction that misfortune might come my way, because a pig followed me one night.

Finally, the officer from Java came in and sat next to me on a bench. His worried brown eyes were fixed on the floor.

"What's wrong?" I asked apprehensively.

"We have made a bad mistake," he said softly. "You must understand that we have had some confusion in communications and other problems. Now we know you are an American student."

I blew my breath out in relief. "Great, really great."

"However, I am required to ask your next destination."

"Sumatra."

"Why do you wish to go to Sumatra?" he asked.

"I want to find the Kubus—you know, the aboriginal jungle people."

"Yes, but take great care. They are savages and still live in trees."

The next day, the military police drove me to a few temples near Den Pasar before taking me north to a coastal village where boats sail across the sea to Java. Because of the confusing arrests and detentions, I was driven through some of the finest scenery in the world and allowed to visit many out-of-the-way temples—all at the expense of the military police.

When I waded toward a Java-bound outrigger, floating at anchor, a police officer hurried down to the water.

"Again, we apologize for the inconveniences," he said.

"It wasn't so bad. In fact, being arrested as a spy has its advantages."

~ 11 ~

Forbidden Jungle Kubus

Throughout Indonesia and other Southeast Asian countries, rumors of the aboriginal Kubus were abundant. They were said to kill most outsiders who found them deep in the Sumatran jungle. "Like savages, they live in trees," one Javanese official told me.

The temperature inside the government waiting room climbed to well over one-hundred-five degrees. A squeaking ceiling fan seemed to intensify the heat and did little to frighten away the flies. I felt as though I were evaporating. For an hour or more I had been waiting in this Palembang, Sumatra, government building. A letter from the Ministry of Information in Java grew damp in my hands.

Finally, a male secretary led me into a spacious office where a rotund official presided over a desk full of papers. With the speed of a drowsy orangutan, he read my letter requesting permission to visit the aboriginal Kubus.

"I should like to give you permission to visit the Kubus, but we cannot assume responsibility for you," he said. *"It is forbidden."*

"Forbidden?"

"Were you aware these savages killed two Dutchmen a few years ago?"

"No, but I'm still eager to make the trip," I said.

"Another difficulty is that a suitable guide will be hard to come by," he said, wiping the sweat from the rim of his *pitchi,* black velveteen cap.

"But if one can be found, and I travel at my own risk, may I go then?" I asked.

"Possibly," he said, as he pointed to a map of Sumatra on the wall. "Some Kubus are said to live in this uncharted jungle north of Palembang City."

"Maybe I could find them. In fact that's why I'm in Sumatra."

"Unfortunately the Kubus do not trust outsiders. Years ago the Malay pirates chased them down with dogs and sold many of them into slavery. Afterwards, the Dutch frightened them. They have been withdrawn from the world for years. No, it's best you do not go," he said, waving his plump forefinger across his glasses.

I gazed with disappointment at the red-flowered trees outside the window. "Sir, if you do change your mind, would you please contact me at my hotel."

"Yes, since you are so interested I shall take the matter to the higher officials. However, for the present, the matter remains negative."

That night I saw a motion picture in downtown Palembang in an effort to keep my thoughts from the denial of my request. With amusement I viewed a propaganda film from Communist China depicting the reputed glories of their system. Whining to a raucous climax, the music underscored the bravery of a farmer who captured a capitalist saboteur from America. Surrounded by family and friends, the hero stood on a tractor with his arms raised triumphantly into the sky.

When the house lights blinked on, the rest of the audience and I filed into the warm streets. A short distance away I strolled by another theater. Its facade was plastered with lewd posters of a scantily clad teen-age girl from America. She held a smoking pistol.

Unfortunately, the impressions both motion pictures left with the Sumatrans were far from typical of life in either country. Yet melodrama and sensationalism were the stuff of commercial films. My embarrassment over the American film turned to anger. No doubt, most of the Sumatrans who saw this film believed this represented life in my country.

I ambled through the dark streets to my small hotel where I shared a room with six other men. On walking up the steps, I noticed a short man around forty who rose from a chair and nodded.

"Excuse. Are you *Tuan* Reeder?" he asked.

"That's right," I said.

"The government now speak that you visit the Kubus. They also want to know more about them. I, Hasan, am your guide."

"Wonderful," I said, pumping his slender hand. "I didn't think they would change their minds. Have you been in the Kubu area before?"

"No, I know of no person who has. If you give me some *rupiahs*, I buy supplies. The day following tomorrow we go."

"Good enough," I said as I reached for my wallet. "I'll give you some more *rupiahs* tomorrow. But please buy everything as cheaply as possible—no luxury items."

"I shall," he said, wiping his glasses on his immaculate white shirt.

"Do you think the Kubus would like gifts of salt and tobacco?"

"Indeed, they might," he said.

"Well, I guess we'll soon find out."

Two mornings later, Hasan and I boarded a bus that rumbled along the unpaved roads to the north. In the late afternoon our bus left a thick jungle area and passed through rice fields before squealing into the village of Bajunglintjir. Hasan and I left the bus with several other dust-covered passengers and tramped down the path toward a wide river.

This coffee-colored river flowed under many unpainted wooden houses rising from low piles along each bank. All of the houses were connected to land by a rear boardwalk while the front porches served as boat docks. Someone shouted. The village headman, dressed in khaki uniform and a sun helmet, jumped into a wooden canoe and skimmed across the river toward us.

"Selamat datang didesa kami," he said, after tying up his boat. "Welcome to our village."

"Terima kasih," my guide said as I mispronounced the same greeting. "Our thanks."

After Hasan explained our mission and presented our identification papers, we rested inside the headman's house where his wife served us many cups of unsweetened tea. Later we changed into our sarongs and stepped onto the front porch. A warm breeze moved down the river as Hasan and I squatted on the edge of the porch to bathe.

After lathering, we dropped into the water to rinse without removing our sarongs. Many women and children across the river were bathing in the same manner. While we bobbed in the water to relax from our jolting bus ride, the headman and a few others paddled downstream in their stubby-nosed canoes.

"Wonder where they are going so fast?" I asked.

"They hurry to rent a boat with a motor for us."

"Good. Do we leave soon?"

"Indeed yes—tomorrow morning. The headman knows the way to Kubus, but they often travel about."

After changing into a fresh shirt and trousers, I gave two tins of Dutch Beef to the shy headman's wife. Soon the aroma of steaming rice, warmed-over meat and wood smoke drifted into the humid air.

We stood outside for a long time watching the amber light fade on the shingled roofs and the darkening jungle beyond. Gradually, the villagers gathered on their boat docks and gazed up the river with a hushed air of anticipation. One boy glided in a skiff across the dark water to join his family. Several night birds punctuated the silence. Softly at first, and then with increasing intensity came the haunting wail of the *Muazzin*, Muslim priest. From a wooden tower his guttural voice lifted in prayer, *"Allah-u-akbar, Allah-u-akbar,"* he intoned. "Allah is great, Allah is great."

With bowed heads, the villagers chanted softly with him before kneeling and prostrating themselves. When the villagers finished praying west toward Mecca, they re-entered their houses as the *Muazzin* descended from his antique tower into the shadows.

Lights from the air-pressure lanterns beamed through the unscreened windows and doorways of the houses and shimmered on the black water. The headman returned in time for the evening meal with news that he had successfully rented a river tugboat. However, the pilot had a previous commitment to drag logs toward the sea and would not be able to take us the entire distance. The last part of the journey, Hasan and I would have to make alone in a small canoe.

One by one, the lights in the quiet houses were extinguished. The headman courteously insisted that my guide and I sleep in his large bed. He slept on the floor. A warm breeze rippled our mosquito net and stirred the rank odor of fungi beneath the house. We fell asleep listening to the murmur of the river which flowed from the far reaches of the uncharted jungle.

The next morning the melancholy cry of the Muslim priest awakened me. Hasan, already dressed, prayed on the porch with the headman. When the prayers ended, we sipped several cups of tea and loaded our supplies onto the twenty-five-foot boat tied to our front landing. The hefty pilot uttered something to us from his narrow cabin in the bow as we sat under a roof shading the rest of the craft. A shrill cry startled us. Fastened to a wooden perch, a green parrot squawked and fluttered its wings as our white tug chuffed into mid-channel.

As we motored up the river, our boat's wake swayed the village canoes and splashed a few women who cleaned breakfast pots in front of their houses. The headman yelled an order. Soon the captain increased our speed as we passed a schoolyard full of small boys playing soccer.

After passing the village, Hasan and I sat on the small bow to enjoy the refreshing breeze. Our boat chugged up the meandering river flowing through an endless mass of scrubby palms and high grass. Occasionally, we saw enormous gray trees that had outgrown the lower vines and had burst into an umbrella of leaves. In the distance, a flight of white water birds flapped along the sky line.

I was brimming over with excitement. If Hasan was nervous, he hid it very well. I felt peculiarly like a soldier or sailor going into an unwinnable battle. If I considered death the outcome of this expedition, such self-deception would mitigate my anxiety. I chuckled when I thought of our craft looking a little like Humphrey Bogart's boat in *The African Queen*. Although my Islamic companions were forbidden to drink alcoholic spirits, they surreptitiously emptied my bottle of Dutch gin. Hasan said it was medicine for his bad stomach.

Around one bend, our motor startled two short crocodiles. On stiff legs they crawled forward and slipped under water, leaving circles of foam on the surface. Yellow orchids curled around the jungle vines. Several times our racket sent packs of monkeys chattering away on their arboreal pathways.

By mid-morning, we swept around a curve and came into a small, unnamed village. The headman called to an elder on one of the boat docks for information about the Kubus while our tug idled in midstream.

"Headman talks of Kubus. They are two days or more away," Hasan whispered. "Now he asks if Kubus are friends."

In a fit of acrimony, the elder stomped around the dock and yelled vile words as he pointed toward the Kubus. He spat betel nut juice and strode angrily into his hut. Most of the other villagers turned their eyes from us and quietly withdrew.

Startled by the elder's response, Hasan looked dejected. The headman and I remained speechless. In a moment, the pilot opened the throttle and our tug surged toward the Kubus.

We anchored the tug in early afternoon; the canoe tied to our stern was loaded with supplies. Both the headman and the pilot gave us more information about the possible route to the Kubus. Unfortunately, the tremor in their voices gave us little confidence. Hasan and I stepped gingerly into the overloaded canoe. When we sat on the bamboo deck slats, water came within three inches of pouring inside.

The large boat turned back and throbbed down the river as the parrot screamed. An anxious feeling made my stomach shrink. I glanced, without solace, at my spectacled companion who made an entry in his notebook; he seemed more in character behind his bureaucratic desk than as a jungle guide. Both of us remained motionless until the sound of the motor was muffled by the dense vegetation. Apprehensively, I dipped my paddle into the river.

We skimmed along the narrow river, stroke by slow stroke. With the absence of the tugboat-created breeze, the heat grew more oppressive. Hasan was partially shaded by a broad straw hat. Drops of perspiration oozed down the back of his neck and saturated his shirt. To avoid the wobbling reflection of the sun, I pulled the bill of my baseball cap down snugly. The high river grass discharged bitter juices which seemed to perspire with us.

Late in the afternoon, a hot breeze moved the charcoal shadows under the high teak trees. A whining cloud of gnats covered us. We tried to wave them off. A spasm shot through my body when several of these black insects clogged my nostrils. In the excitement we almost capsized the boat, an occurrence that could be fatal in crocodile waters. Finally, another breeze came and drew the gnats away with it.

Hours later we located a flat mudbank shaded by palms. Yellow butterflies drifted from the earth and fluttered around us as we beached our canoe. I took the *golok,* or knife—our only weapon—and walked into the jungle for firewood; Hasan filled our teakettle with river water.

After quenching our thirsts with many hot cups of tea, we sat on our blankets and stared with exhaustion at the river. Hasan pulled a bottle of costly French cologne from a cloth sack in the boat.

"Where did you get that?" I asked.

"I buy this with your money," he said, as he dabbed the "refreshing" cologne on his neck and chest.

"But I told you not to buy anything expensive," I said with disgust.

"This is necessary item in the jungle—indeed very necessary," he said with a haughty air.

"Hell, have it your way," I said.

Throughout the afternoon our tempers became increasingly heated. Irritated further by the jungle dangers, we also had the pressure of the Kubus on our minds. Every past injustice or unfriendly act committed against me seemed to reappear and burn in my steaming brain. Apparently, Hasan had been assigned this mission and had little enthusiasm over finding the Kubus. I said nothing when he opened an expensive tin of English cigarettes.

A pair of blue, long-tailed parrots streaked over us in the dusky sky. One by one the insects exploded with their buzz saw noises, until the entire jungle whined. In the shadows, tree frogs chirped like frightened birds. A warm wind moved down the river and refreshed us with its clean breath. My guide swatted a mosquito and lit another cigarette. Now the jungle was almost black.

Hasan prayed quickly toward the supposed direction of Mecca before we heated a tin of beef. With a little food in our tea-bloated stomachs, we relaxed and talked in a more friendly manner. After draping the blankets over our heads to keep some of the mosquitoes away, we sat closer to the smoky fire. Bright fireflies swirling above us made the stars in the Southern Cross seem unreal and inconsequential.

*

In the dimness of early morning we glided through patches of rising fog on the river. The towering jungle was motionless in its cover of monochromatic green. Invisible spider webs broke across our faces as we paddled under overhanging tree limbs.

When the sun covered the jungle in pale yellow, we heard the sound of high-pitched human voices. Around the next curve in the river we approached an elongated raft of over thirty teak logs. The river was almost blocked. Four men scrambled out from a lean-to on the front of the honey-colored timbers of the raft. They spread out and struck menacing poses. Each man pointed a long spear at us.

"Kubus, Kubus," Hasan gasped, startled, almost sinking our canoe.

One Kubu shouted something in an unusual Indonesian accent. In a surprising display of confidence, Hasan stood when we came alongside the raft. With assured gestures, he delivered a bewildering speech. The only phrase I could understand was that we were important people representing the government of Indonesia. As he talked, he repeated his phrases frequently, as though repetition would impress upon them our good intentions. The Kubus studied us with hard brown eyes; I tried to manage a friendly smile. Slowly they lowered their weapons when Hassan passed out cigarettes. They became less aggressive as they appraised our defenseless position. Ultimately, they crouched down on their teakwood barge and arrogantly floated downstream toward the jungle market.

As we continued, Hasan turned to me. "We are close," he said. "Remember this, never smile at Kubus; they think you make joke of them."

"Did they come from where we are headed?"

"No, no, no, those were the friendly Kubus."

"Good God," I blurted out.

"Place where we head—Kubus not very friendly."

Later in the day we saw a Kubu clad in a loincloth dozing in the shadows along the river bank. Near him were two partially submerged fish traps. Hasan greeted him and started another complex explanation of our mission. With a startled expression the Kubu jumped to his feet. Brandishing his spear, he raced into the high grass yelling. His alarm was soon answered by a throbbing drum beat. We exchanged agonizing glances and continued paddling.

At last, we came to a wide place in the river with many huts scattered on both banks, under the mottled shade of enormous teak trees. The drum beat grew louder and stopped. This was our destination—the Kubu village.

Many huts were supported on twelve-foot high stilts with ladders leaning on the open doors. Brown bark enclosed the sides of the huts; sun-bleached palm leaves covered the gabled roofs. No one was in sight.

"Quick, quick—hide in grass. I find the chief," Hasan whispered as he began to hyperventilate.

"The tobacco, the gifts, remember the...," I gasped.

"Indeed—the tobacco," he muttered.

Breathlessly, I watched him swish past several teak logs floating near each bank of the river. I hid in the high grass, but was still able to see Hasan paddle past a small boat tied to a tree.

After sliding the canoe on the river bank, several brown-skinned men in loincloths emerged from the underbrush. Each held a long spear. With bewildered faces, they listened to Hasan while he distributed handfuls of shredded tobacco. A bare-breasted woman peered at him through a clump of banana plants. Other women gradually appeared in the shadows under the tall huts. Suddenly, they screamed and ran up the ladders to their huts; several naked children scampered behind them.

My life seemed as ephemeral as a balloon on a dart board. Perhaps it would be punctured by a Kubu spear. When the men hurried away from Hasan, a racing pulse drummed in my ears. Had Hasan lost his art of persuasion? My legs became heavy. I was completely at the mercy of the Kubus who had killed missionaries and perhaps other visitors.

After a pain-riddled period of time, Hasan finally shoved off from the village and paddled back to me.

"They know us to be of no harm," he said with renewed confidence.

"Good," I sighed. "Very, very good."

"I tell you have no gun and are friend—a friend of Sumatran government."

"Where did they go?"

"You will soon see," he said.

Paddling into the village, we passed a very long house on four-foot high stilts, large enough to hold several families. A rattan clothesline in front of the dwelling held a few faded sarongs. After beaching our canoe next to the grey-hulled dugouts of the Kubus, we walked over to the shade of a pavilion and waited. I was numb; my head was reeling, and I found it difficult to believe that Hasan and I were still alive.

At last, the barefooted Kubu men stepped down their ladders. No longer dressed in loincloths, they now wore brightly colored sarongs. They respected us enough to put on their finest clothes. A couple of the younger men were in light blue pajamas. One boy around thirteen stumbled toward us in oversized tennis shoes. While the men and boys circled around me, I stood rather stiffly, as though I were undergoing an admiral's inspection.

In a moment the bare-chested old chief stepped forward in his sarong with red and gray stripes. Powerful arms dangled from his slumped shoulders. His grizzled mustache swayed as he talked.

"*Ukarkahperdjalanan kemari,*" he asked. "Was the trip difficult?"

"*Ja, sukardjugalah,*" I said several times with the prompting of Hasan. "Yes, it was."

"*Lepaskanlah lelah,*" he said, "*Ini pinang dan tuak.*" "Rest, take a little betel nut and palm wine."

With the exception of Hasan, we all stooped down. I drank a small gourd full of wine and stuffed the betel concoction in my mouth. Hasan passed out more tobacco and some salt to the Kubus who accepted it without thanks. With an air of official dignity, he gave a speech about the luxurious life outside the jungle. As he spoke, he moved his arms like an old-time revival preacher. Although the Kubus listened intently, they displayed no emotion. I was filled with admiration, however, for Hasan's way with people and his fascinating oratory. Our previous quarrels were forgotten.

Although the Kubus bore a close physical resemblance to the Sumatrans outside the jungle, they were shorter and darker. Perhaps disease and poor diet had stunted these primitives' growth through the years. It was apparent that the Kubus could not be considered aborigines like those people found in Australia. The Indonesian Government had been trying to lure many of the Kubus out of the jungle to live a civilized life. Hasan's speeches were always spiced with the promises of good health care, education and better living conditions that could be found in the outside world.

Later we carried our bundles up the shaky ladder to one of the chief's huts. The leaf-filtered sunlight streaked through the small window and narrow door, making the room seem larger. With each step on the matted floor, our feet sagged several inches. Overhead, in the bamboo rafters, were three black spears. Except for a dank pile of sarongs in one corner, the room was bare.

After the afternoon nap we followed the chief through the village toward the rice field. One unusually large hut trembled on its stilts. The chief saw that I was curious and motioned for me to climb the ladder. Crammed inside were women and girls dressed in their best sarongs and blouses. Frightened brown eyes glanced at me while I peered through the door. A girl shrieked, and the females shifted desperately to hide behind each other. When I jumped off the ladder, Hasan and the chief smiled.

"They are superstitious and fear you," my guide said. "Many others hide in the jungle."

"Tell them to come out. I'm harmless," I said.

"Marilah turn kemari," he shouted. "Come down." But no reply came from the women.

The chief shook the stilts and yelped a command. Eventually, a few of them climbed down from the swaying hut and stood near us with their eyes fixed on the ground. Because of the Kubu's prosperous trade in teak logs and rattan, their batik sarongs were of the same fine quality as those worn in Palembang. Hasan delivered another lengthy speech about government progress when the rest of them came down.

After his bureaucratic oratory confused the women, we continued along a vine-covered path to an opening in the trees where green rice shoots lined the ground. In the hot shadows at the far end of the field, a man was napping close to his wooden plow.

"Chief proud of rice. Years ago Kubus had no rice—only tapioca," Hasan said, while scribbling data in his notebook.

"Wouldn't he get a better crop if he flooded the field when the rice is young?" I asked. "The Balinese do that."

After a conversation with the soft-voiced chief, Hasan said "Chief does not know—it is against the spirits to do this."

Turning down a trail near the river, we walked into a grove of rubber trees. I winced on inhaling the fecal stench. Latex oozed down from the gashes in the trees to coconut shell containers on the ground. Outside the grove, in the lower branches of an enormous tree, rested a palm leaf shelter. The chief spoke to an old woman who was snoozing inside. Her flabby breasts shuddered when she sat up abruptly to peer at me. Perhaps she or her relatives had been wronged by light-skinned foreigners.

"She is old," Hasan said, as he continued to make notes.

"Yes, but why is she the only one living in a tree?" I asked.

"The chief talks she always living in tree."

At one time all of the Kubus were nomadic hunters and lived in temporary tree shelters. Whenever a village member died, everyone fled to escape the spirits of death. The gradual introduction of agriculture made the Kubus less mobile, so they began to build more permanent ground-level structures. Now the death spirit forced the villagers to leave only when the chief died.

After bathing in the river that afternoon Hasan and I returned to the chief's hut. His chubby wife served us rice and bits of dried fish. She giggled when I tried to compliment her brown and purple sarong within my poorly pronounced Indonesian. In a very serious manner Hasan dabbed some cologne on the long black hair flowing down her back. She smiled with delight. Soon many of the other village women bent over while Hasan sprinkled cologne on their hair. Even the chief and some of the other men were pleased with the new fragrance. Gradually, the jungle village reeked incongruously with expensive French cologne. Maybe Hasan was right; cologne was necessary in the jungle!

Night came quickly. Hasan and I helped the chief build a small fire under his hut. Similar fires already glowed beneath the other structures, dimly outlining their tall stilts. When Hasan and the chief finished their last English cigarettes, we tossed banana leaves over the embers and climbed into the hut. We pulled up the ladder and closed the bamboo door. Invisible smoke waves filtered through the loosely woven floor of the black room.

"This keep mosquitoes away," Hasan whispered.

"Fine," I coughed.

We seemed to smoke like fish on the bamboo rack of a Kubu cookshed. Scrabbling along the walls, *chichaks,* small lizards, hunted mosquitoes and other insects. I drifted into an exhausted sleep, listening to the hiccuping shrieks of insects, and the snores of the old chief.

We put the ladder down the next morning and climbed into the refreshing air. White vapors rising from the river and jungle made the stilted village appear as though it were some prehistoric community on the edge of a volcano. Two boys in short trousers squealed by us while their playmates chased them with bamboo sticks. Their make-believe animal hunt ended in the misty underbrush when these hunters threw imaginary spears.

The men no longer wore their best sarongs and pajamas to impress the visitors, but walked proudly through the haze in loincloths. However, the modest women were still garbed in *kebayas,* long-sleeved blouses, and sarongs as they hovered around the cooking fires.

After we ate rice with our fingers, the chief led us in his spraddle-legged stride to the dugouts in the river. He mumbled gruff instructions to the men and boys who squatted along the bank smoking tobacco rolled in palm leaves. One Kubu tripped and fell into the water. Jeers and laughter greeted him. With a smile the clumsy Kubu threw water on one heckler and a good-natured water fight began. In a little while all of us were wet and laughing.

Later the chief, Hasan, and I joined several men who were lashing four teak logs together at the river's edge. Each timber was tied to the other by bamboo poles and long vines. On the bank several villagers cut the rattan into twenty-foot strands. Eventually, this rattan would be shipped down river and made into furniture for the world market. And the teak would line the walls of fine homes.

The chief tilted his head back and squinted toward the sky as though he were listening. Hasan and I heard nothing. Then a slow, creaking sound became audible. Leaves on the top of a downstream teak tree shivered. Voices came up in a chorus from the base of this giant tree. Within seconds the teak crashed down through the lower vines and trees with the sound of a waterfall. Blue sky rushed in to fill the freshly formed void. After the trunk boomed to the ground, air currents rippled the river and covered us with hot jungle dust.

When the chief saw me dragging bunches of rattan to the river logs, he snickered.

"Chief talks he did not know Dutchman worked," Hasan said.

"Hasan, I thought you told him I'm an American," I said.

"Yes, but he only knows Dutchman. Indeed, it is good for your life you are not mission-man."

While I continued to help the men with their heat-retarded work, my guide paddled with the chief back to the village to rest and talk. At the end of the logs, I picked up some loose cords of rattan floating in the water. Something stung my left hand. I yelled. A short gray snake was tearing my flesh. I had been bitten, and the snake was still attached!

Angrily, I slung my hand down toward the water. Yet the snake sank its teeth deeper. Again I slung my hand down, and with my free hand yanked at its tail. Once more I repeated the same maneuver. This time it released its grip. Quickly, the snake swam away with its head above water and disappeared into the high shore grass.

Breathing heavily, I slipped across the slimy logs, jumped into a dugout and paddled to the village. Along the way, the betel nut in my mouth grew very bitter and I spat it out. As I hurried toward the chief's hut, the jungle turned gray like a spotted photographic negative. I closed my eyes, and when I reopened them, the hut was outlined in red.

Within a chilled minute I was inside, fumbling in my bag. After burning the germs from the needle of my syringe, I injected five centimeters of antivenom into my buttocks. Quickly, I bandaged my hand and rested while I fought off thoughts of the possible consequences. Since I was hundreds of miles away from Western medicine, I was glad I took my navy friend's advice. In Japan, Dr. Tom Dooley had suggested that I buy, or scrounge around for, a snake bite venom antidote to take whenever I traveled into the unmapped areas of Southeast Asia.

"What is happen?" Hasan asked as he climbed the ladder.

"A snake bit me," I said.

"I call the *dukun*," he said with unexpected excitement.

"What's that?"

"The medicine man; he repairs you."

While I was resting, a gaunt man in a faded, brown sarong knelt down by my side. He was the *dukun*. His slender fingers twisted a black paste in a wooden bowl while he murmured some soothing words. After applying the salve around the bandage, he smeared dabs of it on my temples. Slowly, the poultice burned into my skin, releasing a stench like buffalo dung. His keen brown eyes sparkled reassuringly as he turned me over and rubbed my back and leg muscles. The exorcism

111

ended an hour later when the *dukun* left to talk quietly with the chief, who waited outside.

"He talks to chief you are soon repaired," Hasan said.

"I am feeling a little better," I said.

For the rest of the day I tried to sleep, but this was impossible, as the ladder and hut shook frequently with curious villagers who came to see the *dukan's* patient.

Later, Hasan, the chief, and his wife brought me tea and a few bananas. To entertain them and to keep my mind off myself, I took a three-dimensional viewer from my bag. The chief drew in his breath on seeing a few color slides of New York City. Even though Hasan tried to explain that it was a monstrous village, the old man of the jungle sighed with disbelief and chewed on the end of his moustache. His wife giggled with astonishment over each scene. One slide caused an unusual amount of curiosity between the chief and his wife.

"They want to know why so many poor people live by the water under small umbrellas," Hasan said.

After glancing at the scene, I tried to withhold a smile and said, "Tell them the people are not poor. You see, they are on vacation in Fort Lauderdale Beach. It takes many teak logs to live that way."

I slept soundly that night, and the next morning I suffered no ill-effects from the snake bite. Perhaps the antivenin coupled with the sympathetic treatment of the *dukan* had cured me. To help the medicine man maintain his prestige, I gave him my navy field cap. In a solemn manner, he nodded and walked proudly through the village with the khaki cap slouched over his right ear.

"Chief talks you and one man can hunt wild pig," Hasan said a couple of days later.

"Are you going?"

"No, no. Pig is not clean—I am Muslim."

"I'll see you tonight, then," I said, as I followed a short Kubu in a loin cloth toward the dugouts.

We paddled past a woman who sprinkled rice on a tree limb to placate the evil spirits. A baby napped in the security of a sling that dangled over her breasts. The infant's head was shaved except for a tiny patch of hair remaining to frighten the spirits of death. Nearby, four young girls squatted in a circle to pick lice and groom each others' long black hair.

A bellowing sound startled us. The hunter and I smiled as several boys tried to push the village's only buffalo from its shed. It snorted, lurched uncontrollably, and finally staggered forward, tossing its heavy horns up and down.

After paddling downstream for several hours, we poled our boat up a shallow tributary. In the limbs of one tree stood a decomposing shelter. Perhaps evil spirtis had frightened its former inhabitants to another part of the jungle. We beached the dugout in the high grass of a shadowed area.

The grass hissed in the hot breeze as though it were slowly burning. The Kubu walked along looking for any signs of the wild boars. I followed close behind, until he found numerous hoofprints on a mudbank. He smacked his lips and motioned for me to climb a tree with my spear while he shinnied up another one.

Under the oven-like Sumatran sky, we waited patiently. Now and then, gray clouds floated over us, but did little to stifle the heat. One hour melted into another without any sign of animal life. While resting in the branches, I thought about my disappointment in finding the Kubus more advanced than folklore suggested. The rumors in Bali and Palembang led me to believe they existed on a primitive level below that of the Australian aborigines. Yet, these Kubus were doing well in their timber and rattan trade and could now buy many of the same articles owned by the Sumatrans outside the jungle. Perhaps someday most of the Kubus would live in much better conditions similar to those outside the jungle.

Around three in the afternoon we waded back to the dugout to drain our bucket of drinking water. At this stage of my journey I no longer insisted that my water be boiled. It was impractical and slowed me down. Foolishly, I had stopped using my water purification pills. Somehow I thought my body was invincible. Eventually, I would regret this decision. After the guide and I drank our water, we returned to the trees.

Later, the Kubu seemed to stop breathing. A rustling noise on the ground came closer. We held our spears tightly and hoped the sound was a herd of pigs snuffling for roots. For a moment, the stirring hushed. Again, it started and came toward us. The Kubu raised his spear. I banged mine against the tree. This noise spooked our quarry. A skinny black boar scurried away. The grass rippled toward the teaks. Unseen pigs squealed. Quickly the animals disappeared. After frowning at me, the Kubu broke into a sympathetic smile.

When the tracks beneath us grew dark in the twilight, we left our roosts in the trees and paddled toward the village. My flashlight beam led us up the dark river to our berth.

"What did you kill?" Hasan said as we beached the dugout.

"Nothing—we had bad luck. The pigs heard..."

"Pigs, pigs—they are too unclean to hear."

"Maybe, but I'm not much of a hunter."

"Indeed, but you must now eat and sleep swiftly. We go tomorrow."

"You said we could stay longer. I want to learn more about the Kubus," I said bitterly.

"Impossible. I must return to the ministry with this information," he said arrogantly and held up his notebook. "We meet the tugboat soon and then go to Palembang," he said, as though he were more than satisfied with the entire expedition.

After swelling my stomach with much tea and a little rice, I hunkered next to the chief and Hasan, who puffed on the last of the imported cigarettes.

"Do you know if the Kubus have any dances?" I asked.

Hasan mumbled something to the chief and then said, "Yes, but for now it is time for sleep."

"Tell him he can have my new flashlight if the villagers dance for a short time."

No sooner than this was translated, the chief inhaled with delight, grabbed the flashlight from my hands and hurried to a nearby hut. He shook the bamboo stilts, until the sleepy occupants lowered their ladders. He yelled an order. In a few minutes, a drowsy family descended the ladder. After visiting each hut, he returned to the cleared pavilion area; a dance fire was started. Again, Hasan opened his notebook.

Gradually, around forty lethargic Kubus assembled. Some of them stooped down in the pavilion, while others clustered around the fire. Enthusiasm over the unscheduled dance was missing. A young man slowly thumped a buffalo-hide drum, while the men ambled around the flames in a ragged circle. Dutifully, they followed the chief, who chanted and held out his heavy arms. Now and then the women shrieked a few words above the dull drum thuds.

As the beat quickened, the men jogged along with their chief, whose mustache flowed out in the breeze. One man playfully slapped the dancer's head in front of him and yelled. As the pace picked up, a woman hooted. Two men leaped in the air. I whistled in excitement as the chief twirled in exaltation.

The drum beat was so frenzied that several Kubus tumbled on the ground, and the dance came to a disorganized end. Everyone laughed wildly at the impromptu climax and caught their breaths while sprawled on their dusty stage.

All brown eyes were on the chief. With careful steps he circled the fire to reenact a hunting experience. After stalking his quarry, he heaved an imaginary spear through the air, waited a moment, then hunched over imitating a squealing pig. In a serious manner, the audience shouted its approval. Next, he clutched his neck, expelled a rasping breath and twisted around many times.

"He talks of python," Hasan whispered.

Struggling frantically to free his arms, the old man rolled over and over in the dust. With convincing groans he squeezed the pretended snake's neck on the ground and waited for its constricting muscles to ease somewhat. Soon he squirmed free amid our shouts.

Breathing hard, the chief stood near me and mumbled the same phrase several times until Hasan understood it.

"He talks you take the head of the snake off first. Then the other part comes off," my guide said.

Now the dancers grouped again and allowed me to join them. Giggles and shouts came from the formerly shy women as they saw me skip along with the others. The drummer's brown hands pounded faster when we shuffled closer to the fire. With zest, the chief's wife bounded to her feet and followed us far outside the circle. The chief growled a command to her, and she padded back to the laughing women. Again the rhythm became so fast that we fell over each other and tumbled on the jungle floor.

"Chief wants to know if this is enough dance?" Hasan asked.

"You bet; thank him a lot," I said, as I tried to catch my breath. Emotionless, Hasan looked carefully at his watch and recorded his final notes on the dance.

We lowered the ladder earlier than usual the next morning and loaded our canoe. Rice, wrapped in a banana leaf, was already tied on our bow to feed the evil water spirits. The chief's wife placed a stalk of bananas on top of our bundles and gave us a few dried fish. Hasan seemed disappointed that most of the Kubus were still sleeping. Unfortunately, he could not deliver his official farewell speech. The chief shoved us out into the hazy river, and stood silently while we paddled downstream.

While gliding past the last Kubu hut, I turned and saw the lean figure of the *dukun*. He adjusted his khaki cap and nodded with solemnity. After stroking a few more times, I glanced back again, but the rising fog had blotted the jungle village from sight.

~ 12 ~

Advancing Sumatrans
And Retreating Tigers

In Sumatra, tigers and other exotic animals were killed or driven deep into the jungles by the land-hungry farmers. If these conditions had persisted, most of the wildlife would have disappeared.

After a few days rest in Palembang, I traveled by train to the inland city of Lubuklinggau. There, the Indonesian Office of Information had arranged for me to tour a village of relocated Kubus. I sat in the lead vehicle of a three-Jeep convoy packed with government officials. We wound along the oxcart-worn trails at a relaxed Sumatran speed.

"Many Kubus gave food to our soldiers when our soldiers were driven into the jungle by the Dutch," an official in the front seat with me said. "This happened, of course, at the time of our revolution."

"Did your government have much trouble later in persuading the Kubus to come out of the jungle?"

"Oh, yes, they would not come at first. However, later our government offered the Kubus agricultural aid and medical assistance. This brought a few out."

Hours later we stopped on a hill overlooking a village surrounded by many acres of well-irrigated rice paddies. Identical rows of white houses with shingled roofs lined the dirt roads beyond. We walked down a path, which ran across the rice fields to a house surrounded by slender tapioca plants. In a moment the village chief, garbed in a sarong and undershirt, came out to greet us. Long sprouts of gray hair dangled from the chin of his pock-marked face. With his left hand on his right elbow, he lightly clasped our hands. After each shake, he slapped his chest.

We followed the chief down a wide road; many of the villagers straggled behind us. In the shade of a few coconut palms, he ordered two boys to climb the trees. With the sound of buffalo hooves, coconuts hit the ground near us. Skillfully, the chief carved holes in the coconuts and gave one to each of us. We sipped the warm milk inside, as he led us to the school pavilion. Around thirty boys, seated on wooden benches, faced a young man in a white suit who scrawled an Arabic word on the blackboard.

"This teacher comes here for seven months every year. At one time he told me he was surprised the Kubus learned so fast. Some of them, he thinks, still have strong jungle dreams," one official said.

"Do these relocated Kubus have a doctor?" I asked.

"One comes every month. For the most part the *dukun* treats them."

"I found out first-hand that some of the *dukun's* treatments are helpful," I said, glancing at the snakebite scar on my hand.

"Yes, they often succeed when many European doctors fail."

Later, we strolled out of the village, which, from all outward appearances, was like many others in Sumatra. In just a few short years these Kubus had adjusted rather well to life outside the deep jungle. The chief escorted us to the Jeeps and continued to chat with an official.

"It is said the chief likes it here because life is less difficult than in the jungle," the official translated.

The old chief who had spent all but his last three years in remote jungle areas said good-bye and then hurried toward the rice fields where the men were plowing.

Our official party bounded through miles of unpopulated country; suddenly we entered a vast clearing that contained many white houses. Most of the land had been burned. Billows of thick smoke from a pile of burning logs swept across our Jeeps. We coughed, and squinted at the clouded landscape. Only a few uncut trees provided shade over the houses. To our right, men in broad straw hats were digging an irrigation canal through the charred landscape. Farmers coaxed water buffaloes that pulled wooden plows on a hillside. Rice would soon be planted.

"This village is Sumber Harba," an official said. "The government transported nine hundred Javanese people here to have more land. This will give them a promising new life. In Sumatra, we have much land but very, very few people."

"Does each farmer from Java own his house and land?" I asked.

"Yes. The government gave them this, and free travel. Java is, as a matter of fact, one of the world's most densely populated islands. Lastly, they were loaned seed and various tools."

"You know, this whole Transmigration Program is exciting. In a way, it reminds me of our American pioneers many years ago."

"Yes, at one time you faced some of the problems we now have. Finally, we have the freedom to build our nation in our own way, the way John Wayne helped to build yours."

After touring other sections of the countryside, the officials discharged me in Lubuklinggau. From this city, I boarded a crowded bus that, with thundering backfires, crept up a mountainous road and rolled down toward the western seacoast. As the bright green forest leveled off, the driver kept his bare foot pressed hard on the accelerator. Fortunately, the farmers in oxcarts ahead heard our rattle in time to coax their lumbering beasts off the road.

In the amber afternoon light we rolled into a jungle tract; trees formed a dark overhead canopy, making it appear like an enormous tunnel. The driver flicked on his lights and turned off his motor to save gasoline as we coasted downward. When the fading sunlight again streamed into our windows, we came to a quick and unusually silent stop. Frightened whispers passed through the bus.

"Dato, dato." "The ancestor, the ancestor."

A small tiger was padding down the road ahead of us. After glancing in our direction with an unconcerned air, it bounded into a gully and disappeared. One girl screamed until her mother shook her into silence. As we drove past the place where the tiger had been, an old man shouted angrily and spat betel juice out of the window.

Before darkness covered the jungle, we arrived in the seaport city of Bangkahulu where I registered at a small inn. After changing into a fresh sports shirt, I hired a *bendi*, pony cart taxi, and rode as it clopped toward a Chinese restaurant in the commercial district. Bits of red cloth tied to the pony's mane fluttered in a warm breeze from the Indian Ocean. The scent of flowering trees drifted past me, as I leaned back in the seat to enjoy the pleasant evening.

Quickly I became apprehensive when a Jeep filled with military police stopped the pony cart. "Oh, no. What kind of spy do they think I am now?" I said to the taxi driver as though he could understand English.

A squat policeman examined my papers with formality. His associates frowned at me. The driver sat erectly as though he was ready for a difficult interrogation. After some ten minutes the khaki uniformed officer said, "You are indeed the very American who wants to hunt tigers. The government in Palembang has written us of this."

"I hope you can help me," I said.

"We have been waiting. Will tomorrow night be too soon to go?"

"Great, that's not too soon at all."

"Let us call for you at the hotel some time tomorrow afternoon. Is this convenient?" he asked.

"Very convenient—thanks," I said, before the Jeep drove away. The *bendi* driver grinned at me knowingly as I hummed with delight. He slapped his whip on the pony's rump, and we continued on to the restaurant.

The next afternoon, Darmano, a haughty official, joined me and a young policeman who was driving a Chevrolet pickup truck. After checking the map, the three of us crowded into the cab. Rain began to fall and quickly increased in intensity. Cautiously, we followed a muddy road while peering through the squeaking arc of the windshield wiper.

That night, during a thundershower, we arrived in a small village. After sliding off the road near an elder's house, we ran toward the single oil lamp on his front porch. While waiting for the rain to ease, we ate plates of fried rice; we then pumped bamboo ramrods into the bores of our antique Belgian army rifles.

"The old hunter, Amat, is soon to be here. He comes when the rain slows," Darmano said. "He has killed several tigers around this village."

"Have you killed many tigers?" I asked.

Darmano smiled arrogantly, panned his rifle across the dark jungle and boasted, "In my forty years, I have killed one hundred and sixty tigers. That is the average of four a year! All of this was accomplished in my free time."

"That's really impressive."

"Yes, an abundant number," he said as he stalked around waiting for an imaginary tiger to attack.

"Are there still many tigers around?"

"Yes, they are very plentiful in Sumatra. One killed a buffalo close to here last month. And last year a woman was said to have been killed by a tiger."

"A woman?"

"Do not be misled by the story about this woman. At times, the farmers become frightened—they often exaggerate. They, of course, do not have my hunting experience."

While Darmano stared histrionically into the rain, the young policeman smiled at me and shook his head in disbelief.

Around ten o'clock the moon slipped behind the dark clouds, and the rain on the thatched roof eased to a murmur.

"Is the village elder going with us tonight?" I asked.

"No, only the policeman, you and Amat—no one else. This will give *you* the opportunity for the big kill."

"Thanks," I said nervously, as my hands grew cold.

"To be more than truthful, I tend to grow weary of such hunting. It is my official duty to spend time with the elder. Besides, I have proven my courage."

"You certainly have," I said, as the policeman tried to hide the look of disrespect that came over his face.

Later, the policeman and I sloshed down the dark road behind Amat, the white-haired hunter. Unlike Darmano, Amat said little and seemed very eager to find a tiger. At a downhill curve, he connected his acetylene headlamp to a canister buckled on his short trousers. He reminded me of a coal miner deep in a mine shaft. Slowly, he moved the long beam of light around the underbrush while we raised our rifles. His strong hands turned off the lamp, and we tramped on in the darkness.

Rain again started to splatter the black palm trees as we came to a river. We slung the rifles over our shoulders and stepped onto a bamboo raft. The water rose above our ankles as we poled out into midstream. Gradually, we drifted on the overweighted raft downriver until Amat steered us to the opposite bank. As we tied the raft to a tree, a loud splash followed by a gurgling noise resounded up the river. Hundreds of birds awakened. From their perches they skirred their wings desperately into a prolonged hiss. Yet none of them flew away.

Amat broke our pact of silence. *"Buaja,"* he whispered. "Crocodile."

After climbing a high bank, we passed under the partial shelter of vine-laden trees and emerged into a large rice field. The droning beat of the rain no longer came from the sky, yet the jungle behind us still percolated with dripping water. A faint light glimmered from the moon, giving the landscape a surrealistic quality. While we slopped across the rice paddies, I felt as though I were participating in a bad dream. This was my first attempt at hunting. What an overly ambitious way to begin this sport. My family and friends in Tennessee seldom hunted. In fact, I leaned toward the view that hunting only for sport and not food was wasteful. If we hit a tiger, but did not instantly kill him, the probability of our being mauled was evident. With the passing of each hour, my confidence faded, but I soothed my nerves with thoughts of old Amat's skill.

Finally, Amat yelled something to a farmer's hut which rested on low stilts. Within a few minutes he was answered by a drowsy voice. A soft light radiated through the cracks in the door. Amat turned on his headlamp and led us below the hut where we stooped down to rest.

After the farmer climbed down to join us, we pried the leeches from our bodies. Those leeches, which could not be pulled off, succumbed quickly to a lighted cigar. I pulled the gray parasites from my ankles. Fortunately, there was very little pain involved. Only a few leeches left black scars.

Before leaving, the farmer showed us fresh tiger tracks outside his heavily boarded buffalo shed. With renewed interest we followed the tiger's spoor through the waist-high *lallang* grass. Swishing along, we wove behind the old man, who aimed his headlamp from one side to the other. The trail soon vanished in a wall of foliage that we could not crawl through. We skirted this barrier and came into a large clearing.

Then we saw him.

Our light barely touched the dark form of a tiger, while he ambled across the edge of the clearing. He moved in an imperious manner, as though he had no enemies. The policeman and I gasped with excitement. My heart pounded. Impulsively, the policeman and I raised our rifles. Amat calmly held up his hand to restrain us. I could not breathe. Apparently the tiger was too far away, and we could not be sure of killing him. When we glanced up from our rifles, the tiger slipped into the underbrush and disappeared.

I rationalized my disappointment with a feeling of relief that the tiger was still free. Before I could compose myself, the hunter scampered down a hillside. The policeman and I strained to keep up with him. No doubt Amat was trying to outguess the tiger. Would the tiger ramble down by the river, pass deeper into the jungle, or pad through the rice fields?

Breathing hard, we stopped at the edge of a swamp. This seemed to be a suitable area to intercept our prey. If we were lucky, we might see him again or find another tiger. We rested in the low limbs of a tree but saw no sign of wild life. It began to seem as though our tiger hunting efforts had failed. And I was glad.

About three o'clock Amat suddenly raised his rifle and blasted a gray form blurring past us.

"*Itu kidang,*" the policeman said. "It's a deer."

We scurried after the wounded animal as it thrashed through the swamp and hobbled up a hill. The bloody trail continued for miles. In another rice field Amat thought he saw the deer and squeezed his trigger. After the report echoed and faded into the night, we heard a man shout.

Amat did not answer; the policeman and I stood motionless. A loud splash came from the rice pool near us. Within a second we heard the booming echo of a rifle. No doubt we were trespassing on some farmer's prized rice field. Quickly, the old hunter turned off his lamp, and we raced away with shots hitting all around us.

When the sky grew light, we trudged back to the elder's house and tried to rest on his front porch. Clouds of mosquitoes kept our hands waving continuously.

As I sipped a cup of bitter coffee, I wondered how long the government would allow wild animals to be hunted with such ease. No hunting licenses were required, and there seemed to be no limit on how many animals a hunter could kill. Many Sumatrans existed by trapping or shooting tigers and selling their skins to Chinese merchants.

Somewhere on this gigantic island, orangutans, rhinoceroses and other exotic animals could easily be poached and sold on the international black market. I hoped that in future years the government would take steps to protect Sumatra's wild game from all commercial exploitation.

On Sumatra, the Kubus and the many immigrants from Java were being well taken care of by the government. Obviously, their advancement had top priority; however, it was unfortunate that there was little interest in allowing wild animals to exist in harmony with human beings. Perhaps the magnificent tigers and other animals would eventually retreat into extinction.

"We leave very soon for the city," Darmano said, as we continued to sip the bitter coffee. "My schedule is most crowded."

"Good. I want to start toward Palembang today," I said.

"Did you arrive there by airplane from Java?" he asked.

"That's right, and I guess I'll fly toward India from there. It's much cheaper than waiting around for a cargo ship."

"Will you go hunting there?"

"No. I want to live with the holy men and study the Untouchables. In fact, I might try to meet a maharajah or two."

"You are most ambitious. But I think you had your fill of tiger hunting last night," he said, and laughed. "Tell me, does it cost much to hunt tigers in India?"

"I've read that it does. This hunt cost me around four dollars. In India I doubt if I could even rent a rifle for that."

"In fact, anyone would be wasting time and money hunting tigers in India," Darmano said, and folded his arms pompously.

"Why is that?"

"I have often heard that Indian tigers are as tame as house cats. The only real tigers in the world are found here in Sumatra."

"Oh?"

"Yes, and they are presently being killed in abundant numbers, but only by men of courage, like me."

~ 13 ~

Meditating With
An Indian Mystic

Reading articles and books on Hindu mysticism did nothing but confuse me. Perhaps most religious persuasions could only be experienced in person. While I continued my search to understand different religions, I lived in an ashram in the hills south of Bombay.

As the train rumbled out of the station, I searched through a noisy crowd for the stationmaster. For several days I had stopped at different cities along the railroad line leading south from Bombay. I hoped to find a *sadhu*, or mystic, who was rumored to be living in this general area.

Ultimately, my search led me to the city of Kirkee. After I met the stationmaster, he escorted me out of the cold wind into his comfortable office. While his assistant served tea, he leafed through his collection of books on Indian religion. He also showed me several magazine and newspaper clippings about Indian holy men who were exposed for committing various sins. One article, in the international edition of *Time* magazine, dealt with a holy man who had amassed considerable wealth and had kidnapped women to live in his well-guarded *ashram*.

"Impostors, impostors," the stationmaster blurted out over the crackle of the wood-burning stove. "Too many of our so-called holy men are nothing more than impostors!"

"I've heard that," I said.

"Nevertheless, I think you will find the *sadhu* here an exemplary person. He is encamped at a temporary *ashram* in the hills near here. I know him; he travels from city to city."

"Wonderful! At last, I've found him. Quick, give me some directions."

"Do not run through life. You must just eat here at the station house."

"I'm really not hungry."

He chortled and said, "This will be the last good meal you will have for many, many days."

"You mean the mystic is fasting?"

"He eats little and meditates much. Come now, I will draw you a map while you fill your belly with mutton stew."

After leaving the station, I strode down the city streets into the farming country. Using the map as my guide, I followed a dirt road through the undulating hills and then climbed a trail to a grove of trees that rested on top of an imposing bluff. Afternoon sunlight filtered through the trees and glowed on the mystic, who sat at the base of an enormous tree. An apricot-colored robe draped his slender body. Long black hair and a beard framed his surprisingly youthful face. Sticking up in the ground near him was a silver trident of the Hindu god Shiva. After slowly emerging from a trance, he blinked and grew vaguely aware of my presence.

With eyes that glowed with an inner satisfaction, he gazed at me for a long time. His feel for time was exceedingly slow; it seemed that he had no intention of moving or speaking. I respected his silent countenance and stood immobile as he seemed to return to reality from some blissful trance. At last, he grew fully aware of me and smiled.

After awkwardly introducing myself and explaining my world trip, I expressed my interest in his religion. He searched the sky and glanced at the tree limbs and his trident before focusing his eyes on me. "I can see you are unenlightened," he said in a cheerful manner.

"What do you mean?" I asked.

"You are unenlightened about Baba."

"Baba?"

"Yes, Baba, he is the master of all prophets. It is he who enlightened Mohammed, Christ, Moses and every man of true wisdom."

"Could you tell me about him?"

"You must allow me to be your *guru* or teacher."

"Fine, that's why I came here."

"This I know. Now you must just try to empty your mind of all other prophets and gods. You see, he may just come to you. Baba has lived before time and after time and without time. Presently, he has a body and travels from the jungles to the mountains."

"How long have you followed Baba?"

"For some ten years now. One time I was in the army—a most splendid service, but not God-centered enough. I left and became a merchant. One day, as I washed in a stream, a powerful light filled me. It was like lightning but without thunder. This was the enlightenment of Baba. For days after, I prayed and thought of him."

"Your flash of enlightenment sounds like a *satori*. You know, the sudden enlightenment the Zen Buddhists have."

"I do not know of the Zen Buddhists."

"I learned a little about them in Japan."

"Only true enlightenment comes from Baba. A fortnight after this powerful light filled me, Baba came to me in a dream. He told me to give up all worldly things and walk the country like a beggar. I gave my wife and four children to my brother to care for. From that day on I have been a *sadhu*."

"Tell me, how do you worship Baba?"

"I cross my legs in this pose of the lotus and search the sky or a fire for his face. If I am right, he fills me with his all powerful love—at that time I am peaceful."

Our conversation was interrupted by three young men in long orange robes. After bowing toward the *sadhu* with their hands in an attitude of prayer, they greeted me. Without speaking, each of them went to his own place of meditation near an outcropping of rocks.

"Does Baba have many disciples?" I asked.

"Quite a few the world over. Baba tells us the world will be destroyed in the Christian year of two-thousand. At that time his worldly body dies."

"Does this worry you?"

"No, no. Baba is at all times here, everywhere, nowhere. This body of his is nothing, nothing," he said with gusto as he flung out his arms.

"I mean, are you worried about the world being destroyed?"

He chuckled and said, "Indeed not. The world is an illusion. We are nothing in the eternal."

"Nothing?" I asked.

"You Christians are too concerned about death and nothingness," he said, and laughed merrily. "To us, death is a most happy release from *this* life."

Vultures skimmed across our hill and drifted with the air currents over the low farmlands before converging on the skeletal remains of a wild dog. The wind no longer caused the leaves over our heads to shudder. Now the coolness was more bearable.

"It is time for my disciples to go to the city to beg for food," he said, and smiled.

"Let me go with them and buy some food there."

"*Dhanyavad*," he mumbled. "I am grateful. You shall gain merit for your next incarnation. I remain here and take water and food only at night."

After following his young disciples into the city, where they separated and went from one house to another begging for food, I found a store. Inside I bought rice, flour and firewood from a merchant who had known the mystic for some time and held him in high regard. There was little doubt that this *sadhu* was a man of sincerity. His enthusiasm was engaging, and I looked forward to learning more from him.

The disciples and I arrived back at the *sadhu's* retreat, *ashram*, with food and the supplies that I had purchased. We were fairly well stocked for several days. All of us gathered around the fire to eat our evening meal, the only meal of the day.

Speaking in Hindi to his disciples and in English to me, the mystic led a happy dinner conversation. Religion was not mentioned; it was a natural part of life. This was the time of day when everyone could relax and enjoy each other's company. It was a safety valve to keep us in touch with the petty realities of life. I was delighted to see their lively conversation punctuated by gales of laughter.

Later in the evening, the disciples wrapped themselves in quilts and slept near the fire. Before speaking, the *guru* studied the flames for some time.

"I feel that you are sincere," he said. "Now, if you wish, I shall start you on the road to enlightenment."

"Fine," I said, moving closer to the fire.

"First, you must allow your mind to empty. Think of your head as a vessel and your mind as water. Slowly, pour the water from the vessel. If necessary, think of something pleasant. Perhaps you could think of the red sun over your Tennessee mountains. By all means do not sleep. Relax and breathe deeply, slowly, and you may become as one with Baba."

Gazing with heavy eyelids at the fire, I let the colors merge with the red of my imaginary sunrise. Occasionally, the pleasant heat interrupted my somewhat blank mind and ignited comforting thoughts of warm Bali and Sumatra.

The cold night passed slowly. Several times I walked around to keep awake and to put more wood on the fire. My *guru* seemed to move only to finger the dried berry rosary around his neck; he relaxed with his legs crossed under his body. Although I was unable to assume the rigid lotus position, I was at ease with my arms wrapped around my knees. Fortunately, my religious experience in Japan reinforced my present attempt at Hindu meditation. Now and then I was able to clear my mind, yet a plethora of images drifted back to me.

Initially, I daydreamed of home, while flashes of religious experiences that I had on this journey dotted my mind. Suddenly, I was mentally transformed back to the nocturnal vigil on top of the Buddhist temple of Borobudur. I could visualize the sun rising from the summit of Mount Fujiyama. The old people in the Japanese fishing village drifted into my mind. Yes, they were clapping their hands as they worshiped the sun over the Pacific. I was surprised to hear the ocean and their soft chanting. Gradually, the surf grew louder in my imagination and merged into a pleasant roar as I tried to keep my mind free and open.

Our fire burned lower as the pale-blue morning light slanted across the far hills. The *guru* sneezed. His rheumy eyes were fixed on the embers for a sign from Baba.

"Did you see Baba?" I asked.

"Only for a short time. Things were not right last night."

"I didn't make too much progress in my meditation," I confided.

"Be patient—actually, it will take many days and nights to make progress."

During the next week, I repeated the slow-moving routine of life in the *sadhu's ashram*. I tried to keep my mind open at night while I meditated by the fire. Each day, I strolled around the hillside, napped occasionally in the warming sun, read paperbacks on meditation, and chatted with my *guru*. My nose was running, and I felt as though I were developing a head cold.

In the late hours of the fourth night, I drifted into another dimension.

The only umbilical cord I had with reality was the sound of the fire. My body seemed to disappear. A fascinating lightness possessed me while night turned into day, and I traveled above roads through the Indian farmlands. I was gliding like an eagle over the heads of people going to market, bullocks grazing, and farmers clearing their fields. Softly, effortlessly, I passed over Indian towns, crowded markets, sari-clad women at their wells and camel caravans. A pleasing narcotic numbness permeated these scenes.

The *mantra*, incantation, that I had been chanting, lapsed from my lips and a chorus of muted voices seemed to repeat it. Then "*Aum, Aum, Aum,*" came from a choir in an unidentified realm beyond my understanding. Yet I had no desire to understand. I could visualize no choir but was fascinated with the voices intermingling from major to minor chords as though they were soaring on a celestial wind. The temporal world of people and places dissolved. Now I saw scores of pale colors in a fog bank. Slowly, easily, I felt as though I was rising high, high into a comfortable world of soft, white light. All grew silent.

Seconds, minutes, or hours later, I returned to the darkness of my body and rested by the dim firelight. Time had little meaning. A sense of fulfillment swept through me. When, at last, I felt like talking, I shared my experience with my *guru*.

"Ah, ha. You have been possessed, and your spirit left your body. You have made one of the first steps toward enlightenment," he said with great joy.

"I really don't understand it," I said.

"You should not try to do so. To think too much is bad for the spirit. Western logic is dangerous. You must let things happen to you as Baba desires them to."

Living in this small retreat was exhausting. I was continually hungry, and my head cold was becoming worse. Although I had developed an insight into my guru's religion, and was elated over my out-of-body experience, I felt months, even years, away from any meaningful progress.

Yet there remained within me a quiet knowledge of the very private experience that I would not share with anyone except the mystic, for years. Before leaving the *ashram*, I offered him a few *rupees* to buy more food.

"No, thank you," he said. "You have already made offerings of food and firewood. Baba will provide for us in the days to come."

"You know, I wish I were not so puzzled about your religion," I said, before walking toward the city.

"You will always be until you cast out your old thoughts. Only then can Baba's spirit truly come to you."

After this draining experience at the retreat, I allowed myself the luxury of riding in the comfort of a first-class coach on a train bound for the north. Seated next to me was an Indian government official dressed in a western suit. For many miles we discussed the "great Indian experiment in self-government."

When I mentioned my profound interest in Indian religions, he laughed and said in a cynical manner, "My young American friend, you must not be misled by all this tommyrot of mystics and exotic gods."

"Why is that?" I asked and forced a smile.

"Such beliefs and rituals are nothing more than backward superstitions. We must rid India of these old-fashioned religions. Then and only then can we take our rightful place in the modern world."

Suddenly, the train stopped at a small station. I lurched forward with his words still throbbing in my ears. Anger, then disgust for his lack of religious tolerance overcame me. I bit my lip and thought of the mystic who had transcended many of the evils of this worldly experience. It was evident that the mystic existed on a very high spiritual level, one that this government official could never comprehend.

~ 14 ~

Life And Death
With The Untouchables

In the Indian caste system, the Brahmans were the highest caste; many of them were priests or wealthy land owners. Below them were the warriors, then those in various occupations. Near the bottom of this system were the Outcastes. Detached from all of these people were the despised Untouchables. During this world trip, I intended to live the life of these people. Unfortunately, their future was not promising.

My eyes stung. For a moment I couldn't remember where I was. Slowly, I was awakening. Dawn sprayed through the cracks of the door near me as if diffused through a prism of ice. My overcoat and blanket felt colder than the dirt floor beneath me. Blinking, my eyelids finally stretched apart. In the corner of the room, the gray figure of a bullock appeared. He seemed warm and tranquil under his heavy quilt. From his droppings rose thin currents of steam. At the other end of the room, two black figures slept in their thin wraps.

After I coughed the dank air from my lungs, my mind cleared. Yes, I remembered, I was living in a village of Untouchables in the mountains south of Bombay. The headman and his son were sleeping close to me. Quietly as possible, I slid the door back and went outside. Shivering, I passed a cluster of grass-roofed mud huts, before continuing to the mountain's edge that tumbled down into an immense valley.

By degrees, the ruddy glow of the sun beamed over a distant ridge and flushed the frozen stars from the sky. Sleek crows whirled over the brown, exhausted fields below, piercing the silence with their familiar cries. In a neighboring village, several sari-clad women filed dreamily toward a well. The hammered copper waterpots on their heads caught the sunlight and gave them the aspect of saints with orange halos. Running close to a river, a pack of wild *pi,* dogs, stirred up a plume of dust. The valley echoed with their foreboding howls.

Soon the headman walked with a few other brown-skinned men over to the white-flowered *champak* trees. They seemed uncomfortable in their dirty white jackets and *dhoties,* draped white pantaloons. With shoulders touching to draw warmth from each other, the villagers faced across the valley toward the rising sun.

The slender headman clasped his hands in front of his angular face and then behind his back; he repeated this gesture several times in rapid succession. Praying softly, the others followed his example, a ritual satisfying their sun worship and warming them as well. When the men finished their devotions, I returned with them to a cleared place within the village.

We squatted down in a circle to enjoy the cool morning sunshine. Apparently, these villagers savored long periods of silence, as the talk was unhurried and fragmented. This was the unproductive, dry season, and the men had little work to do until the rainy season drew closer. When the sun floated higher in the sky, I grew restless and left them.

In a couple of minutes, I arrived at the hut where I stayed. Harsha, the headman's eleven-year-old son, led the gentle-eyed bullock out of the hut and toward the pasture. With each heavy step, the hump over the animal's shoulders quivered. Harsha smiled bashfully, motioning for me to follow. I signaled that I would meet him later. Although the breeze was cool, he wore only an orange fold of cloth around his hips and a white headband.

Acrid smoke from a primitive clay stove streamed out of the windowless hut. Inside, the headman's wife swept the floor with a bunch of twigs; her silver bangles and necklace clinked musically. An emerald-green cloth circled her hips and fell to her knees; her short-sleeved crimson blouse covered her breasts, leaving her abdomen bare. I entered and sat very close to the stove. We prattled in our own languages for some time, occasionally laughing at our bold attempt to communicate.

After serving me a cup of tea, the headman's wife carried the night droppings of the bullock out to the sunward side of the hut. She patted the dung between her weathered hands until it hardened, then stuck it on the side of the house to dry, leaving her handprints on each cake. These disks would later serve as fuel. After wiping her hands on the dry grass, she gathered her black, clay waterpots and visited her neighbor's hut.

As the headman's wife gossiped with her neighbor, a faint cry came from another hut. Both women froze, then jumped from their squatting positions, jangling their silver jewelry. The frightened tones of a crying woman grew louder. In a moment, all of the brightly dressed village women ran toward the noisy hut.

They chattered outside the door like a group of nervous myna birds. Soon the headman appeared. While tightening his white headband, he tried to listen to the women. Losing patience with their excited babbling, he pushed his way inside the hut.

Finally, the body of a year-old girl was placed outside the doorway. She was the child who had been coughing fitfully during my entire stay in the village. Now she was dead.

One leathery-faced old woman, whose eyes had seen much suffering, glanced at the girl and yelled something to me in a cracked voice. She began to move toward me with a few other agitated women. I feared the villagers' conception of cause and effect might link the girl's death with my presence in the village. Perhaps they believed I had invoked the displeasure of their Hindu gods. Apprehensively, I strode toward the edge of the village.

Several of the women and children were close behind me. A rock hit me on the leg. The women chanted. I decided not to run out into the fields since my retreat might be an admission of guilt. Quickly, the headman's wife ran between the women and me, waving them back with her muscular arms. At last, they turned and joined the others, who prepared for the cremation. Throughout my stay with the Untouchables, I had tried carefully to honor all their customs. I felt very uncomfortable and sad that I was not fitting in with them on all occasions.

The girl's dark brown body rested on a piece of musty-smelling muslin. She was dressed, as she had been in life, with a band of red and blue beads around her hips. Her neck was bound by a black necklace crafted shortly after her birth. It contained a piece of her umbilical cord as protection against evil spirits and death itself.

One misty-eyed woman tried to comb the girl's radiant black hair. After sprinkling water around the body, another woman fingered the small blue lips and commented with a sense of wonder about the discoloration. Squatting in the shadows, the girl's mother sobbed loudly.

Several men brought a single five-foot ladder to the door of the dead girl's hut. After the headman examined the rungs to see if they were lashed properly, he lifted the limp body onto this bier. On the girl's navel, a woman placed a flat cake of dough, which would feed the spirit on its upward flight. Tenderly, the women shrouded the body in white muslin. Now the girl's features gave the appearance of a marble cherub. Strangely, her hunger-swollen abdomen appeared larger than usual. Harsha picked some white blossoms from the trees, scattered them over the body and meekly stepped back with the curious onlookers.

Two men in gray jackets lifted the ladder on their shoulders and started down a steep path. The old woman, who suspected me of causing the death, ordered the men to lower the bier. She pulled the muslin down and drew a circle on the girl's forehead with orange mud. After replacing the cloth, she chanted a lengthy prayer.

Again the men hoisted the ladder and, preceding the parents, climbed down the long mountain to the river. Flames from an earthenware pot held by the girl's mother, licked the cool air. Her husband glanced back at the long line of barefooted villagers who followed. In the center of this procession the headman thumped a small drum, while he and several others chanted. A few women carried heavy branches for use at the funeral pyre.

At regular intervals, the dead girl's mother wailed. Her echo returned from another mountain like the whine of a lost kitten. As we descended through a shady grove of trees, the mother stopped the procession to catch her breath. Many of the villagers chided her for stopping and not maintaining a continuous wail. In a few minutes she continued the cries expected of her; however, they were less frequent and seemed labored.

The hot sun forced perspiration out of the villagers' slender bodies as we marched onto the floor of the valley. Its brightness seemed too cheerful for such an occasion and made the mourners' clothes seem much too colorful. I shed my overcoat and flung it across my shoulder, as I followed the procession toward the river.

This was January, the dry season, when the eroded earth took on the color of cracked parchment. Only a few hardy trees and bushes punctuated the landscape with splashes of green. The sun-withered grasses had somehow managed to survive.

We hurried down a wide riverbank toward the small stream in its middle. Two men shouldering the ladder laid their burden down near the river and knelt to drink with the rest of us. Now that the villagers were partially refreshed, they piled branches in a mound and stuffed grass between the cracks.

After waving away green flies, the headman and the girl's parents lifted the bier onto the wood. Many of the men and a few women pretended to be in a happy mood in order to ease the spirit's upward journey. The mother held her flaming clay pot as she led the villagers around the pyre in an informal circle. At the end of the third trip, she placed a leaf from the sacred *tulsi* plant over her daughter's mouth. The headman pounded his drum in a fast tempo. After the mother sprinkled the fire from the pot over the branches, she squatted with the others.

White smoke hissed around the body, forcing everyone back. The headman gave a spirited cry. One middle-aged woman began an impromptu dance. With arms spread in awkward angles, she shifted her weight from one foot to the other. Her stylized movements brought back recollections of the Hindu dances of Bali.

Now the smoke turned black and curled into the endless blue tomb of the sky above, where dark kites—those swift birds of prey—soared in the low drafts. I sat a respectful distance from the others, but I could still see their faces. They seemed to search the sky for some sign of the liberated spirit of the girl, as it ascended into another region to await rebirth. Undoubtedly, they hoped for her reincarnation into some higher caste since the life of an Untouchable was difficult.

A low-pitched sound like the pop of an air-blown paper sack told the villagers that the skull had exploded and their duty was done. They arose from the ground and talked animatedly for a long time. After the headman prodded the fire with a stick, he nodded to the others that the small corpse was properly cremated. A body and spirit had been transformed. Satisfaction registered on many faces. With no ceremony, the parents of the girl shoved the coals and remains into the purifying water.

Later, we trudged in a straggly line through the dusty valley toward the mountains. Shadows of the soft-whistling kites swept over us as we quickened our pace to reach the village before sunset. The cooling air did not seem to bother the thinly-clad Untouchables. I felt depressed and cold as I put on my overcoat.

When we climbed up to our village of Raiwadi, the shadows of the houses stretched to enormous lengths. Without hesitation the women stacked waterpots on their heads and hurried to the well. Many of the men hunkered down in front of the houses to chew their *pan-supari*, betel nut, while the boys searched for the cattle.

I walked to the edge of the woods with Harsha where his white bullock was tethered. Speaking affectionately, he entwined his slender arms around the neck of the heavy beast. Carefully, we scoured the dry ground for stalks of grass. The bullock accepted these extra bits with the pompous air of a raja receiving a meal from his servants. After unraveling the animal's blue and white beaded neckband, Harsha and I led him to the village.

A bitter night wind moaned across our mountain top, causing the fire in the headman's stove to flutter and waver. His wife stooped over a flat stone near the flames, while she ground curry paste for the only meal of the day. Since this was the dry season, the villagers could eat very little. As I watched her grind bits of cloves, red peppers and leaves, my mind drifted back to warm Sumatra. Although many of the people there were poor, they could usually keep their stomachs full. If nothing else, they could pick a few bananas or a jack fruit outside their huts. But here in India, the villagers had to withstand empty stomachs along with the depressing cold.

Humming merrily, the headman's wife kneaded moist flour into a large ball and slapped it from one hand to the other. The bangles on her wrists clinked rhythmically before she spread the dough into a large *chapatty*, griddlecake. After dropping it into the frying pan, she coughed from a gust of smoke. In the corner, the headman and Harsha chatted while they smoothed a quilt over the bullock, as he munched on a pile of grass.

Later, the wife ladled out small mounds of boiled rice in our bowls. We tore off sections of the *chapatty*, dipped it in the curry paste and stuffed it into our mouths. In eating, I attempted to use my right hand, as the left was considered unclean. Whenever a few grains of rice fell on my overcoat, Harsha grew concerned and replaced each rare morsel in my hand. Before finishing our meal, we passed the bronze teacup around, and each of us ate a spiced pickle. Harsha, his father, and I left the hut to allow his mother to eat the rest of her meal and to clean up.

In the center of the village, the headman squatted with a drawn face near a bundle of twigs and grass. He remained silent until several other men joined him. His son stepped carefully from the house holding a lighted string; he let it fall into the grass bundle. Flames crackled as the headman tossed in a red pepper to frighten disease and death. Soon his wife passed us on her way to a neighbor's house where she slept while I was in the village.

After feeding the bullock the leftover rice water from our meal,

Harsha closed the door and stirred the dying fire. He and his father curled up in their blankets on the well-swept floor. I loosened my shoelaces, before rolling up in a tattered quilt. Outside, the wind swished against the grass roof and forced the trees to rub their frigid branches together. The scent of the rich curry still lingered pleasantly within the dark hut. While I tried to sleep, my thoughts went back to my trip to this village.

*

Several days before, in Bombay, I had boarded a train, which trundled south through the hill country. I was dozing in a crowded third-class coach, when the train jerked to an unscheduled stop. A tree-lined road and many neat houses looked inviting. It was a typical small Indian village, which seemed to bear few signs of foreign influence. With a carefree air, I snatched my handbag and left the train to stroll around.

After wandering through the noisy streets, I found a young merchant who spoke English. During our long conversation in his modest cloth shop, he told me about a mountain village of *Adivasis*, primitive people, who lived some ten miles away. Sensing my enthusiasm over visiting them, he offered to guide me there the following day. Before going to his small home that night, I bought a burlap bag of rice and one of wheat for these mountain people.

Early the next morning, the merchant shook my *charpoy*, rope-webbed bed. It was still black outside his barred window, but his room glowed from an open mustard-oil lamp. His wife brushed through a curtain from the kitchen area and served us cups of milky tea. Silently, she withdrew to comfort her squalling baby. The merchant put on his Western topcoat, unbolted the door and walked outside, carrying a heavy bag on his shoulder. After hoisting a sack on my shoulder, I followed him outside his home and then through the village. Our pace became labored as we climbed the mountain; we stopped frequently to rest.

"Are these people free from the caste system now?" I asked, as we sat on the sacks and gazed into the great valley.

"Technically, they are free but they will always be Untouchables," he said firmly.

"I thought the law had changed all that."

"Yes, the old law has been changed, but the hearts of people are difficult to change. You see, in the law, they are equal to all others, yet custom forbids them to use these rights. They must use their own wells and are not allowed to enter the temples of my village."

"I understand. In my part of America we have many people who are black. Our laws are changing to give them equal rights."

"Oh, yes, yes. Both our countries have damnable problems. Come now, let's climb up a few more furlongs."

By midafternoon, we passed through the woods on the summit and entered a large clearing. Barking angrily, two white dogs trotted across the farming land toward us. We fended them off with sticks while following a trail toward a village.

"Their lands are barren now," the merchant said. "When the monsoon rains come in June, they grow rice and *nagli*—a sort of maize."

"How do they survive in the dry season?"

"They sell firewood to different villages and buy food. Often they go hungry."

On coming closer to the village, the merchant yelled something. Many of the women and children disappeared into the safety of their homes while the men approached us. The headman stepped forward to greet us. After a brief conversation with the merchant, he knelt before me and touched my shoes before placing his hands on his cheeks, behavior that he had probably learned from his former British masters.

"The headman says no, no. You could bring the disfavor of the gods if you live in this village."

"Tell him I won't be able to give him the wheat and rice unless I can stay," I said firmly.

When this was translated, the headman conferred for a long time with the others, who seemed to conclude that the gods might possibly smile on the food and me.

"He was also frightened of you because he thought you were a tax collector, and they have nothing with which to pay."

"Are you going to spend the night here?" I asked.

"No, I would suffer much criticism from my people. The headman is grateful for the food. You can stay here as long as you desire...."

*

Suddenly, the bullock groaned mournfully and kicked the wall; my mind darted back to my present circumstances. I was lying in the headman's house where I was now trying to sleep, following the funeral.

Harsha padded across the dark room to comfort the sacred animal.

Awake early in the morning, we huddled close to the dung fire. The foul smoke bothered me little, since the coveted heat accompanied it. With mounting intensity, the stabbing pain of dysentery forced me to leave the warm blaze and scurry into the woods. After I made several of these trips, the headman motioned that he would go for some medicine. Soon he returned with a cup of warm cow milk.

On the grinding stone, he pounded several twisted seeds into a powder. I drank the powder and milk mixture and in an hour suffered no more discomfort. The headman's eyes sparkled with delight over the quick results of his potion.

Later that morning, the fretful bullock seemed reluctant to leave the house. Snorting contemptuously, he kicked out a section of the wall as Harsha tried to coax him toward the pasture. The headman uttered some oath. He soon ordered his wife to go for water, as he inspected the damage.

When his wife returned from the well, the headman had disappeared. With little ceremony, she gathered baskets of dirt and stirred it with fresh dung and water. Pursing my lips, I fought back nausea to help her make the wall repairs. We lashed a long row of wooden strips over the hole. I held them down as she smeared the cow dung paste over the area, allowing it to dry in the morning sun. As we finished, the headman appeared and scowled at me for doing woman's work.

Metallic rapping echoed from the edge of the mountain village, where women trimmed their long bundles of firewood with *churis*, sickles. One by one they hoisted heavy loads on top of their heads before leaving for a distant village to trade for wheat. The headman's wife led the procession. Gracefully, their dark figures moved across the blue horizon toward the trees below. Sunlight brightened their colorful saris and polished their silver jewelry. Somehow their clothes seemed to disguise their drab poverty. These stately women reminded me of a frieze on the side of a Hindu temple, depicting life before the British had colonized India.

Later in the morning, I accompanied the headman across the fields. We paused at a large tree that had smoke rising from the knotholes on its trunk. Gesturing simply, he explained how the tree would burn inside and eventually fall. Once it was on the ground, the villagers would cut the wood with knives and sickles. This method was used because the villagers had no axes or saws.

Nearby, several men enlarged one of the fields by pitching small rocks aside and cutting down bushes. The farmers withstood the cold weather very well, although none of them wore shirts or coats. Unfortunately, this new plot would lie fallow unless the villagers could save enough money for extra seed. The men completed their daily work about thirty minutes later. Then they ambled into the center of the village, where, in a squatting posture, they chatted in the sunshine.

Harsha played with several of his friends in the white-flowered trees near the cattle. After I threw several bits of candy to them, they laughed and dropped out of the trees. My pockets were quickly emptied. The men soon learned I was giving away peppermints.

"*Mithai, mithai,*" they pleaded, their eyes bright, while they circled around me. "Sweets, sweets."

I motioned for them to follow me to the headman's house, where I kept my handbag. In a few minutes the village men and women were enjoying the candy as much as the boys. In an area of food scarcity, any treat was greatly appreciated by people of all ages.

While the afternoon sun drifted lower, the men and boys squatted in a ragged circle under the trees. With an air of great dignity, the headman started a long story. He talked slowly in his loose-throated accent, pausing frequently to study the sky for the next part of the tale. Twice his memory failed, yet several men were able to prompt him in the story that, no doubt, came from some Hindu epic. Harsha tried to remind his father during a pause, but was ignored for his efforts. Near the end of one story, the headman evoked lusty guffaws by jerking his arm up and down in a phallic manner.

Finally, the relaxed session ended, and the silver clinks of the women's jewelry grew louder. The women gradually filed into the village from their exhausting trip and assembled near the headman's house to divide the bags of wheat they had earned by selling firewood. With a sigh, the headman's wife dropped a heavy burlap bag in front of me. Her moist necklace smelled briny and strong. Smiling wryly, she handed me a note from the merchant:

> *My respected and revered sir,*
> *I am hereby dispatching an extra bag of rice for you, due to the fact that the headman's wife informed me you told her in sign language to send the same. You may reimburse me when you return to my home.*
> *Your most obedient servant,*
> *R. H. Saraff*
> *Postscript: They are esteemed to have you as a guest.*

I smiled at the note since I had made no request. In a minute I laughed with a few of the men, at the craftiness of the headman's wife. With a happy gleam in her eyes, she carried the bag into the house where she began preparing for the evening meal.

Early the next morning, the old woman who mistrusted me began cursing whenever I passed her hut. This irritated the headman. With his arms flailing, he spoke harshly to her. The gold ring in her nose swung back and forth as she meekly defended her actions. When the headman stomped off, I gave her a small bowl of uncooked rice and a piece of candy. At first, she resisted my gifts. Grunting a few syllables, she seemed to relax. Then, turning abruptly, she shambled back into the shadows of her house, with the rice bowl grasped in her arms. At last she was beginning to tolerate me.

A guttural chant rose from many of the village women as they circled the sacred *tulsi* bush near the headman's house. Their bare feet stirred the dust over the bush, almost obscuring its dark green leaves. Several minutes later, the ceremony ended when one woman raised her hands and squealed. Everyone backed away from her. With arms outstretched, she swaggered around the bush. Soon she bared her teeth to the sky as though she were fighting some bitter-sweet spirit within. Emerging from this brief trance, she shook her head and regained her composure. In a few minutes, she put her water pot on her head and followed the others to the well. This daily ritual seemed to be enacted to pacify some of their gods.

A few days later, Harsha was trimming a few limbs for his mother's bundle of firewood behind his hut. While he hacked on an upright branch, his sickle slipped and cut his knee. Yelping, he flung the sickle down and limped around the hut to his mother. She wiped off some of the blood and led him to the manure heap that was protected by a cover of grass. After mixing water from a bronze cup with a wad of dung, she smeared it on his wound. Her clean hand caressed the back of his neck. A little later, Harsha was able to return to his chores.

It was surprising to see her use the same primitive medication that had proved effective for a friend of mine from the Tennessee mountains. Although I remained somewhat doubtful about the merits of this remedy, my friend had a successful record of preventing infection from cuts and abrasions.

While I helped Harsha chop some rough branches, I wondered if the Untouchables would ever have a chance to improve their living conditions. Many other primitive people were changing slowly under the guidance of the Indian government; it seemed impossible, however, to help all such people in a single generation. Harsha's future would no doubt continue to be austere, with little prospect for improvement.

The next morning I drained my teacup and bowed deeply to the head man. After touching my shoes, he hung a garland made from the blossoms of *shite* trees around my neck. With elaborate gestures he tried to tell me something. I think it was that his village would be more prosperous and fitting for a visitor when the fields became green once more. His wife smiled impishly at me while patting her stomach, which bulged with some of the wheat that I had "bought" for them.

As I left the village, I heard the voices of several women returning from the well. Harsha and his friends waved to me from the far pasture. The men now squatted in the cool sunshine, with very little to do but wait patiently for the rainy season.

~ 15 ~

Developing A New India

Unlike the neglected Untouchable villages, the government was trying to improve the conditions of many. Advances in agriculture and healthcare had come about very slowly. Fortunately, however, these changes were promising.

After the railroad official chatted with me, he summoned a young porter. I followed the porter as he carried my handbag on his head through the dark streets of the commercial district. Finally, we arrived at a building with a sign that read "Community Development Project." Apparently the railroad official was unaware that these offices were closed during the night.

"*Dak bangla dikhao*," I said after thumbing through my dictionary. "Take me to the dak bungalow." After I repeated my poorly pronounced *Hindi* several times, the porter remained confused.

At last he said with a bewildered expression, "Yas, sahib, indeed, yas."

He trotted back through the village and headed toward a few buildings at the top of a hill. I jogged along behind him. Inside one of these buildings, a light from an oil lamp trembled across a wall of iron bars. My porter awakened an old man sleeping in the doorway. The man shouted angrily at him. High laughter ricocheted from behind the bars. We were at the jail and not the dak bungalow. The frightened boy muttered, "Yas, sahib," gaped around for a moment and scurried up to the top of the hill. When I reached him, he squatted timidly in front of the official rest house or dak bungalow.

"Did you think I was a criminal?" I asked with amusement, when I tipped him.

With embarrassment, he smiled and repeated the only English phrase he seemed to know, "Yas, sahib, indeed, yas."

Early the next morning, a stocky government official in a European suit walked down the hill with me toward the village farmhouses. We passed by the dry, brown fields that were sprinkled with herds of grazing cattle. Unlike the farming area outside the Untouchables' village, the land here in Karjat was completely level and yielded abundant crops.

"You see," the official said, "here in India most of the people are farmers. That is why we place so much faith in a development project such as this. It is our way to fight hunger and disease. We do this in a free democratic system as compared to the regimentation of communism."

"Was it difficult to start the project here?"

"At the inception, the people did not trust us. Then we demonstrated what improved seeds, planting methods and sanitation could do. Now they are beginning to change."

"Do you have any irrigation for this dry season?"

"Only a little. Our plans are for better irrigation, so instead of one rice crop a year, the people can have two or more. The rains are heavy during the monsoon, but it drains down to a pitifully low water table—now water is very dear."

We strolled through the trees at the bottom of the hill and stopped in front of a comfortable farmhouse. The house's brown clay walls were capped by a roof of matted grass. After entering the well-swept courtyard enclosed by a low stone wall, we rested on the front steps. Softly, the official called into the windowless house. There was no answer.

"I think the family must be in the fields," he said. "We must wait."

To our surprise, a baby boy, dressed only in a short red shirt, toddled out the open front door. Gibbering happily, he stumbled into my arms. I picked him up as we laughed. In a moment his older sister appeared in the doorway to retrieve her brother.

Across one field we heard high-pitched voices merging with a screeching noise. Clustered around the stone-encased well, women drew their morning water with the aid of a rusty pulley. A cool breeze unfurled parts of their colorful saris, giving the illusion of banners waving out from flagpoles. Near the well, two old women circled the small tile-roofed temple, praying to their gods inside.

At last, the mother of this family returned from the well with one of her daughters. She spoke to the official as she walked up the steps. Her green sari was draped from her head to her knees. Both the mother and daughter balanced hammered brass waterpots on their heads. A gold ring swayed in the mother's nose as she smiled self-consciously at the official and me.

In a little while, she returned from her smoking stove and served us milky tea in antique china cups. Without speaking, she and her daughter carried bundles of laundry to dry on the long poles at the far side of the courtyard.

"Have you taken enough tea?" the official asked.

"Yes, thanks," I replied.

"Then we must go across the fields to see the head of this family and his two sons. They are cutting food for the cattle."

In a nearby field, the young father of the family dropped a stack of yellow grass to the ground from a sling on his back. Mounds of this fodder already rested above him on a five-foot high storage platform. While the official and I walked closer, rich grass dust made me sneeze.

The father brushed off his white shirt and khaki *dothi* before pressing his hands together in an attitude of prayer.

"Namaste, yeh admi." "Greetings," he said.

"America se ayya hai." "This is an American," the official explained.

After an unhurried conversation, the official said: "You are welcome to work a bit with him, but you cannot stay in his house—it is much too crowded. As a matter of fact, the dak bungalow is more comfortable."

"Probably so," I said with disappointment.

"I must return to the office. I am due for a meeting of our adult education program. If you tire here, just have a look around the village."

For several hours I cut grass in the fields and carried it to the drying rack with the father and his sons. My final shove in hoisting the grass up to the platform proved helpful, since I was taller than they. At first, they were perplexed with me, as other people around the world had been. But as the morning progressed, they grew more accustomed to my assistance. They slung the grass about in a spirited way, completely unlike the mountain villagers. No doubt their extra energy came from sufficient food and better health.

Before noon we returned to the front yard where the mother served us tea and *chapatties*. While nibbling on the curry-covered griddlecakes, I glanced into the large room of the house. Two rope-webbed beds stood near an inner door, leading to the grain storage chamber. A picture of the Hindu god Shiva hung on the mud wall. His four blue arms flared out in an arrogant pose as he sat on a jewel-encrusted bull. Pasted on another wall was a faded print of Gandhi at his spinning wheel.

While the mother squinted at the position of the sun in the sky, she whispered something to Vasant, her twelve-year-old son. Suddenly he realized that he was late for something. It was time for him to abandon his chores at home and rush toward the village.

Vasant ran inside the house and soon reappeared in a clean white shirt and blue shorts. After brushing his neatly trimmed hair, the mother wiped a smudge of dirt from his full cheeks and watched him skip out of the yard. Smiling, the father gestured for me to follow the boy. I hurried behind Vasant as he breezed through the village and finally caught him when he turned into a large schoolyard. Vasant hurried to a seat on the ground with his fellow students. Many other classes of the school's second-shift were also assembled outside the stone buildings. In a superior voice the instructor chided Vasant for being late, then the class returned to the mathematics lesson. The class recited the results of the addition on an upright abacus; each time, the teacher clicked several colored beads across the wires of an abacus at the front of the class.

I walked around the primary school for some time, looking at the different outdoor classes. Unfortunately, there were no girl students present. No doubt, in future years, girls would have the opportunity to attend school here as they did now in India's large cities.

While listening to an instructor read to his boys, a slender man in a white jacket and *dhoti* came over to me. Introducing himself as the principal, he escorted me inside the building where the rooms were crowded with classes.

"You understand," he said, "we emphasize reading, writing and mathematics for these boys. Then, too, we have carpentry and agriculture. But most important, we stress citizenship. Now that the old provinces have been merged into the one country of India, the students must be made to feel a part of it."

"Did you have a school here before the government project began?"

"Only a very small one," he said, straightening his white Gandhi cap. This cap reminded me of those worn by cooks behind the counters of American diners.

"Would you tell me about your recreation?"

"Recreation—ah, you Americans are keen on that. We will have a recreation period in about twenty minutes."

Shouting with happy confusion, the children ran from their classes and started playing. A group of boys rattled *lezims*—sticks with metal disks attached—back and forth over their heads as they exercised. A woman in a pink sari counted the slow rhythm to them. In the shadows of the high trees, boys thumped a volleyball across a sagging net while nearby a game of tag called *hututu* took place.

It was heartening to notice that all the students were clean and well-groomed. This was not the case in the village of Untouchables. Here in Karjat, water was available even in the dry season. In the village of Untouchables, there was only one well, and it stood some three miles down the mountain from the village.

"Wonderful," I said and smiled. "This is the first time in over a year that I've seen such well-organized recreation."

"Yes, yes," the principal said. "I can see that you are enjoying it. Children should have the opportunity to just be children even though it interrupts their classes."

Soon we chuckled when a line of six-year-old boys shuffled around a building. Shouting "Train, train," a small boy led this procession across the volleyball court. After the make-believe train filed under the net, with the flagman in the rear waving his handkerchief, the older boys resumed their game. I was pleased to see that they respected the younger children.

"Just see, it is never too early to teach them about modern transportation," the principal said; we both laughed.

Late that afternoon I followed Vasant home from school. He and several of his high-spirited classmates played tag as we took a short cut through the countryside. Entering the woods, we heard growling dogs. Everyone stopped. Impulsively, the boys started shouting and throwing rocks into the shadows. A pack of wild *Pi* dogs emerged from the bushes and ran, yelping, down the path in front of us. Excitement over the dogs quickly subsided since such encounters seemed to be commonplace.

After helping Vasant pull weeds in his onion patch, a project of the Indian 4-H Program, I climbed the hill to the government rest house. That night while lying on my mosquito-netted bed in the warm dak bungalow, I thought about Harsha in the mountain village. His severe life would never improve. He did not have the advantages of education and improved conditions that Vasant now enjoyed in the community development area. Yawning, I felt the security of being in a clean, warm bed as never before. Somehow I was glad not to be sharing the cold, dirt floor with Harsha, his father and the bullock.

*

Squealing, the wooden wheels of our bullock cart bumped over the fields. Vasant and I sat on a load of grass and shouted encouragement to the two bullocks pulling us. When he slapped them, they spluttered and pranced forward, but always settled back into their sluggish pace. Across the fields we heard his mother. Vasant stopped the animals by yanking on the ropes strung through their nostrils. As he listened to his mother, an apprehensive look tightened his face. Motioning for me to follow, he jumped off the cart and began leading the bullocks toward his house. Quickly, we tethered the animals and strode into the village.

Outside the dispensary, Vasant's father stood in line with his left bare foot slightly off the ground. Dust and dried blood covered a gash near his toes. Gesturing, he told me how a log or some other heavy object fell from the grass drying rack onto his foot.

"Dhuki nahi." "No pain," the father said several times in a loud voice to impress the other patients.

"Acchcha." "Good," I said as I examined the minor wound.

After Vasant realized that his father was all right, he scampered away from the dispensary toward the fields. I hurried along behind him. We passed a large maternity home where his younger brother and sister had been born, and then we passed by the veterinary hospital. It was in this building that a veterinarian saved one of Vasant's bullocks from dying with a bloated stomach.

On the day before my departure, the official joined me on the porch of the dak bungalow. While chatting, we gazed at the high-tension power lines dipping on their steel towers toward the industries in the city of Bombay. Karjat's scant electricity came from a spasmodic old generator. Perhaps someday the villagers could tap into these gigantic lines and use some of this electricity for their own lights and power.

"It is pleasing you find our project of so much interest," he said.

"I think it's doing wonders. In fact, in my part of America we have a somewhat similar project. We were unprogressive for a long time; then with the introduction of the Tennessee Valley Authority things began to change. We had new dams for electricity and new agricultural aid, and we gradually became fairly prosperous."

"Yes, yes," he said quietly. "I have read much of this. We must do just a little of the same here—we must!"

~ 16 ~

Within Palace Walls

In 1955, India continued its uncertain experiment with democracy. Many of the Maharajas had been stripped of most of their privileges, including governmental power and funding.

M y **carriage driver reined up** outside the palace gates of the Maharaja of Jaipur, *Rajpramurh of Rajasthan*. White cupolas and turrets soared into the blue sky. Behind the high walls, flags of state flapped in the cool breeze. I wanted to enter the palace grounds to learn more about this flamboyant sovereign whose family rule dated back to the eleventh century. Many of his subjects in the city of Jaipur had proudly told me of his prowess on the polo field and of his expertise in killing tigers. He had two wives, one who was traditional and one who was modern. His modern wife often wore the latest Parisian fashions and traveled with him, while his traditional wife attended to her duties at the palace. Occasionally, he reveled with members of the international jet set; however, he spent most of his time attending to affairs of state.

With an air of diplomatic dignity, I adjusted my necktie, briskly marched past the turbaned guards and muttered, "Official business with the Maharaja." They glanced at me in confusion before snapping to attention. A long office building faced a second gate, which opened into the central grounds. Since the guards there glowered at me very suspiciously, I turned rapidly into the first office. While sorting papers on his desk, one of the male secretaries listened skeptically to my request to enter the palace grounds.

"I regret to say, no person is allowed to enter the grounds when the Maharaja is in residence. Have you seen the old Pink Palace in the center of Jaipur?"

"Yes, I have; but I've read much about the Maharaja's garden here and I'd like to see it," I lied, hoping there was a garden inside.

"I see. Then, I shall permit you to see my colleague in the next office.

I doubt, however, if he will allow you to enter. Give me your card."

"Uh—unfortunately I don't have any cards. Could I have a piece of paper and make one out?"

After lettering my name and country on a slip, I received a belittling stare as he led me to the next office. The official there promptly sent me to another secretary who, in turn, accompanied me into a large modern office. A few minutes later, an urbane man in a blue, European suit offered me a seat. He thumbed through the pages of my passport and questioned me with interest about the different countries I had visited.

"Well," he said, "since you have come this far and have desired to see His Highness' garden for so long, I shall try to arrange it. I shall ring up the officer in charge of the guards. He, of course, must investigate you for security reasons."

A khaki-uniformed guard escorted me from the official's reception room through the inner gate. The white palace stood in imperial splendor across a vast lawn. Tiers of marble steps rippled up to the main portal where a red-turbaned guard with a lance blocked the entrance. Unlike the ornate Pink Palace in town, which also belonged to the Maharaja, this contemporary palace had smooth, uncomplicated lines.

Giggling came from the far driveway. A nursemaid in a blue sari was chasing one of the royal children as he glided around on a tricycle. Several limousines were parked behind them.

As we walked, grandiose illusions twirled in my brain. What if I should actually meet the Maharaja? Undoubtedly he would entertain me with a few chukkers of polo and a majestic banquet. Perhaps he would even give me a handful of rare jewels!

We passed by a building that enclosed a swimming pool and approached the far wing of the palace. On a large, open porch a table was set for the Maharaja's luncheon. Silver bowls and other elaborate tableware sparkled in the noonday sun. Each detail was arranged with an elegance befitting royalty, except one item: standing crassly in the center of the linen tablecloth was an oversized ketchup bottle with a torn label.

The young commander of the guards questioned me very carefully in a palace office about my interest in his ruler and my trip around the world.

"I am satisfied you have no political antagonism for the Maharaja," he said, "so when the old gardener arrives, you may go with him."

"Thank you. Did I understand you to say the Maharaja flies his own plane?"

"Indeed, yes, he is an expert pilot. He flew in from Delhi only yesterday."

"He's in the government there?"

"Of course, he has some responsibility there, but now with our independence his power and taxes from the people have been cut severely. He had well over one hundred polo ponies before. Now, with the decrease in funds, he has about forty."

We chatted for some thirty minutes, but the gardener did not appear. The commander told me to pass down the hall and look for the old man in the garden. After closing his office door, I walked deliberately in the wrong direction. Rich Persian carpets spread over the floor of one room adjoining the hall. The ornately carved wood on the comfortable chairs and sofas had the scent of furniture polish. Their backs were covered with golden brocades. Dark-framed portraits of former monarchs hung on the thickly draped walls.

As I left the palace, I almost collided with a well-groomed man in his late thirties.

"Good day," he said, while loosening the collar of his blue, long-sleeved sports shirt.

"Good day," I said. "Is this the way to the garden?"

"Just ahead—you can't miss it."

"This is certainly a fine-looking palace."

"Yes, thank you," he said, smiling.

In my enthusiasm over being inside the palace I asked, "Who is that monarch in the portrait over there?"

He chuckled at my curiosity.

"Now that is an interesting question. That monarch, as you put it, ruled centuries ago. A truly splendid hunter."

"What did he hunt?"

"Tigers."

"I didn't realize there were many tigers around here."

"Actually, there are very few here now, but in his day conditions were different. He would travel all over his kingdom to his different hunting lodges. Quite often he would spend a month or so away from the palace while hunting."

"Did he hunt them from the top of elephants?"

"Perhaps now and then; however, I think most of his hunting took place in his towers."

"Towers?" I inquired.

"Yes, there were large stone towers. He and his hunting party would shoot down from the tops of them as the natives flushed the tigers from the bush."

"Just like in the movies."

He laughed in a condescending manner. "Yes, yes—just like in the movies."

"Well, the tiger didn't have a chance with all the native beaters and all the marksmen."

"To you it probably does not seem too sporting; however, the rules for hunting were different then. Especially for royalty."

"Oh, I see. You know, when I was in Sumatra, I hunted tigers by lights at night."

He smiled and said, "Now that does not seem too sporting to me."

"Right, but the Sumatrans also have different rules for hunting."

Both of us chortled over the contradictory patterns of sportsmanship. Later he excused himself to stride down the long hall to attend to some other servant who called to him. Slowly, I walked down the side steps thinking what an intelligent and well informed servant he was. Yet I could not understand why he was dressed so casually in the formal palace. Where was his turban?

Finally, I found the gardener who guided me through the long rows of flowers. Even though the winds blew very cold in the winter, all the multicolored blooms seemed to thrive. Carnations and pansies grew in symmetrical patterns between the low hedges. Here and there fountains bubbled into smooth irrigation troughs.

While squinting at the intense colors, I thought about the pageantry of the maharajas. For centuries the rulers put on lavish displays for weddings and other special occasions. Processions of richly decorated elephants, mounted warriors and court ladies in flower-garnished palanquins added zest to the rather drab life of the people. I hoped that some Indian princes could always afford such exhibitions. However, I was glad that the people were not taxed heavily for such displays as they had been in the past.

Several people gathered on the open porch of the palace. The man in the sports shirt with whom I had talked sat down in an umbrella-topped deck chair near a table.

"Do you know who that man is?" I asked the gardener. "I met him inside."

He drew himself up and gave me an astonished look. "Sir," he said, "I thought you *knew*. He *is* the Maharaja."

~ 17 ~

The Cobra
Charmer's Apprentice

One of the oldest forms of show business was Cobra Charming. For centuries, it had existed in India. I was curious to learn more about this dangerous profession.

Melancholy music from the cobra charmer's flute filled the morning air with an eerie tune. Several men in orange turbans and frazzled coats stood in front of the charmer's hut, while he played to an open wicker basket. Squatting closer, the old charmer rattled the sides of the basket to unsettle the cobras. Two snakes slithered up from their lower coils with an inquisitive attitude, quickly flaring their hoods. The scales on their bodies glistened as they hissed. Each time the cobras feinted toward the charmer, he moved his flute to make them withdraw. After keeping the sinuous bodies waving around for some time, he shoved them into the basket with a lid.

He tightened his bulbous orange turban and turned to me with amused brown eyes. *"Aap thaiyar ho, sahib?"* "Are you ready, sir?" he asked.

"Hah achcha." "Yes," I said with a dry voice.

The cobra charmer's son placed an oval wicker basket near my feet and handed me a flute. A five-inch stick was tied to its shaft so the snake would strike at it instead of me. While my hand rested on the top of the basket, I felt the cobra throbbing against the thin wicker sides.

Stroking his beard, the charmer urged me to squat closer and open the cover. This cobra had its fangs fractured to nubs, yet if it tore my skin, lethal poison could throb throughout my body. In an ambivalent mood of both compulsion and hesitation, I lifted the lid.

A stench like rotten seaweed made me cough. For a few seconds the cobra squirmed inside with its hood contracted. I tapped the sides of the basket, and the mirror-eyed snake reeled up, flaring its hood. Excitement buzzed through my body. While I tried to play the flute, the cobra hissed within two feet of my face. My reflection danced in its eyes. Gradually, it settled into a hypnotic state and followed the motion of my flute. Then it reared back as I swayed from side to side. It was under my control. To feel the warmth of my body, the cobra flicked out its tongue periodically. I felt an exhilarating satisfaction, as though I had met death and conquered it.

In a few moments, I stopped playing long enough to cough; yet the lack of music did not bother the snake. I remembered that most herpetologists claim snakes cannot hear sounds transmitted in the air. It was bewildering to find the ancient art of snake charming so easy. The cobra arched up naturally, as it did when searching for prey, and responded well to my steady body movements. However, a cobra in this position was ideally situated to strike—a prospect that kept my knees trembling.

Murmurs of approval and amusement came from the men behind me. After gaining a little more confidence, I tried to move the cobra to the safer backside of the basket. In an attempt to strike, it darted out of the basket and brushed my trouser leg.

With the stick on my flute I lifted the cobra back to its wicker cage. Recovering, it rose up again and fell into a lilting trance. The charmer's son gave me the basket lid, to force the snake down in a coil. After tying the orange cloth around the basket, I paced around the courtyard while rubbing my cold hands to settle my nerves. I gestured that I would return a few hours later, then walked through an alley leading to the noisy streets of Jaipur.

That afternoon the old charmer, his son and I rolled through one of the pink city-gates in an open carriage. The driver, who had arranged for me to study with the charmer, whipped his horse as we trotted past a caravan of supercilious camels, bound together by ropes woven through their nostrils. Our horse clip-clopped, almost in time to the quick hammering from a brass-smith shop. Pedestrians in bright yellow and red turbans slowed us down as we passed a restaurant where the air swirled with thyme and ginger.

Later, the lengthening shadow of our carriage ruffled over a plowed field flanking the country road.

"Sahib, the old man pleases to give you this root and stone," the driver said, as we stopped in a grove of trees.

"What are they for?" I asked.

"The root is from the *aristolochia* plant. It puts fear in snakes. The black stone draws out all poison when you receive a bite. You need only pay him two *rupees* for this, since you did so well today."

We followed the old cobra charmer through the trees into a valley dappled with patches of grass and bushes. Sagging over his shoulder was a pole with snake baskets tied to each end. After lowering his load, he sat on his heels near the driver to rest in the sunshine. The boy and I started poking each animal hole with our long sticks to find cobras. We searched through the brush for over an hour before returning to the charmer. He gave a cackling laugh at our failure, puffed on the stub of his *bidi*, a cigarette wrapped in a tobacco leaf, and led us across the far side of the valley.

The old man sprinkled a brown powder into many holes to pacify the snakes, and then he started a piercing maneuver with a stick. Some thirty minutes later he shouted. His son knelt beside him as they scooped up the earth from the sides of a large hole. Hissing came from within. After hesitating for a moment, they flipped up a writhing cobra. Quickly the boy pinned its neck to the ground with his stick. The old man flung the thrashing coil into a basket, tied the lid down and stooped over another animal hole.

Moving cautiously, the boy tried to stop another cobra that slid up angrily from its hole. It wrenched loose from his stick and periscoped up to attack. I stood out of range beside the driver for a minute while the old charmer played his flute. The late sun turned the cobra's fangs to amber as it bobbed up some three feet from its lower coil. Quickly the boy stepped back. With confidence stemming from immaturity, I walked behind the snake. Now the boy held his ground; rapidly, I slapped the cobra's head down with my forked stick. A spray of dust lashed from its tail, but its head was under control. In a mongoose-like swoop the boy seized its neck and slung it into a basket.

"Old man says you must not interfere again, *sahib*. You just may kill the snake," the driver said.

"Don't worry—I won't interfere," I said, somewhat puzzled by the charmer's covetous attitude.

As we walked toward the carriage, the feeling that the charmer had deceived me intensified. When the boy and I were searching for snakes at the far end of the valley, the old man was out of our sight, hidden by the bushes. Perhaps he had removed the lids of some of his baskets and released the cobras, which we had caught. This, of course, gave me the impression we had captured wild snakes. The eyes of the charmer gleamed with satisfaction as we breezed back to Jaipur. Now his palm was upturned for more *rupees*.

Early the next morning I arrived at the cobra charmer's house while he fed his snakes. His son pitched several stunned mice into the open baskets for the cobras to devour. Grinning with pride, the old man opened the basket of his prize cobra, allowing it to crawl on the ground. The boy shook a waterpot, and a toad leaped out near the snake. Before the toad could hop, the cobra struck. The toad bobbed up and down in the cobra's mouth for some ten minutes before the snake could completely swallow it. I was surprised to see the toad resist for so long.

Because, in legend, the cobra once spread its hood to shade the sleeping God Brahma, it became sacred to the Hindus. Although many Indians simply frighten these snakes away, thousands of people die annually from cobra bites. Often the cobras expend most of their venom on small animals and cannot later administer fatal doses to human beings. Shock, no doubt, is responsible for many deaths.

After feeding the cobras, we rode through the streets in the carriage and stopped in the market place. The old man had little trouble attracting a crowd. At the end of each performance, he twined several of the cobras around his neck and held his palm up to receive a few coins. One young Indian in a European suit seemed unwilling to pay for the show. Pressing close to him with a large cobra, the charmer persuaded the youth to make a hasty contribution.

In another market area the old charmer tied a white turban around my head and beckoned for the crowd to move in closer. I squatted near a snake basket while fingering the flute. Several American tourists snapped their expensive cameras at me. Then, with a great flourish, the charmer lifted the basket lid, and a cobra floated upward. A sudden stab of fear swept through me when I saw this snake was highly nervous and had long, unbroken fangs.

Hoping that this cobra would not strike immediately, I started to play the flute. It bent its hood back and forth for some time before slumping down into the basket. Stroking its head with the flute, I agitated it into rising again. Now the cobra lurched angrily at me. I stopped playing and moved the flute at arm's length for protection. Its fangs streaked toward my knee, but the flute blocked the blow. When its temper cooled, I took the lid to the basket and slammed the reptile inside. Happily, the charmer collected many *rupees* for the frightened showmanship of his foreign apprentice.

As the charmer, his son and I passed along the crowded streets, the carriage driver leaned back to me. "Sahib," the driver said, "the old man pleases to say you were a cobra charmer in your past life. He will make much money for you. He asks that you do not go to Africa but work with him."

"Tell him thanks, but I've had enough cobra charming for this life or—I guess—any other," I said with relief.

~ 18 ~

Mau Mau Terrorism

During the 1950's, the Mau Maus in Kenya, Africa,
were trying to overthrow the British government.
Unfortunately, they resorted to barbaric terrorism.

In Nairobi, the capital city of the Colony of Kenya, I met a police
officer who patrolled a Mau Mau terrorist area. He was a lieutenant
in his early thirties, who wore a sandy mustache that blended with his
tanned face.

"No. Definitely no," he said. "You know it is rather impossible for
me to take you out into the maximum security area. The Maus seem to
have some sort of ambush there every day, really—you..."

"What if we..." I interrupted.

"If something happened to you—say you were killed—it would be
quite embarrassing to our command."

"I don't want to embarrass you," I assured him. "But if it's all right
with you, may I come back later to see if you can somehow take me?"

"Well, if you are so bloody well determined, come back and we'll see
what we can do."

A few mornings later the officer shrugged when he saw me chatting
with his African guard inside the green Land Rover. I held two letters of
recommendation from the editors of my hometown newspapers. Both
letters described me as a student writer but not as an official journalist.

"Very well. Since you have journalistic credentials of sorts, I'll let
you come along on today's run," he said, smiling skeptically.

Our Land Rover pulled into a street humming with British motorcars.
Slowly, we drove through a modern city of high-rise buildings and wide
avenues interspersed with formal gardens.

My preconceived notion of hot, uncivilized Africa was changed by
Nairobi. The weather was as cool and delightful as an Appalachian

spring. It was hard to believe the equator circled only one hundred miles to our north.

The lieutenant slowed down as we approached a crowded intersection. Jaywalking in front of us, an Indian shopkeeper dressed in a long white robe and a European jacket almost bumped into a young lady. She was stylishly clad, English, and was wearing a gun belt around her dainty waist. After acknowledging a greeting from a black African wearing European clothes, she hurried toward her chauffeur-driven Jaguar. Modern shops lined the street behind her. In one sports shop, mounted antelope heads reminded us that we were still in a land of abundant wild game.

Our canvas-topped Land Rover rolled faster as we left the business district. Soon we swept past clusters of trim English bungalows. Stately apartment buildings towered high above the trees and red bouganvillia bushes.

Miles away from the suburbs, wheat fields flanked the road. Resting peacefully under a sun-filled sky, the comfortable homes of the white settlers gave no indication of the atmosphere of terror that prevailed.

Kikuyu women glared at us while they walked along the roadside. Straps across their foreheads supported loads of vegetables and firewood that rested on their backs. Children peered at us with dark gazelle-like eyes. All of the Kikuyus were barefooted and wore sack-like dresses over their raisin-black bodies.

"See that village," the lieutenant said. "That's one of our Home Guard posts. The loyal Kikuyus live in them. Keep them under lock at night, but we let them farm about in the day. Security you know. Now and then a few of these Kikuyus try to smuggle food to the Maus."

"What happens if the Mau Maus have their food supply cut off?"

"They are allowed to surrender. Our surrender terms are a bit too lenient if you ask me. The Maus are put in a rehabilitation camp to cool off for a long, long time. Of course, if we capture them, they are in for a quick trip to the gallows."

We wheeled off the main road and rumbled up a hillside to the Home Guard post, partially hidden by a red clay bank and encircled by a barbed wire fence. From a shallow trench, sharp wooden spikes bristled up defensively, like giant porcupine quills.

Inside, an aging Kikuyu with a spear saluted us. *"Shikammo, bwana."* "Everything is fine, sir."

After asking him a few questions, the lieutenant and I toured the firing posts around the tops of the clay walls. A khaki-uniformed Kikuyu executed inspection arms with the precision of a British soldier. While squinting down the barrel of this Kikuyu's rifle, the lieutenant mumbled, "These blokes learn fast. Rather intelligent for Africans—it's beyond me why their tribesmen started this bloody terrorism."

"Don't they want independence?" I asked.

"Independence! They're years away from that," he exclaimed.

Gradually, the happy jangle of the women's and children's voices in the center of the Home Guard village disappeared as they became aware of us. Now all we heard was the intermittent thumps of long poles as the women pounded maize on short wooden blocks. As we walked through the rows of *bandas*, thatched-roof huts, the people deliberately ignored us as they continued their work. Dark eyes occasionally glowered at us.

"Well, things seem to be right here. Suppose we backtrack a bit and go up-country," the lieutenant said. "Bit more trouble there."

Hours later we entered a lush valley and parked in front of a comfortable farm house. Several honks on the horn brought a chubby, middle-aged Englishman from his whitewashed barn. Waving his tan safari hat, he greeted us with enthusiasm. Slung low over his khaki jacket was a sweat-stained gun belt.

"Good morning to you," he said. "Looks like you have a visitor with you this time. Pardon my greasy hands, been having a bit of trouble with my tractor's carburetor. My boy and I almost have it straightened out though."

"You have a beautiful place here," I blurted out.

"Don't tell me now; I can tell by your accent you are a Yank or Canadian—you're a Yank. Right?"

"Yes, sir, you're right."

"Been a long time since I've seen a Yank. Don't go down to the city too often with the emergency on, you know. Even then I don't see many foreigners. Most of them are coming or going on a big game safari or having a look around the game parks."

While the African guard stood by the Land Rover with its extra shotgun racked in the front seat, we had tea on the settler's porch. The musty odor of sun-ripening wheat blew over us as the settler's cook served us a tray of sandwiches.

"Do you realize," the settler said, "I've worked on this land for the best part of my life. It's my home and a jolly good one, too. Perhaps some of the best farming country in the world. Ah, yes, things here were going along in splendid fashion and then—BANG—those bloody Kikuyu witch doctors started all this Mau Mau business. Well, no one is going to frighten me from my place."

The settler poured more tea and continued talking with the rapid zest of a man who had long been isolated from his countrymen. "Now you won't believe this, but three of my most trusted boys left me. Had to do the planting and harvesting shorthanded. Even two of my neighbors were chopped up one night by the Maus with their damned *pangas*. What could the Kikuyus do without us? We brought law and order and a decent religion to them, even built an expensive railway, introduced coffee and cotton. Why there wasn't a proper road when we came here a century ago, and I..."

"But didn't you take the choice grazing and farming land from the Africans?" I asked.

"Yes, of course, but what would these savages do with it? They don't need or deserve as much land as we do. We should be compensated for protecting them."

"I wonder if something like the Mau Maus will break out in other parts of Africa where the people are advanced like the Kikuyus?" I asked.

"Quite easily," the lieutenant said.

"Right," the settler added hastily, "if an African learns too fast, he develops a touch of brain fever and makes trouble. They have to be watched—always watched."

"I've heard rumors that some of the Europeans have tortured Africans—even innocent ones," I said.

"Good God, no. What do you think we are?" the settler said as he bit down on his pipe. After a long embarrassing pause, he added, "Well, of course, sometimes there is only one way to put fear into them."

After drinking our tea, we left the settler and rumbled swiftly up a road, the color of a lion's back, into the green foothills of Mount Kenya. Overhead, the clouds blotted out the sunlight and left the forest in shadows. Only the warmth generated from the engine made the cool wind outside seem less gloomy.

"Know how to fire a shotgun?" the lieutenant asked.

"I think so."

"Well, if we are 'bushed, this one by my foot is yours—unofficially, of course."

From the back seat, the serious-faced guard let some extra shotgun shells clatter into my hand. The road soon tore into the high grasses. While racing along, I visualized each shadowy valley and wooded hillside as the possible site of our death.

In a dark stretch of forest, the lieutenant stopped to examine a rear tire while the African and I spread out to stand guard. Deciding the tire was all right, he motioned us back to the Land Rover. With a jolt, we zoomed away. In a moment we sighed deeply, glad we were no longer a stationary target.

As we rushed over a hill, the lieutenant switched off the motor, and we glided to a stop.

"Movement down there," he whispered.

We eased out of the Land Rover without speaking. Dust puffed up some three yards ahead of me. A rifle whine stabbed the air. We saw two dark figures bolt through the trees near a dip in the road. Immediately, the underbrush in front of us shivered with the staccato beats of the lieutenant's Bren gun. The African and I squeezed the triggers of our shotguns toward the disappearing targets.

"Hold it," the lieutenant shouted; "think they've gone."

We crouched along the roadside while bittersweet gunpowder swirled around us. My ears were ringing. We continued to listen intently for the Mau Maus but heard nothing. Gradually a few birds in the surrounding trees broke the unreal stillness. I was pleased to hear my stomach growling.

Later we jogged back to the Land Rover and drove toward an object the Maus had left on the shoulder of the road. Lashed by green vines to a wooden cross was the carcass of a dog. Its front legs were bound to the horizontal piece while its trunk and hind legs dangled down the main shaft. The dog's eyes were knifed out and its red entrails flowed into the dust.

"These bloody Maus think it's a jolly good joke to mock the Christians," the officer said. "Must have been killing it when we drove up, and couldn't hear us over its cries; don't understand them."

It was not until we motored on for several miles that I realized my hands and knees were trembling. My tremor did not subside when I thought of this area's many past ambushes.

We visited three more settlers' homes in the district, found things in good order and, at dusk, turned back toward Nairobi. The African night swooped down on us with a chilling swiftness. We moaned along the road at a slower pace than before, hoping that it would be an uneventful return trip. Bouncing over each rut, our headlights jiggled high into the dew-coated trees. The African, who was accustomed to such tours, nodded while a shotgun rested across his lap. Fatigue had numbed my brain, and I now thought very little about being in a dangerous zone.

Some time later our lights swept across a pickup truck blocking the road.

"Jump in the bush and cover that lorry," the lieutenant said as he skidded to a stop.

We stumbled into the underbrush, holding our guns in a firing position. From the dark came a muttering voice. At first I could not understand it. Then an English settler stepped out into our headlights.

"Thank God—someone's come," he said.

"What's the trouble?" the officer demanded.

"Some bloody Maus—dirt in my petrol tank, trying to 'bush me. Would you give me a lift to my farm? It's not too far."

Turning into the front drive, we saw the figures of his wife and two sons standing anxiously on the porch. Each of them held a gun. When we stopped, they embraced the settler. His wife's eyes were moist with tears; his sons' faces were ashen. Soon they whisked him toward the safety of his home.

"Very—very decent—chaps—good night—to—," he stammered, while trying to hide his embarrassment.

In Nairobi we passed several patrol cars and skimmed through the back streets to my inexpensive hotel. The city had withdrawn into its protective shell. While the African guard knocked on the hotel door for me, the young officer said, "Best you don't tell anyone you have been up country with me. It's a bit against regulations."

"All right," I murmured with a smile.

He looked at me suspiciously and added in an amused tone, "Well, that is, of course, not until the emergency's over."

A few days later, in the lobby of a first-class hotel, I took tea with a gray-haired businessman from London who had been traveling to Kenya for years.

"You see," he said, "the way I look at this whole business is that the government here has got to make more changes. Certainly, it gives the Asian and the African a token place, but that's not enough."

"But do you think the Africans are capable of governing themselves?" I asked.

"Not for a long time, but some of these Kikuyu chaps are extremely keen. When I began coming here, they did nothing but farm and servant work. Now many of them do highly skilled tasks."

"What's this about land reform? Do you think the African will ever get some of the good land back?"

"Possibly, in the future, but it will raise a loud fuss with the settlers. This is a black man's country though, and one day soon he must have his rights. Of course, this Mau Mau terrorism has stifled all development toward multi-racial government and opportunity."

"I've heard that if the Mau Maus are brought under control, another secret organization will just spring up in its place."

"Perhaps so. You see, the Kikuyus are strong ones for secret cults, and it's a possibility."

"You know, I like Kenya, but I'll be glad to leave this atmosphere."

"Do you still plan on going to Uganda?" he asked.

"Yes, sir, in a day or so."

"Ah, I am sure you will like it there—a lovely spot. That's where we are making real progress in bringing the African 'round. Perhaps the locals there will be running their own show someday."

"I hope it works out well."

"All of us do, but things move slowly," he said as he gestured to a Kikuyu waiter to refill our teacups.

~ 19 ~

Uganda: Country of Peace And Promise

Unlike Kenya, there was no terrorism in Uganda. Law and order prevailed. This country had the mineral resources and the rich farming land that rivaled some of the world's most prosperous nations.

After traveling by bus through the green highlands of Kenya, I proceeded by train to the port of Kisumu on Lake Victoria. There I boarded a steamboat bound for the British Protectorate of Uganda.

Churning slowly past the marshes of an inlet, the steamer gradually picked up speed. Ahead of us the lake merged with the horizon. While a fellow passenger and I leaned on the handrail of the main deck, he handed me his leather-scented binoculars.

"Quickly, now, quickly," he mumbled.

Focusing back and forth, I found a pink cloud in the distance. It floated high over the hills, trembled in a dark pink mass, wheeled around, then drifted into the marshes—a flight of flamingos.

Reaching the main body of the lake, the fierce equatorial sun plunged below the horizon. Now it seemed as though we were afloat in a bubbling red caldron. In the warm night breezes of the afterdeck, I relaxed and fell asleep listening to the mesmeric throb of the steamer.

After landing in Entebbe, Uganda, a lake town three miles north of the equator, I tried to hitch a ride toward the city of Kampala. Finally, an African driver stopped for me; his truck was loaded with vegetables.

"Jambo, kimbiza Kampala?" "You drive to Kampala?" I asked, reading from my Swahili phrase booklet.

He chuckled and said, "Bwana speak Swahili like the baby. Nice you try. Yes, yes, I give you a lift."

I felt relieved to talk with an African who was neither surly nor obsequious like many of those I had met in Kenya. Here the people seemed as warm as the Ugandan sunlight.

Along the twenty-one mile trip to Kampala, we roared over the tarmacadam road, passing thatched farm houses, freshly-hoed fields and neat rows of cotton plants. Women on their way to market smiled at us. On their close-cropped heads rested loads of vegetables and sacks of cotton. Their intense orange, yellow and red dresses seemed to shriek out in competition with the sunlight.

In the African and Indian district of Kampala I found a grubby hotel that looked well within my budget. After I asked the plump Indian manager for a room, he sighed and wiped the sweat from the edge of his turban.

"If you wish to stay, it is permissible," he said. "But it is most unusual for an American—most unusual."

The following morning an African student who lived across the hall offered to show me around Kampala. We strolled up a warm street filled with slow-moving Africans. Some of them dawdled through the open-air market while others glided past the crowds on bicycles. Laughter mingled with the scratch of bicycle bells. In the front basket of one bicycle, a baby dozed while his father pedaled; his mother rested over the back fender. A large truck honked its way into the heavy traffic. Several bikes, wrapped in tape to protect the enamel from the sun, rolled past us. Spokes glittered in the sunlight. Beneath the droning rubber tires came the constant patter of bare black feet.

"Sar, this you will not believe," the African student said, wiping his steel-rimmed glasses. "Only three generations ago we had no wheels in Uganda."

Climbing up a narrow street, we approached the Indian and African shopping area. Cacophonous sounds peppered us. Minor-keyed sitar music drifted from an Indian hardware shop; tapping and hammering noises emanated from a bicycle store.

"Ribbid, ribbid, ribbid"—murmurs from foot-pedaled sewing machines—pulsated out of dress shops, and happy voices merged with the piping whistle of a traffic officer.

At last, we arrived at the top of the hill where the European district wound through the trees like strands of royal pearls. We glanced in the display windows of elite shops that glistened with luxury goods from London. Then we entered a park. Resting in the shade of a yellow-flowered *acacia* tree, we gazed over the city of Kampala. While the breeze ruffled the purple bouganvillia bushes near us, the proud student said, "Sar, Kampala is upon seven hills, the same way Rome is. In addition to the mosque on that hill, there is an English cathedral on another hill. Also, there is the Catholic cathedral and my university."

"Could I see your university?" I asked.

"Very well. You must be obliged to like it. It is the only one in this part of Africa."

The University College of East Africa, an affiliate of the University of London, was housed for the most part in a white four-story building. The student and I ambled down the halls, occasionally peering into the modern classrooms. Later we strolled across the shaded hillside to a smaller building.

Inside a turpentine-scented room we saw many students painting scenes of African life in a style that resembled the European realists. A pounding racket came from an adjoining class. We walked over and watched students chisel traditional masks out of long ebony logs.

The colonial overlords in some African countries demeaned parts of the local culture, such as the artistic heritage. Here, however, the old arts seemed to grow creatively with European appreciation and guidance.

"Sar, that building behind the trees is the Institute for Social Research," the student boasted, as we strolled down the hill. "Some of the teachers are from your country. In addition to sharing their knowledge, they encourage us to learn from our past."

I wondered what would happen to the many students I saw studying in the classrooms. Perhaps they would become the leaders of Kenya, Tanganyika and Uganda and would have the difficult job of guiding their people toward a more progressive position in the twentieth century. If they failed, their countries might fall into turmoil.

Several days later, the student escorted me to the offices of the Ugandan Community Development Program near the business district of Kampala. With much enthusiasm, a British official drove us through the lush hills to a village of whitewashed houses. Near one house a group of men sat in the shade of a red-flowering tree while attending an outdoor class.

All eyes focused on a young African in a white shirt standing by a poster filled with Swahili. Each time the African pointed to a word, the older men pronounced it rhythmically. Most faces registered seriousness. After reading a difficult sentence, a gray-headed man chuckled with pride over his accomplishment.

"Sar, this is part of the Adult Literacy Campaign," the student whispered.

"It seems to be working well," I said.

"Right you are," the official added. "The literacy rate is increasing day by day."

"The campaign taught my uncle how to read," the student said, and smiled.

On the way back to Kampala, the official briefed me on the Ugandan Community Development Program, which gave the people valuable assistance in the fields of agriculture, health and general village improvement. Fortunately, this program was well-received by most of the Ugandans.

Late one afternoon I joined a large group of Europeans in a luxurious hotel. They clustered around the bar for their "sundowners" with the enthusiasm of thirsty lions at a water hole. White-robed waiters sporting scarlet fezzes rambled around with trays of cocktails. I sipped a gin and tonic, enjoying the atmosphere. In a little while the couple at the next table invited me to join them.

"Oh, we are quite glad to find you are an American," the man said. "You see, we have a relative who lives in Detroit. Always wanted to visit him, yet when one has home leave, it's only natural to stay in England and see old friends," he continued. "We were noticing the surprised look on your face when you saw those two African couples seated across the lobby. Don't believe you expected it."

"No, I didn't. Is that always the case?"

"Well, it's rather common here in Kampala," the lady replied. "Actually, we have no objections to the African coming to hotels just as long as they are properly dressed and behaved."

"Yes, I am afraid this is their country," he said wistfully. "We have worked quite hard to help them. Things are different here than they are in Kenya."

"There's no race restrictions here at all?" I asked.

"Yes," he said, "there are no legal restrictions, but there is an invisible one which will take years to erase."

"Actually, many of them are quite intelligent; but some servants are quite impossible, yes, quite impossible," she said, drumming her swizzle stick on the table. "If they think the spoons look best on the left side of the plate or even in it, they will place them there. My patience wears rather thin when they use this sort of silly imagination. Oh, but don't let me go on about the servant problem."

"Still, we are proud we don't mistreat the natives as they do in South Africa," the man said. "An old friend of ours there insists with the clap of his hand that his boy will race into the room—even to pick up a match or cigarette he drops by his shoes."

"Come now, won't you be our guest for the evening meal?" she asked.

"Of course, I will," I said, remembering my low funds.

"I believe they are having some of that roast duck tonight," she added. "And I'm certain you will like the wine."

That night I left the elegance of the colonial British district and strolled down the hill toward the drabness of the Indian and African sector where my hotel was located. I had the buoyant feeling of being in a safe and pleasant environment completely unlike terrorist-ridden Nairobi. I passed Indian families sitting on benches in front of their shops while children played around them. Minor-keyed music blended well with the faint drumbeats from a distant section of the city.

At the foot of the hill, I grew confused. Where was my hotel? The roast duck and wine had dimmed my memory. I stopped a couple of young Africans and asked them for directions. Instead of drawing a map for me, they courteously escorted me through the dark streets to the front door of the hotel.

My brief stay in Kampala stimulated my interest in exploring more of Uganda, this fascinating country of peace and promise.

~ 20 ~

Deeper Into Africa

Wild animals were abundant in Uganda just after the Korean War. Very few poachers invaded the game parks to kill the rhinoceroses and elephants, even though their horns and tusks commanded a high price on the world market.

From the noisy city of Kampala I traveled by train to the north, where I boarded a turn-of-the-century steamboat. Slowly, it chugged along the grassy shores of Lake Kyoga to Masindi Port.

There I met a young British army officer who was driving to the Murchison Falls Game Reserve. Since he was alone, he offered to take me with him in his Volkswagen. After buying supplies from an Indian trader, we drove to a side road leading toward the outskirts of the reserve. The first twist in this road was blocked by a wooden barricade. A sign was nailed on it:

ROAD CLOSED—TRAVEL DANGEROUS

"My furlough's rather short," the lieutenant said. "What do you say we give it a go over this blasted road to save time?"

"OK by me," I said. "Let's try it."

We backed away and swished around the fence into the ten-foot-high grass. Somewhere the road disappeared. For over ten minutes we circled at full speed, trying to find it. Suddenly we burst out of the brown grass, rattled down a rough knoll and skidded onto the dirt road.

At last we entered a large valley that reminded me of an abandoned sawmill site. There were no trees; the road was neglected. Here and there, light-brown cones tapered to points like piles of sawdust.

Driving closer to the first man-high cone, the lieutenant said, "That's a tall anthill for you."

"It sure is," I said. "Hate to be around when those ants go on the march."

"So would I. A friend of mine had his house cleaned out by them once."

"Was he hurt?"

"No, but he had to buy new furniture. Actually, those tiny blokes can make elephants stampede."

"That would be a strange sight," I said.

"Yes, very strange indeed."

Around noon we entered a short grassland and parked in the filigree shade of a flat-topped *acacia*, thorn tree. We munched our sandwiches outside the car and relaxed in the drowsy breeze. Several flies whined close by, but did not bother us. When more of them swarmed around, we jerked up long shafts of grass to wave them away. Flies spread over my sandwich. I shook it, and they fizzed on my face, needling my skin. Then they stabbed the skin beneath my shirt. Nervously, I brushed some of them off and ran toward the Volkswagen. Now the lieutenant's face looked as though it were covered with a black veil.

"Bloody tsetses!" he yelped.

"Let's go," I gagged as one flew, whining, into my mouth.

With our bodies quivering, we reeled into the car and cranked up the windows.

After swatting the last of them, he said, "Didn't know this region was under the fly. Can damn bloody well see why no one lives here."

Breathing hard, I cradled a dead tsetse in my hand. It was only slightly larger than a house fly. "Hard to realize a fly this size can do so much damage," I remarked.

"Indeed, yes. They can move into a primitive area such as this and infect both man and beast with the ruddy sleeping-sickness. It's a tough problem to kill them. Anyway, they're not decent company for an Englishman."

Late in the day we drove down a hillside to an enormous river. Ahead of us lay the famous Victoria Nile. Its murky-blue current flowed patiently past us as though it were in no hurry to turn brown and merge into the Mediterranean, half a continent away.

A primitive ferry boat rested on the banks of the river. A sign tacked on its wooden stern read:

NOT IN OPERATION

Not deterred, we brashly drove down the shoreline until we found a cluster of huts. We located the ferry boat operator and persuaded him to steer us across. Even though we paid him, he seemed very reluctant to help.

On the other bank, we drove to a settlement of white huts. From one large hut, which stood aloof from the others, came a brawny English official dressed in white shorts. With arms akimbo, he scowled at us.

"Indeed, I trust you chaps had a pleasant trip over the closed road," he said sarcastically. "If you had had motor trouble, you would be days away from help. You have remembered to bring your food?"

"Errr—yes, sir, we did," I replied, avoiding his frown.

"Well, then, the boy here will show you a tent up at the top of the hill, and he will look after you. You may pay him for the rental when you leave. Remember this area is not officially open. Good afternoon to you."

After unloading our scanty provisions, we chartered a game department launch at a village; it throbbed up the Nile into the marshes. Our driver steered a winding course to avoid the propeller-clogging river plants while we searched the banks for game. Gradually, the setting sun burnished the sky with its warm colors. The lieutenant's white shirt turned orange, and his sunburned face seemed to glow. We both leaned forward in anticipation.

Ahead of us the river was cluttered by a large herd of bulbous hippos. Sputtering and belching, they floated along the surface. Periodically, they bobbed out of the water from the river bottom where they had been feeding. As the noise of our craft grew louder, over fifty pink and gray faces turned toward us. In panic the hippos fled; they churned across the river, sloshed through the shallows and disappeared into the papyrus reeds. Only two hippos remained near us. They snorted scornfully while twitching flies from their pig-like ears.

When our launch bobbled over the rough water, we saw a lone hippo yawning in the grass. His cave of a mouth stretched with such enthusiasm that I sighed and yawned with him. A bushbuck flicked up his curled horns and froze. Sensing that he was safe, he lifted his nose into the breeze and continued to feed. Several dog-faced baboons hurled dabs of clay at a crocodile. Without glancing back, the yellowish-gray reptile scampered into the water. Gleefully, the baboons turned their slick, pink posteriors to us and loped back into the trees.

"Mooned by the baboons," I quipped.

"Rather beastly," he said and smiled.

As we swept around a wide bend in the river, we saw movement in the distant hills.

"Wonder what that is?" the lieutenant asked.

"Looks like wind in the trees," I said.

"Oh, I think I see...," he said, squinting through the sun.

"What?"

"Good God, look at them..."

"WHAT?"

"Elephants—must be more than a hundred!"

On the far bank, nervous tickbirds stepped cautiously around an open-mouthed crocodile. They pecked insects on the reptile's back while we circled in the water. One bird peered into the jagged mouth. Annoyed, the crocodile cracked his teeth together, frightening this bird and others into the air. After flapping and croaking, they drifted back to the bank. Hesitantly, they approached the crocodile, which now seemed to grin as though he enjoyed his unnerving joke.

We were in a game country of unbelievable abundance that had changed little during the centuries. Wild beasts belonged here; men were the intruders. The grazing rhinos with their primordial horns, the mastodontoid elephants and the Nilotic crocodiles made me feel that life must have been like this when man was in his infancy or even before he existed.

Circling back, we startled a small herd of elephants soaking in the river. Their wrinkled skins were bronze in the late sunlight. White birds fluttered from the elephants' backs and drifted in the breeze as though they were drugged. Now, huge elephants folded their ears outward. With siren squeals the herd stampeded toward the riverbank while two bulls stood firmly in the shallows.

Their trumpeting blasted us. Before racing away, these bulls lowered their trunks and charged a few steps. All of the running elephants humped their shoulders defensively and bent their heads unusually low as though they were anticipating some aerial attack.

Our driver opened the throttle, and we smacked across the choppy water. Around the last bend, many crocodiles aligned themselves with the lengthening shadows of the bushes, waiting for some thirsty buck to trot their way.

That night we bathed in a portable tub, ate two tins of meat by the fire and turned in early. Our sun-baked tent was filled with the powdery aroma of canvas. From our cots we heard an unusual sound; it drifted like a tinkling doorchime from the African huts near us. It was our guide playing his handmade music box beside the campfire.

"You did fasten the tent opening?" the lieutenant asked over the whine of the mosquitoes outside his net.

"Yes," I said.

"Yet, a lot of bloody good it would do if a leopard would choose to pop in."

"I know, but at least we would have the satisfaction of slowing him down."

"Some satisfaction," he grumbled. "Good night."

"See you tomorrow."

"God, I hope so."

That night the river pulsated with the "umm-aaaah, umm-aaaah, umm-aaaah" bellows of the hippos. I was only partially conscious when a lion's roar rolled through the dark hills.

*

After gulping down our morning tea, we motored deeper into Africa to search for game. The game park Ugandan in the back seat guided us through the wooded hills, past the high grasses and onto a plain scarred by the hooves of countless animals. A tart, grassy scent lingered in our Volkswagen. The lieutenant drove toward the misty horizon in a carefree, almost reckless, manner.

Somehow the earth and sky seemed to expand to unconfined proportions, dwarfing the scattered herds of game. In the far grass stood many species of animals. They were no more than a slight blemish on the curving face of the plain. Even the elephants along the far hills appeared small and unimportant in this endless landscape.

A warm breeze rushed across our sweaty faces. Without warning, a brownish blur vaulted over the bushes, swerved past us and then merged into a jumble of frightened bushbucks. These antelopes ran across the skyline and receded into the bright haze. Later we watched a herd of approximately sixty dangerous buffaloes trot across a clearing and crash into a thicket.

With our windows up to seal in our scent, we motored close to a herd of long-faced kongoni. In a little while these shaggy antelopes, their horns nodding in curiosity, marched over to inspect our gasoline-odored shell. One male stamped with his front hooves; something about us disturbed him. Then he galloped toward the woods, drawing the others along with him.

We chuckled while a family of plump warthogs raced away on their stubby legs with an urgency not fitting their lethargic appearance.

"Bwana, hunter Hemingway who write book, him plane go down there," the African said while we bounced along. "Him American from state of Cuba."

"You mean in the far jungle?" I asked.

"No, Bwana, him plane go down on *laini majani.*"

"*Laini majani?*" I asked.

"Means 'smooth grass' in Swahili," the lieutenant explained.

Several accounts I had read of the well-publicized crash led me to believe it occurred in some impenetrable jungle, and the famous author had to hack his way out. I suspected the modern news services, and not the jungle drums, garbled the information. These drums had always seemed to beat long and loud and true.

As we walked around the car to stretch our legs the next afternoon, our guide whispered, *"Tembo, tembo."* "Elephant, elephant."

Cautiously, we drove up a trail winding through the high grass until we saw the backsides of two gray beasts.

"From here it looks like an elephant with a calf," the lieutenant said.

One of the huge animals switched its tail and slowly turned.

The African gasped, *"Kifaru."* "Rhino."

Our motor stalled as the lieutenant attempted to turn us around. Now the weak-eyed rhino left her calf and trotted inquisitively toward us. She snorted as she bobbed her head. After deciding we were undesirable, she lowered her horns and charged. I felt as though we were stalled on a runway where a jet plane was touching down.

"You damned, bloody car, start—start!" the lieutenant yelled.

In a minute, our car roared down the hillside into the rough grass and careened back onto the trail. As the rhino pounded closer, we accelerated to thirty—forty—fifty miles per hour, realizing the beast could rip our car apart. The African moaned.

Glancing back through the dust, we saw her stop. Now the mother rhino stood arrogantly in the trail with her curving horns tilted upward. We were safe.

In the early morning stillness, I awoke before the lieutenant and followed my flashlight beam across the bluff. After sitting on a huge rock, I clicked my light off to watch daylight drift down the Nile.

Through the dimness I saw the hippos snuffling around on the banks in easy, moving patterns like black, prehistoric monsters. Their periodic grunts broke the stillness. A herd of silhouetted antelopes pranced along the shore and disappeared into the foggy underbrush.

Upstream, some animal shrieked. Then the waters momentarily churned as he fought his last battle. Perhaps he was now on his way to the underwater lair of a crocodile.

The sky slowly grew violet, blending into gray. High above came the whish of geese as they pointed their spear-headed formation across the hills. Perching haughtily on the low bushes were several snake-necked cormorants. These birds arched their wings to dry in the cool morning air. Other birds chirped wildly. In a bewildering shower of blue and yellow, many of them burst from the trees when a pack of monkeys swung closer. With a deep sense of wonder, I continued to gaze into the early morning light.

Now daylight shone on the Nile with the polish of pale-green jade. Downstream, the elephants enjoyed the pleasant coolness while spraying water on each other and tramping through the papyrus reeds. A herd of waterbucks stepped toward the river. Frisking behind the others on unsure legs was an immature male. As he scampered away, an old buck circled back and frightened him into the safety of the herd. Surprisingly, a playful hippo burst up from the river bottom. After bolting back for a moment, the waterbucks spread along the shore in groups of twos and threes to lower their quivering lips into the water.

Without glancing aside, a lion ambled out of the high grass near the river. Flicking their horns up, the waterbucks studied him for a few seconds; then, sensing that the lion's stomach was full, they continued to drink within a gap of only fifty yards. Many of the hippos luxuriated in the shallows. A breeze from across the river dissipated the mists, stirring up a foul, mossy odor.

There seemed to be a truce among all animals now that the violence of the night was over. Even the crocodiles upstream lounged quietly on the banks as though they were contemplating the calmness of dawn. When the lion and waterbucks withdrew toward the hills, I walked back to the tent for morning tea.

As we packed our Volkswagen, it gleamed in the orange sunrise like some lonely animal misplaced from its honking herd of traffic.

"You look a bit tired," the lieutenant said.

"Guess I got up too early."

"A nice cup of English tea should set you right. But hurry, we must leave for Kampala with all its heat and hubbub."

"You know, it looks like a great day for traveling," I said.

"Right, it's almost as lovely as a summer's day in England."

~ 21 ~

The Ancient Kingdom of Toro

Although Uganda was a British protectorate, its few remaining kings had some power and much prestige. I was determined to find one of these kings and learn something more about ancient African monarchies.

"Young man, think of your place and dignity and do not ride in those indecent African buses."

I recalled this admonition from an English woman while I rolled away from Kampala on such a bus. Dark clouds boiled over; rain rattled our tin roof with a sound of snare drums.

Each time we skidded on the muddy road, the passengers laughed with excitement. Soon we rolled into an unpopulated forest. On one downhill curve our bus skimmed into the bushes but somehow veered back onto the road. Then we hit a rut and thudded into a ditch.

As the driver raced the motor, our bus squealed like a wild boar stuck in a marsh. For several hours we tried to pull the bus, push it and even dig it out; however, we could not dislodge it. Nothing could be done until the rain stopped and the mud dried. We tore off banana leaves to use as umbrellas and began walking toward the next village some ten miles away. Frequently, laughter rose above the moan of rain. Everyone seemed to accept the weather and the accident as only minor inconveniences.

A short time later, I hitched a ride with a young Indian lawyer who was driving to Fort Portal in his vintage Ford.

"You'll like it in Fort Portal," he said as we bounded along. "Wish I had a bit more time to relax in the area, but I must defend an African there tomorrow."

"What did he do?" I asked.

"Oh, another witchcraft trial. This bloke was put under a magic spell by some witch doctor. Of course, now, he didn't like it so he kills the witch doctor. You see, this mumbo jumbo is very real to the Africans. A man with a spell on him is quite often frightened out of his wits."

"What about the sentence? Is it very stiff?"

"Indeed, yes, for murder it's usually sixteen years in prison. That's a bit stiff for an African who believes in black magic. Of course, now the courts are usually more severe on Asians and Europeans who commit murder."

In the afternoon we drove into a coffee plantation that reminded me of Isak Denisen's memoir, *Out of Africa.* Countless rows of trees and white huts surrounded us. As we sped forward, the workers and their children smiled and waved.

On the next hill, white smoke drifted into the clouds. From both sides of the road men burned off their fields to clear ground for new crops. One farmer, whose body glistened with sweat, put out a small flame with his staff and watched us speed forward.

Later, the road bent down toward the city of Fort Portal. Somewhere beyond this city, on the Congo border, stood the cloud-hidden Mountains of the Moon, with some peaks rising higher than the Matterhorn in Switzerland. As the mists thinned, we glimpsed a snowy peak. Before the Indian could stop the car, billowing clouds swept past us, and the fabled Mountains of the Moon vanished.

Later that day the lawyer found a small hotel for me in the city of Fort Portal; there, I heard many rumors about the King of Toro who resided in a neighboring village. Several people told me he ruled a million Africans with the aid of many chiefs, all under the supervision of the British District Commissioner.

One crusty Scotsman told me, "The ol' boy has one wife, the queen, but he has quite a few concubines. It's the custom for African kings, and a damn good one if you ask me."

I was determined to meet this king. At last I met a prosperous Indian merchant who offered to introduce me to the king's secretary at the palace in Kabarole, a few miles from Fort Portal. The merchant drove me up to a commanding bluff, where an impressive red-roofed palace was encircled by trees. After parking, we walked through a concrete archway and past a tall reed fence that enclosed the palace grounds.

The merchant left after introducing me to the king's secretary, a scholarly man dressed in a European suit. He questioned me carefully for a long time. Then we strolled past two khaki uniformed guards who wore blood-red fezzes, and we entered the inner courtyard.

The palace was a two-storied, white stucco structure with eight square columns across the front. A green railing partially enclosed the upper porch; the lower porch remained open. Under the entrance columns stood a wooden throne draped with dried lions' skins.

I felt like some early explorer who had trudged across the continent of Africa to sign a world-shaking treaty. The waist-high ceremonial drums in the dark hallway seemed to pulsate with the rhythms of ancient festivals. I visualized the upright spears as being coated with the dried blood of tribal warfare.

At the doorway to a large Victorian parlor, the secretary fell to his knees. I offered him my hand in assistance but quickly realized it was the custom to kneel before the king. Across the room, seated on a couch, the Omukama of Toro occupied himself with the *London Times*. He was a stout man in his late thirties, with smooth coffee-colored skin. The six-foot three-inch king rose slowly from his sofa when he heard his secretary mumble something in the Toro language. After adjusting the necktie and his short-sleeved shirt, he approached me in a manner that was strong and masculine, yet there was an unhurried softness in his movements. He knew his unique position in life and accepted it calmly. After shaking my hand lightly, he said, "Be seated; please, be seated. I understand that you are on quite a long journey. Tell me, how do you like Uganda thus far?"

"Very much, it's a wonderful country," I said.

"Thank you. I have read much about your country. Someday I hope to go there. Tell me, do you have any friends in the District of Columbia who perhaps might arrange an official visit for me?"

"Uh, no, sir, I don't. But perhaps I could work through my congressman and arrange something. I heard you spent some time in England," I said, to change the subject.

"Only a year and a half. Lovely country—the people there are quite nice. I received excellent training there. When I returned home, I served as a member of the police and later became a member of the King's African Rifles. I still carry part of my military title. Let me just see now; I have one of my cards here. Keep one if you wish." The elegant gold-engraved card read:

Rukirabasaija
Lieut. George D. K. Rukidi, III
Omukama of Toro

After a brief and rather formal audience, his secretary came for me. He knelt in the doorway.

"I say, why don't you come 'round tomorrow afternoon?" the king said. "And I shall show you the palace and introduce you to my queen."

"That's very kind of you."

I was overwhelmed that such an important sovereign had received me so well, and I was pleased he was interested in visiting the District of Columbia. Perhaps this curiosity about life in the United States had led him to grant me an immediate audience.

On returning to the palace the next day, I found the king near the front entrance arch. He was inspecting his green Chevrolet that had the royal coat of arms fastened above the back bumper. A Land Rover stood in a nearby reed shed.

"You see, I use my green car for state affairs," he said. "It's driven by my chauffeur. But my Land Rover is for safaris to the more remote parts of my kingdom. And, of course, I drive it myself. I rather like to drive, don't you?"

"Yes, sir, I do, but I haven't driven for several years."

"Come now, I should like you to meet Her Majesty. I think she's unoccupied now."

From a side entrance to the palace the secretary escorted the tall queen. Her nubbly hair was cut short; her brown body was covered with a pleated black skirt and a white embroidered European blouse. She walked gracefully on white high-heeled shoes.

"Welcome to Toro," she said, shyly twisting her lace handkerchief.

Her dark, brooding eyes followed the king's shoes as we started a brief tour of the palace grounds.

"Ah, here is an old hippopotamus skull," the king said, touching a massive set of bones propped apart in a yawning attitude. "My younger brother and I killed him some time ago."

"Your Majesty, what is that thatched-roof building over there?" I said, pointing to an open-sided hut with a conical roof.

"Oh, yes. That is where my coronation took place some years ago. You see, the late Omukama of Toro, my father, passed away, and as is the custom, the ceremonial drum was turned upside down. A year later the British commissioner in Fort Portal proclaimed that I was to succeed my father. At the appointed time we came here with all my many chiefs and subchiefs. I made the ceremonial walk on a grass mat that ran from the palace to the coronation hut."

"Could I ask what you wore?"

"Yes, of course. I wore my coronation robe and crown with a long beard fastened to it that came to here," he said, patting his collarbone. "The drums, of course, were playing, and when they had finished, I made a short address to my subjects. Later I met with the chiefs and other nobles back in the palace. It was a magnificent day—yes, quite a magnificent day."

"Your Majesty, may I take a few photos of the palace?" I asked, with some hesitation.

"Certainly. I am rather keen on picture-taking myself."

Inside one of his modern office buildings, he showed me a number of his snapshots. "I suppose this could be one of my main hobbies as well as music."

"Music?"

"Yes, music of all kinds. But it must have a good rhythm to it. Then, too, another hobby of mine is spear throwing—quite an art in that. Unfortunately, I have been too occupied lately to practice it."

After spending several hours on the palace grounds chatting with members of the royal staff, I located the king and told him good-bye.

"Tell me," he asked, "where do you go after you leave Uganda?"

"I'm on my way to the Congo tomorrow."

"Ah, the Congo—a lovely place. Don't miss the Pygmies, very friendly little chaps. Difficult to find though."

"No, sir, I won't."

"Have a good safari," he said and smiled as I walked toward the main archway. "Oh, do what you can for me. I still intend to visit your country and see the District of Columbia."

~ 22 ~

Predators And Prejudice

Unfortunately, there were no buses in this western sector of Uganda and the eastern Belgian Congo. As an impoverished hitchhiker, I had many unusual adventures riding to out-of-the-way locales.

From Fort Portal, I thumbed a ride with an Indian trader driving a truck. We followed a road into the Queen Elizabeth Game Park where gentle hills and plains seemed to doze peacefully in a heat haze. No animals were in sight. It was around noon, and I was enjoying the breeze from my perch on top of his load of trade goods. In a moment, the trader stopped at a crossroads and motioned for me to climb down.

"Sahib, I turn to the right here to make a delivery at the next village. You just walk down the road to the left. In due time, I will motor in your direction, and if you cannot get another lift, I will stop for you."

"OK, thanks. I'll be looking for you," I said.

Sleepily, I walked down the road toward the distant horizon. A lazy breeze did little to ease the heat. Although excited about visiting the romantic Belgian Congo, I was surprised to find the equatorial interior of Africa so quiet and peaceful. Yawning, I tossed my tote bag under a tree and sat down to rest. While daydreaming about gorilla and Pygmy country, I allowed my mind to melt into a pleasant state of semi-consciousness.

A heavy breathing noise startled me out of my reverie. Squinting into the sunlight, I saw two black animals stepping out of the high elephant grass. What are cows doing here? I thought... no, they aren't cows... they must be wild animals... yes, they're buffaloes... dangerous Cape buffaloes....

Gasping for breath, I jumped to my feet and slithered up a tree like a lizard. Glancing down, I saw one of the enraged buffaloes thunder past the spot where I had been sitting a few seconds before.

The tree trembled. Curved horns of the second buffalo were scraping against the trunk. When the first buffalo recovered from his charge, he trotted around the tree with another one. A stench like burning rubber floated toward me. One buffalo flung my bag into the air with its horns, scattering my clothes, books and camera. For a long time they circled under me, pawing the ground and snorting angrily. On the mud-caked flank of one buffalo was a bloody slash which, perhaps, accounted for some of its truculence. Finally, they crashed back into the grass and disappeared.

After climbing down, I found everything peaceful. Soon I noticed a section of the high grass trembling. Again I scrambled up the tree. Now the grass shuddered like a breaking wave as the same two buffaloes raced out. In a moment they pranced around as though they were confident I would eventually surrender to them. My only option was to wait.

A metallic clatter in the distance froze the beasts. Carefully, with quivering nostrils, they faced the noise, snorted and then bolted away to find the rest of their herd. The noise came from the Indian trader's truck. I dropped from the tree, picked up my broken camera and gathered my other belongings. Blocking the road, I waved him down.

"Just tell me what you are doing?" he asked when he squeaked to a stop. "You should be in Katwee Village by now."

With a hand scratched by thorns, I pointed to the buffalo droppings.

"Oh, indeed," he gasped. "It was just fortunate you had a tree nearby." He shook his turbaned head in disbelief while I climbed into the back of his truck.

That evening I left the village on a truck packed with dried fish for the Congo. A young African student and I rode in the cab with the black driver. Eventually, we all reeked of fish. I hoped that lions and leopards did not have the same taste for fish as their more domestic feline cousins.

Hours later our motor sputtered and clanked as though it were splitting apart. We stopped on the dark road. With a flashlight we tinkered with the fan blades and checked out the motor until we heard a loud roar from some beast. We scurried into the safety of the cab. Laughing nervously, we rumbled away with the hood up. The driver stopped, slammed the hood in place and drove on toward the Belgian Congo. Now we pretended to ignore all the irritating motor noises.

Some time after crossing the border, we arrived in the town of Beni. The truck disappeared down the road, leaving the student and me in front of a settlement. Lights sprayed out of the windows of a small inn where a couple of Belgians hovered over a bottle of wine.

"May I stay the night with you?" the student asked me. "Perhaps you can make some arrangement for both of us."

"I'll try," I said.

Inside, a heavy-bosomed woman glanced up from her comfortable chair with the air of a drowsy hippopotamus and said, "*Oui, oui, monsieur,* there is a room available. Come to the desk for registering."

"There's an African with me. Do you know where he can sleep?"

She arched her brows and threw her hands up indifferently. "Is he your servant?"

"Well, err—yes. He's my personal servant."

"Oh, well, it is late. I shall permit him to sleep on your porch. Where is your automobile?"

"Uh, it's down the road. It's broken. I'll have it repaired tomorrow."

The student followed, carrying our bags on his head. We walked slowly through the lobby toward one of the cottages in the sideyard. While passing some of the guests, I nodded with the air of a distinguished white planter on vacation from my estate. Little did they suspect that I was an impoverished hitchhiker and did not share their prejudice against the Africans.

~ 23 ~

God And Gorilla

My enthusiasm over trying to locate the Pygmies and the gorillas led me deep into the Belgian Congo. At some places and times the missionaries were ubiquitous and seemed to outnumber the Africans.

Two American missionaries drove me up a narrow road in a Ford pickup truck. The mountainous country near Lake Kivu lay ahead. The fleshy woman who was squeezed between her gaunt husband and me said, "I do hope you like it here in Africa. We sure do. Haven't been here too long, but make no mistake about it, we've had the call to serve for years, ever since we heard a missionary speak at our church meeting back home."

"Yes, sir," the husband said. "Then and there we made the decision to save these black folks."

"That's fine," I said.

"Why most of them dance naked and don't come by the true meaning of our message," she added in a confidential tone. "You won't believe this, but some of them worship the devil, and they..."

"Reckon you'll find those gorillas near Kivu?" the man interrupted in his southern drawl.

"Well, sir, I don't know, but I'll try."

"Instead of looking for them apes, you should be doing the Lord's work," he said in a quivering voice. His face seemed paler than ever under his broad-brimmed hat, and I feared that his trembling hands might slip from the steering wheel.

"Yes, indeed," she said. "We need more help here. I read somewhere the black brain is smaller than ours. Scripture backs it up. It must be, because they can't memorize the Bible verses we give them. They fight one another behind our backs—even after we preach to them. Then we have to go bandage them up and hand out penicillin pills. They're simply un-Christian."

"I gave up my street revival work and started selling furniture to make ends meet so as we could come here. We're not going back to Carolina until we've saved our quota. Right now, I'm bad sick with malaria. That's why we're going down south to rest."

After climbing down from their truck in the rugged mountains south of Rutshuru, I saw the woman raise her hand in a pontifical attitude. "Don't forget that which I have told ye, young man, and you will be right with God," she said.

"Yes, ma'am, I won't forget."

I felt a strange mixture of disgust, dismay and sympathy for them while the sight of their truck grew smaller and disappeared into the mountains. Turning, I climbed a path toward a village of round huts.

Several days before, a young Belgian told me that I could perhaps find a guide to the gorillas in this area. He told me that a safari with official sanction would be costly and improbable. Only Belgian scientists and officials were allowed to study these rare beasts. I was willing, however, to risk arrest and a stint in jail for the privilege of seeing a gorilla in the wild.

With a surprised expression, an old man in khaki shorts greeted me in front of his grass-roof hut. After showing him a photograph of a gorilla and a few Congo francs, I was pleased that he nodded in understanding and smiled. Yet he seemed apprehensive over my being there. Finally, he waved his hands at me in a negative fashion, as we squatted down in the shade of his hut.

One by one most of the people in the village gathered around me. I untied my blanket, which was filled with tins of food for my proposed expedition. A few of the men examined my food supply while talking to the old man. Still the feeling they conveyed to me in a mixture of Swahili, French and their own language was that my trek was not official and therefore doomed.

From my bag I pulled out several typewritten letters from home and said, *"Lettres officiel de Belgian Congo."*

"Bon, bon, c'est bon," the old man murmured. Apparently, he could not read English or French but was somewhat impressed by the letters and my passport.

Immediately an eager young man stepped forward and volunteered to be my tracker. Since I had no maps, he drew a sketch on the ground concerning our proposed route to gorilla sites. With enthusiasm, the other men offered advice, and a lengthy palaver or "official discussion" was under way.

At last they resolved our proposed route. In a moment my guide and I agreed on a sum in exchange for his services—approximately ten American dollars; all of them seemed delighted that the palaver ended with success. The villagers and I laughed when one man wearing a torn sun helmet frolicked on all fours and beat his chest like a mountain gorilla.

My muscular guide handed me a spear for self-protection, tied his bundle with mine and somehow balanced both of them on his head. He led me up the terraced corn and bean fields toward the forest. Children, singing a folk song, ran behind us for a while before returning to the village.

We climbed quickly up a steep mountainside for several hours. After following the forest trail over this incline and hurrying down into a green valley, we then ascended another path. The farmer-turned-tracker strode along with the confidence of a man long accustomed to rugged terrain. Occasionally, I had to jog. My chest pulsated with the same fatigue I had often experienced when running track or cross-country for my alma mater, the University of Tennessee.

Crackling through the reeds rimming the dark waters of a marsh, I became more acclimated to the altitude, which was around ten-thousand feet. The guide continually accelerated the pace. Perhaps he was trying to discourage me from continuing with this safari because he wanted to return to his *shamba*, farm, and family as soon as he could.

The tracker slowed down when we entered an animal trail. Above us the trees interwove into a thick roof, blotting out the Congo sun; below us our path was wet and narrow. Frequently, my shoes caused me to slip; his bare feet, however, negotiated the trail with confidence.

Nearing the mountaintop, we passed an intercepting trail filled with the prints of cloven-hoofed buffaloes. My guide motioned me on with great concern, as the soft dung meant these brutes were still in the vicinity. I had learned how dangerous they were and needed no prodding to walk faster. The long black spear felt comforting in my hand; it excited some primitive urge to defend myself or to kill some wild beast.

Leaving the dark trail of animals, we entered into an unbelievably bright meadow, reminding me of a golf course. Beneath us the grass smelled like a freshly peeled orange. A cool breeze scattered clusters of yellow hibiscuses and refreshed us. We sat down at the bottom of the meadow to rest from our long climb.

"Kwenda rugano." "Let's go toward the bamboos," my guide said, pointing his spear to the right.

"Bon, bon," I said and smiled.

Walking down the meadow toward the forest, we saw the clouds dramatically part, revealing a savage landscape.

A forest of giant trees covered an enormous valley. Each dark-gray trunk in the foreground was covered with vines, and rose from a sea of thorny underbrush. Beyond the forest one mountain after another arched its rugged back toward a mammoth volcanic peak that disappeared into the high clouds. We were somewhere in the central part of the Virunga volcanoes. Suddenly a cloud blew across our view as though it were pushed by the Lake Kivu wind-god, who felt he must guard his domain from foreign eyes.

For an hour or so we took bounding steps down a moss-cushioned trail, slithering around huge trees. Then we climbed up a mountain rising above a fog-filled valley. Far below us came the rushing sound of a stream. Wiping the sweat from the band of my baseball cap, I peered down for a glimpse of the water. After several impatient sighs, the African continued, and I had to abandon my sightseeing efforts.

As the twilight turned into depressing night, we built a fire in a clearing near the bamboo forest. Eventually, the cool earth circling the fire grew warm, and we sat down on our blankets. After each of us ate a can of tuna, we gazed into the flames for a long time.

In this primeval forest I felt more isolated from the outside world than ever before. The somberness of the night increased my desire to communicate in some way with my civilization. It would be good, so very good, to talk to my friends, family and shipmates.

I unfolded an old copy of *Time* magazine and browsed the advertisement-laden pages while my guide looked over my shoulder. We chuckled over a photograph of fashion models wearing flowered hats.

"La fleur faux," I said after looking in my French dictionary. "Fake flower."

"Ahh, ahh," he murmured.

Although I tried to explain in sign language that the flowers were artificial, he did not seem to understand why American women would wear artificial blossoms when they could easily wear real ones.

Piping birdcalls and unidentifiable shrieks resounded through the forest as my guide curled up in his blanket. I leaned closer to the fire to dry my socks. As I yawned at the sky, I had the momentary illusion of being in the chamber of a large cave. Vines cascaded down from the trees like stalactites; the stars overhead seemed to reflect our campfire. Drowsily, I wrapped myself in a blanket and fell into a deep sleep.

We awoke the next morning to a cool breeze and followed the trail toward the bamboos. During the night some insect had splotched my hands and neck in red. My tracker paused and examined the bites. Deftly he tore off several leaves from a papery-barked tree. After mashing them in his hands, he smeared the peppermint-smelling juices on my rash. We smiled at my instantaneous relief. I filled one pocket with the leaves, for future use, and hurried behind him into the bamboo forest.

Our animal track rambled through the tall bamboos that filtered out much of the sunlight. We sloshed across a clearing of knee-high ferns, still wet with the heavy dew, and entered a higher path. Frequently, my guide bent over broken stalks of young bamboo to search for any marks left by gorillas.

"La chambre a coucher, a chambre a coucher," he whispered. "The bedroom, the bedroom." Scattered on the forest floor were oval gorilla sleeping nests composed of branches and leaves. I picked up a patch of black fur from one nest. My body hummed with apprehension. Any second I expected to see a black gorilla charge through the bamboos and twist us apart. Yet I comforted myself with the knowledge that gorillas were extremely shy and perhaps never attacked human beings.

Finding no more signs of gorillas by mid-afternoon, we tramped down the mountain to our camp for the night. I sensed my guide was growing disgruntled over our pursuit for an animal he had seen many times.

A distant belch of thunder reverberated over us when we walked into the bamboos the next morning; rain fizzed on the thin-leaved bamboo tops and dripped coldly on our faces. Several hours later we heard a swishing sound.

Ahead, the grass suddenly trembled. Quickly hurling his spear, the tracker grabbed mine and chased some squealing animals.

While jumping over a fern-covered log, I slipped and tumbled into the grass. After flexing my stunned arm, I walked down to see what the African had killed. Proudly he stood over a black forest boar. Its small ribs labored for breath; blood spurted out of its carotid neck arteries. My guide's bare feet and the grass near the dying animal were sprayed with blood. He shouted with glee. Gradually, my atavistic hunting instinct surfaced, and I was somehow transformed. Laughing, we held our spears up triumphantly.

Around the fire that night we stuffed ourselves with the sinewy pork. For the first time in weeks, my stomach was filled. The boar's head with its tusks gleaming in the firelight gave me an uncomfortable feeling. It was unusual for me to aid in the butchering and cooking of an animal that pulsated with life only a short time ago. I was conditioned to eating pork and other meat without thinking about its preparation. Hunger kept me from exploring this thought.

When we awoke the following morning, both of us shivered. During the night the temperature had dropped to a near freezing level. While we hovered over the fire, I thought about the irony of being in "Darkest Africa" where the weather was cooler than many high locations in Europe or America.

Later in the morning the African found several broken bamboo stalks along a narrow trail. Both of us froze.

"*Ngagi, ngagi,*" he whispered. "Gorilla, gorilla."

He pointed to gorilla dung which seemed to be fresh. Our fatigue seemed to vanish; we now followed the gorilla spoor through the bamboo forest with renewed enthusiasm. We strode into a clearing where the welcome sunshine warmed us. High above us the forest disappeared into the mist. We entered a dark trail.

Overhead the bamboos seethed with a fresh wind. In a moment a white cloud scudded across their high leaves, giving us the illusion of walking into a green sea. Suddenly, the wind drifted to another part of the mountain, and there was a strange silence. We occasionally heard bird cries above our muted footsteps.

"*Monsieur, Bwana,*" my guide whispered. Breathing rapidly, he held up a tuft of black fur. I started to speak; he pressed his fingers on my lips. Quietly we climbed upward. Now and then we passed large knuckle-and-rear foot depressions in the damp earth. Swirling around us in the cool air was the rank odor of perspiration. My heart was thumping. The clatter of bamboo leaves falling to the ground seemed much louder than ever. My guide froze. From a sunlit area of the forest came pig-like grunts, high-pitched hoots and thrashing sounds. Instinctively, we crept forward.

Crawling, we entered a trail in the underbrush and soon stopped at a point overlooking a sunny clearing. We peered beyond the heavy leaves

Occasionally, the author would travel second-class to meet more prosperous Indians. Usually, however, his meager budget forced him to squeeze into crowded third-class coaches.

After searching villages south of Bombay, the author finally found a respectable holy man. He meditated in an ashram to experience the life of a mystic.

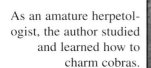

As an amature herpetologist, the author studied and learned how to charm cobras.

With Mau Mau terrorism in Kenya at its height, two African members of the British Home Guard stand by their lorry before going on patrol.

This urbane African king entertained the author and gave him insight into changing Uganda. Since the author's inexpensive camera had no flash, the king was good enough have his guards move the lionskin-covered throne outside into the sunlight.

A mother and her child from the then-prosperous country of Uganda pause as they wande through their village. Decades later their peaceful land disintergrated into ruin from years of civil war.

Emu, a friendly Pygmy, invited the author to live in his village of leaf huts in the Ituri Forest.

Pygmys gather outside their Mongongo leaf huts.

In the vast Ituri Forest of the Belgian Congo, the author lived and hunted with this Pygmy gr

Temu, a full-grown man whom the author nicknamed Giggles, always enjoyed playing tricks.

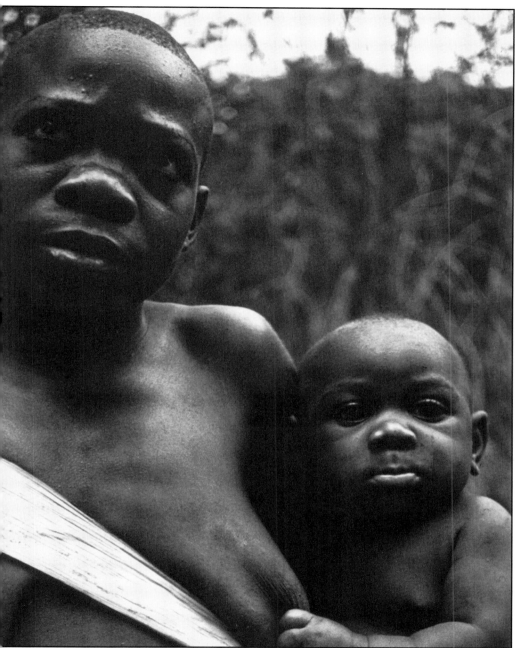

A Pygmy baby clings to her mother's breast as they wait for a hunting party to return.

A father participates in daily archery practice with his two sons. Monkeys and small antelope were the principal game.

Outside his hut on the shores of Lake Edward, a fisherman mends his net.

Both men and Maribou storks fish along the shore of Lake Edward in Uganda.

The author lived and worked with this fisherman and his family. Eager to learn more English, allowed the author to live under the eaves of his crowded hut.

Originally from Palestine, this grandmother moved with her family to a small village near Amman, Jordan.

In a mock Lawrence of Arabia pose, the author brandishes his pistol before riding with a polic lieutenant to several villages. During this inspection tour, the lieutenent arrested two drug smug glers who were disguised as pilgrims to Mecca.

In the springtime, two men enjoy black coffee.

Jordanian teacher amuses children on a village rooftop. Several of his tales had origins in the _Arabian Nights._

In a coastal region of Attica the author became friends with this carefree shepherd.

The rugged beauty of coastal Attica provides a routine backdrop for this Greek shepherd as he herds his flock on their daily rounds.

ce dogs did most of the work, sheep herding was relatively easy, allowing the author to pass e time reading Greek mythology and sipping resinous wine. Here, the author pauses in his duties to cuddle a playful lamb.

During his stay in a Belgian Trappist monastary, the author paused in his work to pose with a humble lay brother.

Several times during the day, Trappist priests went on solitary walks in the woods. Life in this monastary was austere but rewarding.

but could see nothing. My guide lifted his binoculars, which had a cracked right lens, and panned carefully across the clearing.

He gasped and whispered, *"Iko Ngagi."* "It's a gorilla."

After he gave me the binoculars, I focused on a black furry mass which, at first, seemed like part of the dense foliage surrounding the clearing. When I located a gorilla, I lowered the glasses and found that I could see it without binoculars.

It was not one gorilla but a family enjoying the noon-day sun. Three shaggy adults huddled together while several adolescents seemed to play hide-and-seek in the lush greenery of the clearing. To the far left a solitary gorilla seemed to be standing guard over the resting family. Near the three adults, I finally saw an enormous silverback, partially hidden by the foliage. He was lying on his back with his legs crossed.

Squinting, I had the illusion of seeing a family on a picnic in a park. In a moment one adolescent chased another past the silverback male who ignored their frolicking. He circled around and beat his chest in a mock threat to his playmates. With shrieks and pig-like grunts they tumbled out of sight into the underbrush.

Somehow I had the urge to join them. This looked like a friendly group, which would perhaps receive me as a distant relative in nature's chain of evolution. The faces of the older gorillas seemed almost human. Their low sounds could have been part of a relaxed conversation. I was overwhelmed by this peaceful scene of the so-called "savage beasts."

Some fifteen minutes later a doleful cry originated from the distant bamboos. The male who was lying down rolled to his feet. Defensively, he strutted back and forth on all fours in front of the others. He was an imposing, masterful animal. Again the cry echoed throughout the forest. The old silverback faced the direction of the noise while the other gorillas scampered away. Briefly, he stood up on his legs and beat his chest before following his family.

A fascinating scene had suddenly disappeared from the bright clearing. I was exultant over seeing these rare animals in their mountain habitat. My tracker was beaming and chattering away in his native tongue. We slapped each other on the shoulders and stood up. Our mission was more successful than expected.

On our way back toward the village, I hummed frequently with satisfaction. My guide also seemed content. Perhaps he could buy a cooking pot for his wife or a new khaki jacket for himself with the extra francs I gave him. We climbed down a path and strode into a field dappled with reddish orchids. While he rested, I picked a bunch of these flowers, worth about forty dollars on the American market.

My guide, who also seemed giddy from the abrupt changes in altitude, took out my copy of *Time* magazine and pointed to the pictures of the ladies in the flowered hats. Smiling, he grabbed my flowers and put them on his head and skipped around our baggage in a gleeful parody of fashion models. We both laughed. In a moment he became so exhilarated with his makeshift hat that he tripped and fell into the grass.

We continued clowning around for some time until we recovered our composure. Then, with spears over our shoulders and contentment in our hearts, we hiked down the mountain. As we strode through the dim woods approaching the village, we smelled smoke from evening cooking fires. Soon we heard children singing. I could not understand the words, yet the melody seemed very familiar. While we trudged down through a cornfield, one boy met us with a canteen of cold water. With excitement, more children surrounded us. They refused to let us move until my guide told the story of our search for gorillas.

Some of the children expressed disappointment that we had killed no gorillas. My guide avoided my faltering questions. I was shaken at the thought that he and others in the village might have been involved in poaching. Here in the Belgian Congo, the situation was somewhat like that in Sumatra. The farmers, hungry for both land and meat, were gradually hunting their exotic animals into extinction.

We finally continued with the children following us in the cool twilight. Drawing closer, we could see the cooking fires that appeared unusually bright and welcoming in the early evening. Drumbeats resounded over the mountainside. One by one, the children joined in the song they had been singing earlier in their own language. It was "Onward Christian Soldiers."

The guide laughed at me when he noticed my puzzled expression. *"Missionnaire de Dieu,"* he said. "Missionary of God."

"You mean they've come this far?" I asked, pointing to the village.

"Fuite de missionnaire est impossible," he added with amusement. "Escape from the missionary is impossible!"

~ 24 ~

Forest People

In my search for a hospitable Pygmy village where I could live and hunt, I encountered some high-caliber missionaries from the United States.

After meeting several missionaries, I strolled around grounds spotted with grass-roofed huts. Inside one large pavilion, a group of Africans sat on whitewashed, mud benches waiting for treatment. A motherly, pink-cheeked American nurse spoke to them in Swahili while two Africans in white shorts handed out pills to those with minor ailments.

Squirming self-consciously on a rear bench was a Pygmy family. A quiver of arrows hung over the shoulder of the father, and a child-sized bow wrapped in monkey fur rested on his lap. The mother cradled a baby whose face was pimpled with pink sores. Except for tan loincloths around their groins, the couple was naked.

In the hospital's unpretentious main building I met Dr. Carl Becker, of the American Inland Mission, who had spent much of his life helping the Pygmies and other Africans. He was a lean, soft-spoken man in his early sixties.

"Doctor," I said, "I'm surprised to see all of these huts. Guess I expected to see an American-style hospital."

"I know what you mean," he said. "We built our hospital and school here to look as much like an African dwelling as possible. Makes the patients more relaxed to be in familiar surroundings."

"Do you always have so many patients?"

"Oh, yes," he said and smiled. "This has been a light day so far. On some days we have as many as five hundred patients. Of course, now I see only about seventy a day; my staff handles the others."

"In Bali, I saw a lot of leprosy. Do you have that problem here?"

"Unfortunately, yes. We have a lepers' village not far from here. We're making fair progress with some cases. Here, of course, we treat yaws and many other skin diseases. Then, too, there is much tuberculosis."

An African in a white coat stepped inside the office and mumbled something to the doctor.

"Excuse me," the doctor said. "It's time to take a cast off a boy's leg. Make yourself at home—see whatever you want."

After enjoying an American meal in a staff member's brick bungalow, I stretched out on a comfortable bed in the guest room. A breeze refreshed the otherwise hot Congo night. While trying to sleep, I thought about the vigorous and dedicated work my countrymen were doing here. In a little while my mind merged with the blackness of the forest encircling the mission. I slept.

Several days later I hitchhiked with a Belgian who was driving from Beni toward the center of the Congo. Our car followed a dirt road winding through the vast Ituri forest. On each side of us, masses of vegetation rippled down the enormous trees. Periodically, vines scraped across our windshield. Here and there mango trees wrenched free from the lower vegetation to luxuriate in the sun while less powerful trees remained stunted in the shadows below.

"You say, *monsieur*, that you wish a discharge from my autocar on this road?" the Belgian asked.

"Yes, sir, I thought I could find some Pygmies in the bush and live with them. Should be cheaper than staying in a hotel!"

"*Oui, oui*, you must at first find them, but is not difficult—Pygmies are everywhere," he said, gesturing with both hands off the wheel.

Near the bottom of a hill we frightened a pack of black-faced baboons that were ambling down the road. With twittering shrieks, they scurried into the underbrush. Their fetid odor soon blew into our windows, making us cough. When the road uncurled for a few minutes, we saw an old Pygmy man carrying several bamboo poles on his head. He wore a bark cloth apron; under his arm was a pouch. We stopped near him and left the car.

Gesturing eloquently, the Belgian rattled off a bewildering mixture of French, Swahili and the local language. The little man became amused. In fact, he became so tickled that he let his bamboo poles clatter to the ground while giggling like a schoolboy. When the Pygmy stopped dancing around, I tried to gesture my desire to live in his village.

"Is enough," the Belgian said. "I believe I know this old man. He is Temu. Forever and ever he giggles."

"Temu does seem happy," I said, and laughed.

"He is intelligent enough to know what is said. Give Temu some cigarette packs, and he will give aid to you. Remember, if he decides not to give aid to you, is necessary to walk back to the last village."

"You mean the one ten miles back?"

"*Oui,* and *monsieur,* please stay close by the fire at night. The leopard is—I do not know how you say in English—but he is *le gourmet.*"

After the Belgian drove away, I gave the Pygmy several packs of cigarettes and showed him a tin of salt and the canned food in my bag. Sighing with delight, he pressed both my feet on the ground as though he were telling me not to move. After zipping up my bag, I turned around. The old Pygmy had disappeared.

The tropical twilight came through the trees and quickly drained away the countless shades of green. Perhaps I had misunderstood the Pygmy, and he did not intend to return. After dragging several branches into the center of the road, I built a fire which made my defenseless position seem less severe. Thus far in my travels I found that if I met people in a friendly manner, they usually allowed me to visit their families and appreciated my interest in them. However, I feared the Pygmies might react differently.

A dankness gradually settled over the forest, releasing rotten odors from the vegetation. I ate a Cadbury chocolate bar, waved gnats and mosquitoes from my face and waited.

Hearing a loud whistling sound, I suddenly bounded up from my seat. Standing below me was the old man, Temu. With him were two younger Pygmies.

"*Ami,* friend, *rafiki,*" I blurted out in a mixture of languages.

The old man giggled over his prank.

"*Rafiki.*" "Friend," he said in Swahili as he introduced me to his companions who were also smiling.

After the Pygmies smoked several cigarettes around the fire, they helped me smother it with dirt from the roadside. With an effortless grace, one of the Pygmies lifted my heavy bag to the top of his head and led us into the forest. Even though I held the flashlight, I stumbled behind them like a clumsy elephant following a herd of gazelles.

Their flaming torches aided in keeping any predators away from us.

Along the way the old man giggled and talked as though I understood everything he said. Eventually, I nicknamed him Giggles.

As the trail widened, the three Pygmies whistled like alarmed birds. In a moment, shrill replies came from deep within the forest. Several miles later, a pale light wavered out through the night, outlining the bushes and the high trees. Turning down a smaller path, we entered a clearing illuminated by a large campfire. Forming a ring inside this clearing were around twenty dome-shaped huts made from *mangungu* leaves. Each hut shimmered in the light of its own tiny fire. In front of the far huts stood a group of fifty or more Pygmies. I felt as though I had passed through a time warp into a magical Stone Age encampment. A sense of wonder swept over me, and my nervousness abated.

All eyes, sparkling in the firelight, moved up and down my six-foot-one-inch frame. The tallest Pygmy was around four-and-one-half feet high. For a moment the only sound came from a whimpering baby who twisted in a sling on his mother's side. A few men continued to hold their spears.

Then Giggles spoke to the wrinkled elder who seemed to be disturbed by my appearance. This elder's face possessed a calmness and dignity only years can bring. Bowing like a clumsy servant, I presented him with the tin of salt, many canned goods and more cigarettes to the others. Several shy women and children turned their eyes away from me.

With cigarettes smoldering from their dark lips, the men chattered in a relaxed manner and put down their spears. A few potbellied children wearing red and blue beads around their hips seemed to fear me. Occasionally, they would peer at me from the rear of the huts. Their eyes bulged with curiosity.

Turning quickly toward the children, I made a face. They screamed and ran off into the forest while their parents laughed. Giggles howled. I was being accepted. When the cigarettes were smoked out, the elder sprinkled salt, a rare trade item, into the pink palms of all the people. Each Pygmy, including the children, licked it up and sighed with much satisfaction.

Here in the Ituri Forest, as in other parts of the world, salt was indeed a rarity. I felt sorry for the Pygmies, who craved an item that I had always taken for granted. I lighted my half-filled pipe while squatting down with the others. Giggles took a puff and smiled impishly. From his hut he brought a small pouch of dried leaves. Nimbly, he packed my pipe with them. He and the others studied my face as I forced myself to smoke the bitter mixture. Several times I choked on the fumes.

"Bangi, bangi," he murmured.

"Muzuri." "Good," I said.

Glancing around me, I saw several other men puff away on their clay pipes with long reed stems. Giggles inhaled the smoke from his pipe. I was growing very tired. My mind seemed to slow down, and the entire scene of the activity in the Pygmy village seemed to flow in a disjointed slow motion dance.

Later in the night, the Pygmies laughed, chatted and continued smoking. My head was reeling; I felt giddy. *Bangi* must have been a variety of marijuana. It was Pygmy party time.

The village elder pulled me to my feet and tried to entice me to follow him around the fire in some dance. With abrupt gestures, the elder motioned for all the men to join us. A man skipped out of his hut with an animal-skin drum and thumped it with the rhythm of a slow heartbeat. The women and children smiled their approval from their seats in the background.

Grasping a long stick, the elder stalked around the fire as though he were searching for the tracks of an animal. Now I was fully at ease. It was as if I were dancing again with the primitive Kubus in Sumatra. For some twenty minutes we followed him around the fire, to the throb of the drum. Three times he stooped over and explained the details of the hunt. Excited murmurs came from many lips when he found the spoor for which he was searching.

Leaping in the air, he twitched his head from side to side. Now his dignity vanished, as he seemed transformed into a ferocious beast. Beating faster, the drummer found a rhythm that palpitated through the villagers and made them nod in time. From the wavering shadows, one man stepped forward and raised his imaginary spear.

"Tembo, tembo." "Elephant, elephant," he cried.

"Kufa, kufa." "Kill, kill." *"Kufa, kufa."* "Kill, kill," the Pygmies chanted.

All of the Pygmies swayed to the throbbing drum while we circled the fire. One man raised his arms up like the trunk of an elephant and gave a frightening, realistic cry of alarm. The elephant imitator tore off an imaginary tree branch and curled it into his mouth, making loud chomping noises.

"Bwa, bwa," Giggles said. "Dung, dung."

All of the dancers picked up imaginary handfuls of elephant dung and spread it over themselves. This would disguise their scent. Now the drumbeat slowed down as the Pygmies and I moved forward in stealthy, staccato steps. The drumbeat stopped.

Quietly, the elder pretended to spear an imaginary elephant in a vulnerable area of its underbelly. Again the drumbeat continued and grew faster as the other hunters threw their spears. In a moment, the drum built to a crescendo as the imaginary animal staggered forward; the beat kept pace to the elephant's dying steps. The elder yelled. Happily, he and the others danced around and stood triumphantly on the dead elephant's corpse.

An aged woman whose breasts drooped like strips of warm tar smacked her lips, perhaps recalling similar elephant kills. Tears of joy filled the elder's eyes. He went through the motions of cutting the meat and dividing it equally among all the villagers. After gorging on the simulated flesh, the elder rubbed his stomach, belched and sat down with an air of superiority.

Soon, the younger men capered around the fire to a quick drumbeat, while they told the story of a bow and arrow hunt. Laughter and comments came from the audience when one young Pygmy boasted of killing some large monkey. He held his hands three feet off the ground to indicate the size of his kill. Several Pygmies howled in disbelief. With lusty good humor, the audience made him lower his hand to the two-foot level. Initially, this enraged the hunter, but he forced a smile, and the story continued late into the night.

Most of the dwarfed people withdrew into their leafy huts while I sat down by the fire. The elder rimmed my blankets with ashes to keep away the ants and protect me from the evil spirits. In sign language he promised to build me a hut if I shared more of my trade goods with him. Before toddling off to his hut, Giggles encouraged me to smoke another pipe of *bangi*.

*

A cool mist drifted over the trees the next morning. Hidden birds chirped loudly as a gray light filtered down on the small village. One by one, the elfin figures strolled toward the main fire to re-examine me. Everyone seemed amused when I gestured how the marijuana had made me dizzy. After I gave out some more cigarettes, Giggles enacted one of his *bangi* smoking experiences. Waves of laughter came from the

Pygmies when he told the story of his tripping into the fire and burning his rump. His scars proved his story.

After I drank a gourd of murky water and ate a few bananas, the elder motioned for me to leave with them on the day's hunt. I hurried down the trail following a single file of men and women. The mirth of the night before had vanished. None of the Pygmies spoke; hunting was a serious, life-sustaining endeavor.

Turning onto a wider trail, we could still hear the voices of the children in the village. Their days were filled with helping the old women and playing games. Now the hunters seemed exceptionally small and vulnerable as they padded beneath the lofty mahogany trees. Soon the brush grew thicker, and I could see only one man in front of me. Each time he moved his pink-soled feet, a quiver of arrows swayed on his back. Bramble scratches on his legs recorded his previous expeditions. Several times I cracked twigs on the path. Finally, the Pygmy stopped and hissed at my unwieldy shoes.

Seeping through the fog, the sun illuminated the wet foliage with a wavering, phosphorescent light. Now my companions stepped into dark tunnels within the forest underbrush. To keep up with them, I had to crawl or bypass these passageways. They were all under five feet, and I was well over six.

I was relieved when we entered a large clearing. After the elder swept his spear over his head, the Pygmies spread out. The bare-breasted women leaned over to pluck yellow mushrooms and edible roots. Tenderly, they placed this food into leaf baskets which, suspended from forehead straps, dangled onto their backs. One woman beckoned to the others. With nimble fingers they gathered another large cluster of mushrooms and walked away from the men to search for edibles near a stream.

Miles later we heard a chattering noise in the forest ahead. The Pygmy near me stopped; his shoulder muscles grew taut and seemed to quiver. When an unusual bird call soared over us, he slipped an arrow into his bow. We stalked to the far side of a thicket and crouched.

In the trees above us was a pack of dark-gray monkeys. They frolicked in the mossy branches completely unaware that poison-tipped arrows were pointed in their direction. In unison, a series of arrows flew into the trees.

One monkey, with a stunned expression, scrambled down a vine, lost his grip, and crashed into the underbrush. Swinging back and forth on a limb, another monkey fell into the thicket. A mother holding a baby tottered slightly before falling. Another monkey keeled over. Shrieking in alarm, the others jumped from one tree to another in a bewildering blur.

Grinning Pygmies popped up from the shadows like blackened coal miners emerging from a mineshaft. The elder was only twenty yards away, but I could not see him during the hunt. After recovering the bodies, the men yanked out the arrows. Carefully, the elder severed the right paw of each animal with his spear. Perhaps this ritual appeased the spirits of the dead monkeys and insured successful hunts in the future.

When we ambled into the camp, I heard muffled laughter, which confused me. I looked ahead, but could see nothing funny. Smiling, a small boy pointed. I glanced down at a toothless old woman who was imitating my long-legged stride. She strode arrogantly past me while clicking her tongue. When the others heard me chuckle, they laughed boisterously.

That night the air around the little huts was thick with the smell of wood smoke. The monkey meat, which had been divided with much ceremony by the elder, bubbled in caldrons that sat in front of the huts. I ate my meager share of the meat and ended my meal with crisp caterpillars simmered in palm oil. After eating, I stood up to play with the good-natured children who flocked around me.

One boy, wearing only a ficus-bark loincloth, handed me a monkey's tail. I examined it with admiration. Then another boy let me look at his bow and arrow while gesturing how he had killed a bird. Giggles could not be outdone. He elbowed the children aside and puffed across the top of a thin bamboo reed with the sound of a person blowing across the lip of an empty beer bottle. When I tried to make the same sound with his flute, the children laughed with Giggles.

To tease them, I turned on a flashlight under my chin, casting my face in weird half-shadows. "E-EEE-YAA, E-EEE-YAA," the children screamed while running away. The old man clapped his hands and chuckled. Discovering that the flashlight was harmless, the children returned. After allowing each child to play with the light, I moaned as it grew weak, flickered and faded out.

Around ten o'clock the drowsy Pygmies regained a bit of their vigor, and the drummer started an easy beat. At first they seemed uninterested in dancing, but the savage "boom—lub, boom—lub, boom—lub" lured the men close to the large fire. They moved in a slow circle. From their seats the women swayed with bouncing breasts. Gradually, the men and I moved in unison to the rhythm of the Congo night.

Feeling like a clown on stilts, I impulsively pranced around with them. Mirthful cries greeted my performance. When the rosy palms of the drummer pounded a quick, angry beat I withdrew, since this was their own impassioned expression and not mine.

Arms bent by their sides, the men shuffled and skipped into the air. The drummer's eyes shone fiercely as though he were relaying the heartbeat of an animistic forest god. From outside the village came a scream followed by a loud rasping sound. The drummer's hands stopped; all the Pygmies listened. I held my breath. Perhaps it was a leopard. Then the drummer began to pound away with a fear-inspired intensity.

Gradually the rhythm slowed, and the men fastened their eyes on the women. Quickly they joined the men. A feeling of sensuality swelled within the bodies of the adults. Shifting their weight from one foot to the other, the women danced up to the men. Perspiration-polished bodies touched and withdrew to the "boom—lub, boom—lub, boom—lub" of the drum. Pounding louder, the drummer reached a climax, and the dance ended abruptly. With an air of relief, the tired men and women strolled around the fire. Some of the men nudged their wives toward the leaf huts.

I tossed some more wood on the fire and rolled up in my blankets. After many of the voices grew silent, Giggles stumbled toward me with a pretty young girl by his side. Firelight shimmered across her ripening breasts as she gave me an embarrassed smile. He muttered a few words making signs toward her body and mine. While I pretended not to understand, the girl stepped back. With surprising anger, Giggles flung her down on my blanket.

A resigned expression came over her face as she bent her head. Restrained laughter emanated from the huts.

"*L'amour,*" Giggles cooed.

"You're kidding," I said.

I took out my passport case and showed Giggles a picture of my mother and of a Portuguese beauty whom I had met in Japan. After squinting at the pictures, he chortled as though he understood. The girl fled into the shadows. Most of the men stood outside their huts. In a moment, Giggles scampered from one hut to another, holding up two fingers to tell everyone that I had two wives. He seemed perplexed that

I wanted to remain faithful to them. Little did he realize that I was an officer and a gentleman.

*

Padding down a wide trail the next morning, everyone stepped abruptly to the right side. Since I was tired, I continued in the middle. Growling, one Pygmy shoved me to the side of the trail. A few feet later we passed a pit camouflaged with leaves in the center of the trail. Hissing, the Pygmies pointed to the animal trap.

"Merci, merci," I mumbled. "Thanks."

If I had not been warned, I could have fallen into a very deep pit.

In the shadows of the afternoon, the men tied several *liana* vine nets across a trail while a group of women filed deeper into the forest. After smearing a light mixture of animal dung and dirt on themselves, the men motioned for me to do the same. Reluctantly, I dabbed a little on my hands and trousers to disguise my scent. The odor made me retch.

Then we stretched a long five-foot high net from one tree to another. Quickly the Pygmies camouflaged this net, designed for trapping animals, with branches and leaves. Waving his spear, the elder signaled for everyone to take cover.

Dark hornbills flapped across the gaps in the treetops as we waited for the women to frighten some animals into our net. Unfortunately, no breeze came to dissipate our fecal odor. Now and then the Pygmy next to me stood up and flicked his head back and forth like a startled gazelle. Yet he saw nothing.

Later in the afternoon, a flock of green parrots flew over us. In a moment, the Pygmy murmured knowingly as though he heard something. An unusual noise reverberated through the forest. Several minutes later I recognized the faint, high-pitched chant of the approaching women and older children.

A rustling noise approached our net. Breathing rapidly, the men rose with their spears and poison-tipped arrows aimed at the net. The cordon of chanting women grew closer. Impulsively, I stood up. I noticed a savage look on the elder's face. The Pygmies were immobile. The noise grew louder. Someone pulled me down into the bushes. Now the rustling noise merged into the crashing and squealing sounds of a herd of frightened beasts. Perhaps it was a herd of forest boars.

Abruptly, the squealing animals turned away from us, and their sounds grew fainter. Possibly the animals sensed our trap and made a last-minute escape. Chanting loudly, the women and children arrived at our net. When they converged with the men on the trail, a spirited discussion began. With precise gestures the Pygmies traced the route of their quarry in this unsuccessful hunt. Together, the stoic little people took down the net to repeat the same operation elsewhere.

Following the silent commands of the elder, the Pygmies undertook the same hunting procedure in a different part of the forest. Again, no animals were caught in our net. The men and women accepted the long day's hunt calmly, with no apparent grumbling. Giggles sniffed my foul-smelling trousers, slapped his hands and laughed. I smiled as he said something in a brazen manner that made the others chuckle.

There was no meat that night, but the black pots bubbled with greens. Whenever the Pygmies had an abundance of meat, they would trade it with the African villagers outside the forest for salt, vegetables and other goods. Sadly enough, these villagers were notorious for cheating the Pygmies in such transactions.

After eating, the elder called everyone to the middle of the village. From an antelope skin pouch he withdrew a green wine bottle and held it over his head. I smiled in astonishment. The elder and Giggles removed the cork from the bottle. Carefully, they removed a photograph of some villagers with two Europeans. Everyone was standing still as though they were at attention. Their rigid stance indicated that the antique camera which took the picture could not tolerate any motion. If anyone moved, a blurred image would result.

Obviously, they had enjoyed some pleasant interaction with these Belgians some time in the past. Perhaps this relationship had made them accept me more readily. Proudly, the elder pointed out the living members of the group. Several old women had tears in their eyes when the dead villagers were named. With great care the elder put the picture into the bottle for preservation.

After the bottle was put inside the elder's hut, the children started to play. Yelling, the boys raced outside the camp, chasing some make-believe animals. The girls frisked about in leafy skirts and elephant grass blouses. With this disguise, they pretended to frighten wild beasts into the nets while they banged sticks together and chanted in minor-keyed voices.

When twilight turned into darkness, the children did not have to be reminded to return to the safety of the camp. They were well aware of the dangers of playing too far away from the campfire.

I sat by the small fire in front of Dephu's hut. Dephu was a very friendly man about my age. Earlier he had seen me give Giggles and the elder a few aspirin tablets. Gesturing slowly, he spoke to me as though I understood everything he said. Finally, I learned that he would like to trade for my aspirin bottle. It was a pleasure to exchange my bottle for two of his Pygmy flutes. In a few moments he tied the bottle around his neck with a vine. Now he could proudly combine the foreigner's medicine with his own more ancient remedies.

During the next few days he gave me flute lessons. *"Merci, le docteur,"* I said when we finished one lesson. He beamed with pleasure, thumped his chest and, in a deep voice that could be heard around the village, proudly proclaimed himself *"Le Docteur du Aspirin."*

One afternoon when we returned from an unsuccessful hunt, Giggles led the way back to the village. Gradually his depression over the results of the hunt changed. His eyes sparkled as though he had some secret. Soon he began to chatter away gleefully. I had trouble keeping up with him when he quickened his stride to a jog. Now the elder joined us and seemed to share Giggles' high spirits.

When we entered the village, I saw several women and children building a new hut. The saplings had been lashed together in a dome shape; however, the leaves had not been gathered to complete the framework. Both men smiled and told me that this was my hut. I was happy that the elder had finally kept his promise. Clumsily, I crawled into the small door of my hut as everyone laughed. When I sat inside, they were more astonished than ever that I was such a large and ungainly creature.

Again, I felt that I was being accepted. I was humming with happiness. Perhaps I could now live longer with the Pygmies and explore their mores and folkways in greater depth. Giggles and the elder promised to accompany me to the nearest trading post outside the forest. There I could buy food and other items the villagers needed. Since I was an ineffective hunter, these would be my contribution to them. Maybe, in a few days, the women and children would begin draping the leaves over the framework of my hut.

*

Early the next morning I awoke when the wind blew a billow of smoke over me. My eyes smarted. A cold rain had almost extinguished the main campfire. During the night, sparks from this fire had burned small holes in my blanket. My teeth began to chatter. Fortunately, I would be inside the warmth of my hut within a few days. As I marveled over its construction, several Pygmies slid their doors aside and joined me.

After throwing wood on the fire, they studied the giant trees creaking in the high wind. This would be a bad day for hunting. Delicate arrows would miss their marks, and the shifting winds would alert the animals to the hunters' scent. Most villagers appeared dejected with this unlucky hunting season. I felt uneasy, since the foodstuff I had given them was running very low.

Giggles, the elder and I rested by the main fire while most of the villagers remained inside their huts to keep warm. While we discussed our trek to the nearest trading post to buy food, we were interrupted by a shrill bird call. I was surprised when both of my companions sprang to their feet and returned the same call. Immediately the entire village of men, women and children scrambled from their huts and gathered by the main trail.

Soon two hunters from our village appeared and ran through the cheering crowd as though they were marathon runners finishing a race. They dropped their spears and sat down near the big fire. While the hunters caught their breaths, girls served them water, and I gave them some peppermint candy. Eventually, they told everyone about their trip through the forest to find new areas for hunting. During this long report I watched the enthusiasm of the villagers mount. A strong, restless feeling permeated the brave forest people. They were eager to move on.

With a morose look, Giggles left the others and stooped down next to me. We closed our eyes while the wind blew dust across our faces. He remained silent for a long time. Then he drew a map of the entire forest area on the ground. He scattered pebbles on the map to represent other Pygmy groups. Artfully, he cut vines and placed them where the rivers and trails were located. I was fascinated as he built up handfuls of dirt to indicate the hilly country. He flattened small plants to show where dangerous parts of the forest existed. Miraculously, his map developed a three-dimensional quality.

Using his finger, he drew the route the villagers would take to set up a new camp in a better hunting region. Not far from this spot was another Pygmy group. He made a guttural sound to show his anger at this group and indicated that both groups had quarreled over hunting areas for years. Also he made it clear that his village must move at once.

Hesitantly, I asked if I could go with them. Again he lapsed into silence. Then he pressed down on my feet and waved his hand to say no. I was hurt but attempted to hide it. After Giggles hurried away, a gust of wind destroyed the map. My dream of learning more about the Pygmies quickly faded.

The elder shouted to the villagers. Quickly, with much happy chatter, the forest people began packing. Within twenty minutes everyone gathered their few belongings. The women bundled up their cooking pots and baskets while the men collected their spears, nets, bows and arrows. With no ceremony they left their *mangungu* leafed huts and turned toward a forest trail. Their huts were in good condition but soon they would fade into the thick vegetation of the forest floor. My unfinished hut stood alone and naked in the morning sunlight.

I never liked goodbyes. However, the Pygmies had learned that the *muzungu*, the white man, had the custom of shaking hands. With an unusual solemnity they approached me. Almost every member of the Pygmy group touched my hands.

"*Kwenda nzuri,*" the elder said. "Go well."

"*Kwenda, kwenda, kwenda...*" I mumbled in a confused fashion. The moment was filled with emotion; I hated to leave these people whom I admired so much. They were indeed brave forest people.

With the exception of Giggles and two other men, the group turned down one fork in the trail; we four hurried down a twisting pathway leading toward the edge of the forest. The high winds followed us through the trees and churned up dust as we reached the road.

After I had waited by the roadside with the three Pygmies for a long time, a truck rumbled into sight and stopped beside us. Giggles muttered something to the black driver who opened the door for me. Chuckling and chattering away, Giggles gave me a hand slap. Arrogantly, the driver said something insulting to the little men, who were beneath his social class.

With their eyes on the ground, the Pygmies made a quick, awkward departure into the green haze of the Ituri Forest. The driver put his truck in gear, and we droned forward. Within five minutes I had returned light-years ahead to the harsh, mechanized world.

*

I left the Congo and returned to the village of Katwee, Uganda, in an unusual style for a jungle hitchhiker. An elderly American couple, making a tour of the game parks and other sights in the area, asked their chauffeur to stop for me. It was a strange yet pleasant experience to relax in the comfort of a late-model Chrysler.

"By the way, son," the man said, "did you hear about the Rose Bowl game this year?"

"No, sir, I didn't," I said.

"Well, we did pretty damn good—that is, with the material we had. Our star player got hurt in the first half and..."

I was only partially listening, for my thoughts were still with my guide to the gorillas of the Congo mountains and the Pygmies of the Ituri Forest, people and places that now seemed centuries away.

~ 25 ~

Cold Sun Over Lake Edward

An African fisherman invited me to stay in his mud hut and teach him a little more about the English language. Foolishly, I had ignored conventional western medical wisdom and failed to take all my medication. Such oversight caused me great pain.

Lake Edward slumbered within a rolling bed of green Ugandan hills under the midday sun. A breath of hot wind ruffled the waters and soughed across the grasslands.

Near one shore the hippos snoozed like contented hogs in a pond. Occasionally, one of them sprayed up water, creating ripples against the grassy shoreline. I walked along with a burly African whom I had met south of the village of Katwee. He agreed to let me stay with his family for a few days if I helped him fish and taught him a little more about the English language.

Gradually, we approached a cluster of whitewashed mud huts near the lake. The humid air was rank with the smell of fish. Waist-high drying racks, filled with the pink, opened bodies of fish, stretched behind each hut.

"Bwana," the fisherman said, "my three sons and I and you go for fish very soon. Is that not exclaimed in first-class English?"

"Very good for now," I said. "Tell me, where are the other people?"

"The men go out to fish; the women remain at the house. It is too hot to remain in sun now unless you go out to fish."

He bellowed a command to his sons who dozed under the wide eaves of the house. Yawning, they eased up, draped heavy nets over their bare shoulders and ambled toward the canoes.

In a moment we pushed the hot gunwales of a wooden canoe into the shallows while his sons followed in their craft. A flock of black and white marabou storks waded through the shallows. We paddled quickly toward them. Several flew out of the water and flapped away with dreamlike wingbeats.

When we saw bubbles rise to the surface, the fisherman and I back-paddled. Surging out of the water about thirty yards ahead was a hippo. He floated motionless while twitching his tiny ears at us. Then he plunged toward the other "river horses," leaving a white wake behind him.

"They no kill, Bwana," the fisherman said. "But they drown boat if you remain too close and—may Allah be merciful."

Suddenly, a draft of wind rolled over the hills and churned the lake into hundreds of whitecaps. The scent of bananas, parched grass and fish passed over us. Lushly, the waves gathered, swelled and sprayed our craft. After hoisting a torn sail, we rose and fell over the swaying face of the lake toward its far reaches.

Squinting back toward the shore, I could no longer see the settlement. The fisherman shouted orders to his sons. Leisurely, we joined nets and let them sink while our boats drifted apart.

When the burning winds skipped away from the lake, an hour later, we lowered the sails and tugged the nets in. Tattoos of fish fighting vainly for life came from the bottoms of each canoe. The fisherman and his sons broke into a deep, satisfying chant.

After heaving in our nets, we scooped the fish into baskets and paddled toward the settlement. Along the way I felt woozy. My head seemed to be expanding with some hot gas. Perhaps fatigue and the long exposure to the African sun had drained my energy and given me a fever.

The fisherman's wife, wearing a long yellow dress striped with red, met us as we skidded onto the muddy beach. Without speaking, she loaded a full basket of fish on her head and started toward the house. While we carried several loads of fish to the hut, the hump-shouldered storks converged on the canoes. Croaking and squawking, they fought each other. Greedily their long beaks snapped up the remaining scraps of fish.

After eating fish stew and roasted plantains, starchy bananas, we hung our nets along the thatched eaves of the hut to dry. Proudly, the fisherman put on a clean T-shirt decorated with a picture of two helmeted spacemen.

"You see, Bwana," he said. "I buy this shirt of Flash Gordon at the Indian's shop. I take care the sun not steal the color; I wear only at sunset and night. Do you have such shirts in America?"

"I think so," I said, "but yours is among the best ones I've seen."

"Ahh, Bwana, that is first-class," he said and grinned.

While the lake swallowed the afterglow of a feverish sunset, the father and his sons faced to the northeast. Standing, they uttered a prayer toward Mecca. Then they knelt and finally prostrated themselves on the warm beach.

I sat down on my blankets that were enclosed by a makeshift shelter under the eaves of the hut. Since it was too crowded to sleep inside, the fisherman had built this for my comfort and safety. It was designed to discourage the night-foraging hippos from stepping on me. My blood pulsed hotly through my temples. From somewhere in the dark lake came the familiar umm-aaaah, umm-aaaah, umm-aaaah bellows of the hippopotamuses. Before squirming into an exhausted sleep, I heard the snorts and thuds of a hippopotamus passing through the settlement.

My blankets and khaki clothes were soaked with perspiration the next morning. I walked along the shoreline for a long time as I tried to fight off a headache. My body started shivering. A cool wind huffed across the lake. Goose pimples covered me. Suddenly the sun was cold.

"Bwana, Bwana," the fisherman said anxiously when I returned to the settlement. "You look like malaria. May Allah be merciful."

"Let me rest for a while. I think I'll be all right."

"Yes, Bwana, yes."

"Could I have some water?"

His wife rushed up with a gourd of water and stood by gravely while I swallowed a couple of malaria pills. I rummaged through my bag for my bottle of aspirin, but remembered it was tied around the neck of my Pygmy friend in the Belgian Congo. After reassuring the fisherman that I felt better, he left with his sons for the canoes. Perhaps I should have boiled my water and also taken more of my malaria pills as the Ugandan king had suggested.

I lapsed into a hot dream in my outside shelter. Black and red splotches burned through my closed eyelids in flickering patterns. Disjointed thoughts of my parents, brother and friends swirled through my brain. Was Dr. Tom Dooley still in Japan? Where were my whiskey-crazed shipmates? They were probably with dates in the air-conditioned comfort of a nightclub in San Diego.

Enraged flies, drawn by the odor of drying fish, stung me. I felt as though some African demon were surreptitiously filleting my body, leaving only my hot flesh to simmer in the heat. Where were the girls I knew at the University of Tennessee? No doubt they were all married. Where were the people I had met in Asia? Where were the friends...? Where were...? Gradually, my thoughts fell into a steaming, white-hot limbo.

*

The acid smell of thatch and wood smoke pressed down on me as I tried to open my eyes. Light from some doorway swept through my trembling eyelashes. With increasing pain, I grabbed at my blankets and touched a cool dirt floor. After shaking my head, I realized I was lying inside the hut. The doorway turned black when a figure approached.

"Oh, Bwana, Bwana," the fisherman's wife murmured in a solicitous tone as she squatted beside me. She handed me a sweet-scented gourd of water, then gave me a bowl of fish soup. Afterward, I leaned back to sleep.

With frightening speed, my heart seemed to grow cold; it pumped glacial fluids into my arteries and tangled veins. Cold, trembling waves passed through my body over and over. The dark woman gently covered my shivering frame with blankets and stood watch over me.

As I began to feel warmer, my thoughts flowed to this Ugandan family. Perhaps some of their forefathers had been captured by Arab slave traders and shipped to my country. Then one of my great grandfathers in Tennessee might have purchased some of the same people to work on their land. I would like to think that my ancestors treated them with the same kindness I was now being shown.

One afternoon the fisherman surprised me with the news that I had been delirious for a couple of days. Several mornings later my bout with malaria seemed to be over. At last, I was able to leave the hut and stroll along the shoreline to watch the canoes troll beyond the playful hippos.

While sitting near the shore of Lake Edward, I thought about the future of some of the Africans I had met. I hoped these slowly-progressing people would not let their craving for independence lead them into dangerous actions. If they progressed carefully and took advantage of good European and world guidance, they could reach a higher level of comfort and prosperity.

After giving the fisherman a tattered volume of Emerson's essays to help with his English studies, I hiked back to the road and waited.

Finally, the driver of a heavily loaded cotton truck stopped and gave me a ride back to Kampala, Uganda.

Several days later, I located the good-natured African who originally drove me in his vegetable truck to Kampala. Gladly, he offered to drive me to the airport in Entebbe.

"Bwana, why must you fly away?" he asked as we skimmed over the smooth tarmac road.

"Well, I was going to take a Nile steamer to Egypt, but I got sick and missed it," I said. "Now it's cheaper to fly. Anyway, I flew into east Africa; I might as well fly out."

"Do you still go to the Arab country?"

"Yes, I plan on living with the Bedouin nomads."

"Do they speak Swahili and English there, Bwana?"

"I don't think so; I think they speak Arabic. But listen to my new Swahili sentence," I said, glancing at my notes: *'Watu walinipendeza sana, na destur zao pia.'* 'I like the people and their customs here very much.' How's that for improvement?"

"Bwana," he said with much hesitation, "you still speak Swahili like the baby."

~ 26 ~

Americani Arabi

In Jordan, I was escorted by a police lieutenant through the hill country to check on the welfare and security of different villages. Smugglers and other lawbreakers had been reported in his district.

A cool March breeze stirred up dust on a barren mountain in the Hashemite Kingdom of Jordan. Cautiously, I rode behind Lieutenant Othman, my police patrol escort, as we made our way to several isolated villages to meet with the mayors and to check on security.

We descended a narrow pass between two towering cliffs. A sudden gust of wind forced us to wrap red Arab headdresses, *kaffiyahs*, around our faces. Squinting in the dust, we continued into the shadows.

With saddles creaking, our white Arabian horses clopped down toward the distant opening. Their hooves slipped on the loose ground, knocking pebbles into a bottomless crevasse with rat-tat-tat drum beats. Outside the exit of the pass, we reined up in the blinding sunlight. At last, we were on the valley floor. By degrees, the aroma of spring grass and leather filtered into our headdresses. When our eyes finally adjusted, we saw a series of hills rolling out to a far mountain.

Snorting and whining, our restless mounts wanted to run. Othman's steed was prancing uncontrollably. An excitement was surging within me that seemed to match the spirit of my horse.

"We race—the next hill," Othman called out through his headdress.

"When?" I yelled.

"At once, at once..." he shouted as he started some fifteen yards ahead of me.

"Hey, wait," I moaned, but he was already galloping away.

Leaning forward in the saddle, I slapped my horse's flank; within

215

seconds I was racing into Othman's dust. My brown robe ballooned out as one tip of my *kaffiyah* fluttered behind my head.

I gave my horse free rein. His strength and speed were amazing. Bending closer to his neck, I merged into his booming, galloping stride. His snorts kept cadence to his rhythmic hoof beats. Beat by quick beat we closed the gap on Othman and his horse. The brown and green earth seemed to shake with staccato movements as we raced ahead.

Together we reached the next hill and reined in our steeds. Othman adjusted the rifle that rested over his shoulder and tucked his khaki trousers into his black boots.

"Race a bit more?" he asked.

Before I could answer, his horse whinnied and galloped down the trail. I crouched over and raced behind him. The shoes on Othman's mare flicked up the sunlight in a quick, shimmering pattern. We streaked by a man riding a prissy-stepping donkey and then by a goatherd who lifted his cane in salutation.

Othman's horse pranced around on the next hill as I pressed forward in my stirrups to stop nearby. Neighing and rearing up, our mares showed their anxiousness to continue running. However, we held them to a walk. I untangled the sticky mane on my horse and calmed her with a few strokes.

After riding throughout the day, we approached a bluff honeycombed with caves. We dismounted and led our mares to a grove of trees near the largest cave. Hastily, we made camp and built a fire. At sunset, Othman prayed southward toward Mecca. Not to be outdone by his show of religion, I finally knelt and prayed silently. Gently, Othman turned my shoulders toward the east.

"Jerusalem is that way. You must pray there. Only Muslims must pray toward Mecca," he said with irritation.

"Right, I wasn't sure where Jerusalem was," I said, before continuing with my worship.

"Roman soldiers once made camp in these caves. For years they governed all of this land. Now from time to time smugglers stop here. It is my task to police all of this area," he said, flinging out both of his arms.

"Have you arrested any smugglers here?" I asked.

"Yes, only three years ago a small caravan was apprehended here on its way to Saudi Arabia. They had hashish, opium and firearms."

"Smugglers must like these back trails."

"Indeed, but do not trouble yourself with them. You are now under police protection. It's the will of Allah."

After spending a cold night sleeping close to a smoky fire, we broke camp early the next morning and rode into the sunlight. During the afternoon we passed a farmer plowing behind a lethargic team of oxen. I also noticed a few stone houses on the horizon.

Later, we rode toward a hill in the distance that seemed to be cluttered with fragments of brown pottery. As we drew closer, the forms merged into a village worn by time. A crumbling stone wall encircled the houses and appeared useless for any protection. We saw no one and heard no sounds. It seemed as though the inhabitants had abandoned it many years ago for perhaps a more fertile location. The only movement on the hillside came from a dusty whirlwind outside the open gate.

Othman guided his horse alongside me. "This village, called *Main*, was old when the armies of Rome conquered this country," he said. "Now observe that tower over there."

"The one on the left?" I asked.

"That tower is the mosque. The Christian church is on the right."

"How do the Muslims and Christians get along?"

"Splendidly. There is no trouble," he said, waving his hands toward the heavens.

Our horses puffed up an eroding trail and entered the gate of a hard-packed courtyard.

Shouting happily, small boys tumbled out of a school and ran toward us. One lad, wearing shorts and a long-sleeved shirt, talked with Othman while several men came into view at the upper section of the village. After straightening their white headcloths, they threaded swiftly down the narrow lanes that separated the houses. As they entered the courtyard, their faces and stately robes gave them a determined, martial bearing. The mayor stepped ahead of the others. A shadow from his aquiline nose almost hid his thin mustache.

"*Marhaba.*" "Greetings," I said, while removing the part of my headdress covering my face.

The mayor's dark eyes flashed with surprise as he smiled. "*Americani Arabi,*" he said. "American Arab."

Laughter rose from the boys; the men smiled indulgently. To fulfill my lighthearted role as an *Americani Arabi*, I jerked back my reins, forcing my mare to rear up on her back legs. As she descended, I reeled forward, shuddered, and nearly toppled over her neck onto the ground.

217

Brownish hands shoved me back into the saddle. Recovering, I pulled out my dagger and held it up in a theatrical manner. I laughed with the others. My poor display of horsemanship and bungling attempt to imitate the stereotypical Arab proved that I was no Lawrence of Arabia.

After dismounting, Othman and I followed the men up to the mayor's single-room house. As my eyes adjusted to the darkness inside, I saw a faded Arabic inscription on the back wall. Ornate stacks of pillows and rugs rested on the floor below it. Standing in one corner was an alarm clock. It had only one hand, and its glass face was cracked. The mechanical recording of time seemed to have little importance in a slow-moving village such as this; there was little need to have the clock repaired.

Twelve men and I sat with crossed legs, around the smoking coffee brazier like worshipers at a low altar. A rich scent of coffee steamed out of a bronze pot. The mayor filled a small handleless cup and presented it to me. Sipping loudly to show my appreciation, I drained the cup. After I drank two more draughts, the headman filled a cup for Othman. An unhurried chat in Arabic commenced. Frequently, the doorway turned black when women and children peered in to see their guests. I was pleased with my first taste of Arabian hospitality.

"They talk of a scuppering of years ago," Othman whispered.

"Scuppering?" I asked.

"That was a surprise raid of this village made by the Bedouins. You see, over a hundred of these nomads came. They came at dawn and stole many horses. In addition they stole many bags of wheat."

"Many killed?"

"Only a few, but many rounds of ammunition were spent. Such scupperings seldom occur in this day and time."

Later the headman took his World War I vintage rifle from the corner and thrust it into my hands. He smiled proudly as I clicked back the bolt and remarked on its well-preserved condition. The others withdrew and soon returned with their firearms. For some reason, they considered me an experienced judge of rifles, so I inspected each piece carefully. Even though they were proud of their weapons, I felt these farmers were not very aggressive. Perhaps most of their interest in warfare stemmed from their proud tradition of resistance against all invaders.

In front of the house a man splashed water over my hands from an *ibreek*, large clay jug. I rinsed my hands. Then he began pouring water on the hands of the others as two black-gowned women carried a large platter of lamb and rice inside. Without speaking, the veiled women hurried to another house. The mayor called to the others, who feigned little concern over the feast given in our honor. Othman motioned for me to look with indifference toward the fields. After hearing the third invitation, the men slowly filed into the room with reluctance that custom dictated.

"B'ism'illah." "In Allah's name," the mayor uttered as we squatted around the platter. This lamb had been slaughtered and cooked especially for us. Smiling, the mayor cut the tongue from the lamb's head and handed it to me. While I gazed at it, my stomach chilled, and I almost retched. With reluctance, I bit into the tongue. Surprisingly, it was delicious.

A flutter of hands reached for the aromatic meat. One chubby man offered me a morsel and beamed at the improvement in my appetite. Several minutes later we consumed the flesh and fingered the buttery rice into golf-ball shapes and plopped them into our mouths.

Walking around the village that afternoon, Othman and I found a group of children listening to an old storyteller. They sat on the flat roof of a stone house near the outer wall. One girl in a red-checked dress and green sweater held her squalling baby brother. Because the story was so spellbinding, no one noticed us or seemed disturbed by the baby. Finally, the storyteller winked in our direction. Small faces turned and stared at us while we stood in the background.

"I believe he tells them about a *jinn*, an evil spirit, who takes away bad children. Actually, an old story—I believe it is from the *Arabian Nights.*"

"Those stories have been popular for centuries," I said.

"That is so. Do you see that field down there?"

"Yes."

"You see, for many ages the wheat there has been good, but not good enough. Recently, the government has distributed new seed, and the yield will be excellent when summer comes."

"Doesn't look like there's much irrigation here."

"Good irrigation is a thing of the future. Meanwhile we must rely on Allah to provide rain."

When the wailing voice of the *Muazzin* called the Islamic sector to prayer, a fat man with a khaki coat worn over his robe entered the village. He prayed with the others. After the evening prayers ended, he climbed slowly up the village streets in the twilight.

In a moment, the Christian church bell reverberated over the village. A number of dark-gowned men and women with white headdresses ambled toward the church for vespers; they resembled a procession of white-wigged English judges.

The man who had just entered the village walked toward us. At last we recognized him. He was Ragheb, the owner of the horse I was riding. His unshaved face blended perfectly with his soiled clothes. We had not seen him for a couple of days.

"What's he doing here?" I asked Othman.

"Oh, he took a short cut, so he could meet us. The horse is Ragheb's most precious possession. Of course, he is a poor man and wishes to receive the hospitality of this village," he said.

We sat around the coffee brazier with the leaders of the village to enjoy the warmth of the coals that night. Melancholy notes from a long bamboo flute rose above the whining wind outside and left us in a contemplative mood. The mayor poured another cup of coffee for me. Blowing over the top of his vertical reed, a musician continued with the quivering melody. When the music ended, an old man began a story.

Since my Arabic was almost non-existent, I attempted to follow the story by observing the gestures of the storyteller. At times he was firing his rifle as though he were part of an army fighting the Turks. Later in the evening, his voice tremored with emotion as he seemed to relate some religious experience he had while leading his camel out of a desert storm.

Dreamily, I puffed on the orange cord of the mayor's *narghile*, water pipe, which made sounds like cooing pigeons. The cut glass bulb of the pipe reflected a crisscross light on the rugs. With the self-indulgent air of a wealthy sheik, I leaned back on a luxurious pillow. I felt an inner peace. Somehow the gentle blend of coffee and smoke gave me a gratification that no wine could offer.

As the cool winds swelled from the direction of the Dead Sea, we stretched out on the comfortable quilts which covered the dirt floor. Soon our rest was interrupted when the door banged open. With fingers interlaced over his enormous belly, Ragheb spoke in a pleading voice. It seemed that he wanted more money to buy another blanket for his steed. After a long argument, Othman reluctantly asked me to give the horse-owner a small amount of money. Ragheb bowed to me and left the door ajar as he rushed down a narrow lane.

Later that evening, Ragheb returned singing a merry song. Both

Othman and I laughed when we realized that he used the money to buy *arak*, an intoxicating beverage much like paregoric, instead of a horse blanket.

"Do not trouble yourself," Othman said. "Allah has provided a warm stable for his horse. This is the longest journey Ragheb has taken in many years."

"Oh," I said and smiled. "Guess he does deserve to enjoy himself."

We chuckled while watching Ragheb wrap a quilt around his heavyset body. He yawned, belched and eventually passed out. Within minutes the chamber was filled with his fitful snores. Lingering in the air was the smell of charcoal, damp wool and paregoric. I wrapped my headdress loosely around my face and soon forgot the name of the country in which I was trying to sleep.

A rhythmic clatter awoke me the next morning. Yawning, I watched the mayor pound a small pestle into a brass mortar as he pulverized roasted coffee beans. After drinking several cups, Othman and I saddled our horses and led them down through the village. We mounted them in a courtyard near a group of children. One small boy smiled; others giggled and clapped their hands. As we trotted out of the gate, the children started a friendly chant: *"Americani Arabi, Americani Arabi."*

When we curved down a narrow path, Othman and I passed the farmers who were already plowing their fields. Turning, I saw Ragheb rushing behind us.

"Othman, I wonder if other foreigners, say, like Lawrence of Arabia, were followed like this?" I asked and grinned.

"No, I think not. He is eager for more hospitality. Do not trouble yourself."

In the early afternoon we approached a settlement of flat-topped houses jutting up like white tombstones in the green countryside. A blue tractor, driven by a man in an Arabic robe, chugged down a nearby field. Wheeling around, the driver adjusted his sunglasses and waved. We saw a herd of sheep floating like fog across the crest of a hill.

While climbing into the settlement, we heard a clanking noise above the crunch of our horses' hooves. In a minute we passed a group of unveiled women and girls seated around a pile of rocks. They froze as we passed. Then with a lackadaisical rhythm they continued hammering the stones for use in a dwelling. We dismounted near a house where a woman was sweeping her dirt yard with a twig broom. Shyly, she greeted us. We stood near a door chalked with Arabic words which protected the household from evil spirits existing before the time of Mohammed. Slowly, the door opened, and the headman escorted us inside.

We sat around the coffee brazier with several other men while the cup was passed. Their discussion about building the new house gradually trailed into the purpose of our visit. Two smugglers had been captured by the men and were being held for Othman. It was our job to take them back to the officials at district headquarters in Madaba.

From a nearby house, two men in their late teens were brought out into the sunlight. Their wrists were shackled together; their eyes squinted as they held their heads down submissively. At the side of the house a brown Arabian horse and two donkeys were tethered to iron rings anchored in the walls. Several bags of contraband stood near these animals.

"At last, may Allah be praised; we have captured a few of them," Othman said with relish. "They will be well punished. Do not trouble yourself about this."

"What were they smuggling?" I asked.

"The headman tells they have opium and firearms. They stopped here disguised as pilgrims to Mecca."

"How were they captured?"

"The headman and others became suspicious. After the smugglers finished their evening prayers, the headman and the others pointed guns on them and searched their cargo."

"These villagers showed a lot of courage."

"Yes, and by giving them a fair reward, we will be sure their courage continues," Othman said and smiled.

That night we were treated with another feast of lamb and rice. After a few of the men smoked water pipes and listened to several stories, Othman told them of my interest in archaeological artifacts of Roman times. With little hesitation, the headman and others moved the Oriental rugs on the floor and swept part of the dirt away. In the dim light, an ancient mosaic came to life; the blue form of a chicken appeared on the white tile floor. After removing a little more dirt, we saw Roman soldiers and a temple on a hilltop. Ragheb emerged from the shadows, pointing to the Roman temple. *"Mosque Roma,"* he said and chuckled. His mouth and whiskers were shining with grease from the evening meal.

Our procession left early the next morning. The headman led us down the hill on his horse; behind him the two prisoners walked. Their donkeys were loaded with the contraband. Othman and I rode behind them. In the rear, Ragheb sat pompously in the saddle of an Arabian horse belonging to one smuggler. No longer did he have to walk. He smiled at me and broke into a boisterous song.

After paying my respects to the superintendent of police, who allowed me to travel with Othman, I followed Ragheb to his house and stable on the outskirts of Madaba. With the aid of his three young sons, we fed and curried his horse. As we drank coffee inside his house, Ragheb stood up suddenly and paced around the single room.

"What's the trouble?" I asked, as though he could understand my language.

"Mosque Roma," he said with inspiration.

Before I could say anything else, he called for his wife and sons. Bustling around, they picked up the brazier, rolled up the rugs and carried the household goods outside. He then ordered his sons to shovel the dirt off the tile floor. Heavy dust forced his wife out of the house. Crying, she fled to a neighbor's.

His sons removed the dirt off the floor and shoved it back and forth. Dust shrouded me. Apparently, Ragheb was trying to find another mosaic from Roman times that resembled the one we saw in the last settlement. His efforts were unsuccessful. All that he could find was the Roman numeral "XI," which perhaps was the number of his house.

In disgust, he ordered his sons to cover the tile and walked outside with me. After he recovered from a coughing fit, we sat down in the sunshine. Soon his wife, accompanied by several neighbors, returned to witness the hubbub. Ragheb seemed to explain that this rude *Americani Arabi* insisted on seeing if his house had a Roman mosaic hidden under the insulating dirt floor. Angrily, the neighbors surrounded me and muttered oaths about my uncalled-for behavior.

To appease them, I gave Ragheb several Jordanian dinars. As he greedily counted these bills, his wife snatched them from his hands and vanished into the dust of the house. Jeering remarks and laughter followed Ragheb as he retreated to his stable.

Later, I squeezed into a crowded bus bound for Amman. I chuckled when I glanced at my reflection in the window. My Arab headdress and robe were dirty and flecked with straw; my face was smeared with dirt as though I were a commando in combat.

As we roared down a narrow road, I heard a pulsating siren behind us. A red light was flashing. Our bus driver slowed to a bumpy stop off the road. To my surprise, I saw a police car filled with the lieutenant, two guards and the drug smugglers. Othman acknowledged my presence with a salute. I was amused at the urgency of their mission. Since I had learned that few people were arrested in this district, I felt that the police were trying to impress everyone with their importance.

Later our bus met the police car again, which was blocked by hundreds of sheep on the road. The lieutenant and his aides shouted oaths at the shepherd, who seemed to give only token cooperation. When the sheep completely encircled the police car, our driver started the bus and drove slowly around this scene. Before we left, I saluted the lieutenant and smiled.

"Do not trouble yourself," he shouted. "It's the will of Allah." In exasperation, he held his hands up and forced a half-hearted smile.

~ 27 ~

Valley of the Bedouins

Brahim, in his new taxi, drove me from Amman, Jordan, with all of its twentieth century amenities, to the desert where his family followed the harsh, age-old life of the Bedouins.

My **antique Ford taxi rattled** down one of Amman's narrow streets before turning into a crowded thoroughfare. To avoid hitting the Jordanians milling around us, my driver, Brahim, braked frequently. Walking would have been faster. As we swerved around a donkey that was pulling a yellow kerosene drum, the pungent odor of lamb and garlic swept through our windows.

Hesitantly, we motored down a long row of shops with blue and green awnings. We then pressed on through the shadows of modern office buildings. A group of businessmen wearing tailored, western suits walked in front of us. Behind them stepped two ladies clad in fashionable European dresses. As we stopped at another intersection, a cluster of gowned farmers with white Arab headdresses passed by.

A cacophony of sounds filled the air. Guttural Arabic music blared from loud speakers in a second-story coffeehouse where men clustered around tables to argue politics, sip coffee and smoke their water pipes. Bus drivers cried out their destinations at a boarding area. Auto horns echoed relentlessly. Street vendors shouted as they held their wares up to our windows.

Glancing up one hillside, away from the center of Amman, I saw many tiers of contemporary homes and apartment houses. On another hill, stacks of buff-colored homes reminded me of the ancient cliff dwellings of the New Mexico Indians. Our taxi scattered a herd of dusty sheep. An advertisement in Arabic script for a British motion picture flashed by us as we rolled out of the city.

"Do not worry," Brahim said. "In a few hours we will be with my tribe on the desert."

"You said you were forced to leave the desert," I said.

"Oh, dear me, yes, yes. Allah did not provide enough rain one season. Most of our sheep and goats died. I came here to drive taxi, make money and learn more of the world away from the desert."

"You made a smart move," I said.

"Yes, that move was smart. I spent a few years in a boarding school when I was a young boy. Many Bedouin boys of good families attend such schools. I speak English nicely, but I am still troubled with the reading and the writing of it."

"Do you plan on moving back to your tribe someday?"

"Oh dear me, yes, if Allah permits me to make enough money—the desert is possessed with a beauty like no other place in this world."

We sped over the hills for hours. Ultimately, the landscape rolled out into the eastern desert like a billowing, endless Oriental carpet.

"This is Allah's gift to the Bedouin," he said with much enthusiasm.

"Great," I said.

"Before midday prayers, you will be under the protection of my tribe—you need not bother about official papers and red tape."

As we raced down an ancient caravan trail dotted with withered clumps of grass, we flushed a bustard from its perch on a thornbush. With slovenly wingbeats the turkey-like bird brushed along the ground and curved toward the distant hills. At last, three dark blurs hovered on the horizon.

As we drew closer, these blurs merged into the shape of three black Bedouin tents. Squinting through the bright windshield, I could see black goats and several camels bobbing along like driftwood in an ocean. Brahim honked his horn three times and stopped about a hundred yards from the tents.

"Automobiles just might frighten the camels away," he explained.

After adjusting my Arabian clothes, I walked with Brahim to the large tent in the center. He was greeted with embraces by an old man in a black robe. I assumed that he was the sheik or leader of the tribe. Brahim explained that I wanted to travel with them for several days to learn more about the Bedouin way of life. My acceptance was automatic since Brahim was a member of this tribe.

Inside the sheik's tent I sat around the coffee brazier with Brahim and several other men. We were in the *raba's*, the place of men, located on the right side of the tent. The women were hidden behind a partition on the left—the harem area.

A young man brewed a fresh pot of coffee while adolescent girls peeked at me from their side of the tent. Brahim and the other men enjoyed an animated conversation; news was exchanged about life on the desert and in the city of Amman. When the sheik poured the first cup of coffee for me, everyone grew silent.

Dutifully, I savored the first cup alone and expressed my appreciation to him for his hospitality.

"*Deyf min Allah*," I said with authority. "By Allah I am your guest."

The others joined me as I drank two more cups with the required formality.

"By Bedouin law you are his guest; you are under his protection until I collect you in due time," Brahim said.

"When will that be?" I asked.

"Oh, dear me, you Americans worry too much about time. Maybe a few days, a week, a month," he said and smiled knowingly.

After the prayers at sunset, Brahim and I brought in food staples from the taxi and relaxed in the men's quarters. I was pleased that the nomads appreciated my gifts. Soon a woman brought a large platter of lamb and rice for us. She was unveiled, yet part of her face was hidden by a wreath of silver coins; delicate tattoos marked her chin and cheekbones. After we had eaten our share, the woman carried the leftovers to the harem-side of the tent.

Around the fire that night the sheik told stories of raids and desert warfare. Now and then Brahim translated for me. The stories continued past midnight. A man whose face was framed by a white headdress played the *rababa*, a single-string violin. Gradually I fell into a deep sleep.

Awaking the next morning, I was startled to find the tent had been removed; it was packed in baskets hanging on each side of the camels. With embarrassment I stood up. Brahim patted me on the shoulder.

"Do not look so forsaken," he said. "You had a difficult trip yesterday. Now I drive back to Amman and will meet you some days later."

"Is the caravan leaving so soon?" I asked.

"Yes, hurry along now. You just follow them and do not drink too much water. Water is dear—very dear."

Our caravan consisted of some eighteen men, women and children, six camels, four horses, three greyhound dogs and two donkeys. The goat and sheep herds were already moving toward the undulating horizon. With reluctance, the lead camel grunted and followed the sheik who held him by a guide rope. Slowly, the Bedouins and the animals fell into a ragged line.

Even though the sun pressed warmly on my headcloth, the air was cool and bracing. The hooves of the camels scuffed along the dusty trail and struck the rare patches of grass with the sound of eggshells breaking. Frequently, the lead camel stopped to chomp on small bushes. However, if she tarried too long, the sheik would prod her forward with a stick. I soon learned that one of the most comfortable places to walk was with the women and children in the shade of the camels.

Now and then the children left the shadows to pick up twigs and roots for use in the evening fire. The women's bracelets jangled pleasantly as we ambled along to the plodding pace of the camels.

After walking to the head of the column, I gave the sheik and several men pieces of Cadbury milk chocolate. Cackling with pleasure, the sheik halted the camels. He dispatched one of his children to the back of the column to bring me a piece of cheese. With feigned appreciation, I nibbled on the rancid goat cheese. An hour or so later I gave him some more chocolate; however, I politely refused any more cheese.

In the late afternoon the sheik waved his camel stick toward the horizon. His son, Mohammed, did not see the signal. Then the sheik yelled a sharp command that swept out into the desert and faded without an echo. Slowly, Mohammed turned his black mass of goats back toward the caravan.

"Barak, barak," the sheik commanded, while tapping the legs of the lead camel with his stick. "Kneel, kneel." Its front legs went down first, kicking up the dust; its back legs soon folded. When the other camels knelt, the women unstrapped all the bundles and stacked them neatly. With quick kicks from the Bedouins, the camels stood.

After hobbling these beasts with woolen ropes, so they could not graze too far from our camp, the women put up the tents. The sheik mumbled something to his wife. In a few minutes she returned from one of the camels with fresh milk. As she offered the bowl to me, her brass nose ring and pendulous earrings caught the glow of the afternoon sun. I drank from the bowl and passed it to the elder. Although the camel's milk was bitter, it quenched my thirst.

When a girl released a white baby camel, it frisked around us like an elated puppy. This was the family pet. Its fluffy hair and long eyelashes seemed artificial. It nibbled at my long robe and almost knocked me over. All of us laughed at the high spirits of this baby.

The staccato bleating of the goats drew closer and closer to our tents, as the sun washed the sky in orange. Our breaths grew white in the cooling air. Across the horizon a dust whirlwind appeared like a trembling flame as it caught the tint of the sunset. Soon Mohammed arrived with the goats and greeted me warmly.

Moving quickly, Mohammed and his father, the sheik, grabbed a kid goat and flung it to the ground. With his curved scimitar, the elder slashed its neck. Then they held it down, as Muslim law dictated, to let the blood drain away. While they skinned it, the other goats ambled dumbly around us, unaware that one of their herd had been killed.

On the harem-side of the tent, Mohammed's mother kindled a bunch of twigs with a silver Zippo lighter. Along with the other women and girls, she prepared the meat. Soon aromatic smoke came from beneath the cooking pot.

My reading was interrupted in the main tent when I heard the elder and many of the others praying outside. Through an open partition, I could see them wash their hands in the air, a substitute for the purifying water used in the mosque. They chanted their prayers over the grumbling sounds of the camels. As they returned, I knelt on the luxurious Oriental rug and prayed silently toward Jerusalem. Respectfully, the men waited until I had finished before entering the tent.

Our evening meal was served quietly by the women. I was offered the first morsel of the goat and rice dish. With little conversation the others joined me. Standing around the platter, the men were eager to see that I had the best pieces of meat. Later, I was first to drink coffee around the brazier. Bedouin hospitality was sincere; I felt their warmth in seeing that I was comfortable. Indeed, I was attended to with more conviction here than in most places I had visited on my long journey.

During the evening, the men told stories, chatted and laughed; the women remained on their side of the tent. I puffed away on the sheik's water pipe, which was relighted for me several times by one of his older sons. In turn the sheik smoked my pipe filled with British cavendish. The water pipe was bitter, yet it left a pleasant twang in my mouth.

To add something to the evening, I traced my world trip on a worn *National Geographic* map. The men and boys were highly interested in the account of my journey. Even though they understood few words in

English, and I understood little Arabic, we communicated satisfactorily. When I showed them a few photographs of the bare-breasted women of Bali, they were at first stunned. Then as I described this exotic island, they seemed to comprehend more about the Balinese and their lifestyle. There was very little laughter. I interpreted the sheik's gestures as one of tentative acceptance for Balinese culture. After all, infidels have strange customs.

Suddenly he shocked all of us. Standing quickly, he took his curved sword and flailed the air in the direction of the harem-side of the tent. His message was unmistakable. If any of his women dressed as the inferior women of Bali, they would be banished or killed. The other men and boys nodded in agreement; the women who were hidden on the other side of the tent displayed their agreement with shrill, gobbling war cries. I was amused that they had been eavesdropping with such intensity.

As the fire burned low, the men who lived in the other two tents said good-night. Those of us in the elder's tent rolled up in our blankets. All of us left on our robes and headdresses for added warmth.

Outside, the camels and the goats continued to make their raucous sounds. The greyhounds seemed to bark at every real or imagined object. The snores of the men added to the noise and made it impossible for me to sleep. A donkey started braying. I was angry. This was a typical Bedouin bedtime.

Something hit me in the dim light of dawn. I sat up. Reaching out, I felt a furry object. Some animal was sniffing me. Before I could open my eyes, a wet tongue slurped the side of my face. It was the baby camel. As I led him outside the tent, I stroked the dew-curled hair on his neck.

"Mohammed, Mohammed," I whispered.

"Americani." The young goatherd jumped to his feet and assisted me in tying the hobbling rope around the camel's legs. Both of us laughed at the antics of this playful pet.

After morning prayers and coffee, I helped the Bedouins roll up their goathair tents and strap them onto the horses and camels with their other belongings. The women did most of the work; the men did the heavy lifting and inspected their horses and rifles.

Shouting and kicking, the sheik and the others made the camels stand. Although the sheik seemed to enjoy leading the first camel, he turned the guide-rope over to one of his older sons. Mounting one of the horses, he bade me to mount another one. He shouted some command

and made a flamboyant gesture toward the distant hills.

"Inshallah," "As Allah wills," he said, as our long caravan resumed its trek along the hilly desert floor. Mohammed herded the goats far out to our left flank where the tan grass looked somewhat promising. Soon the sheik and I trotted on our steeds to the head of the caravan. I was delighted to be at his side as he led his tribe into the far reaches of the desert.

In mid-morning we stopped, and the sheik's wife offered me water from a goatskin bag. All eyes studied my face; I realized that I was being tested. Politely, I refused the water, even though I was very thirsty. The sheik and a few others smiled in approval. While our caravan was stopped, a few of the girls added fresh horse and camel dung to their baskets. This dung would be used for fuel at the evening campfire. As we trudged along, I had the mounting illusion that we were the only beings in the universe. Nothing seemed to move around us; the wind had disappeared. I looked for the familiar sight of brown lizards skittering from one pile of rocks to another, but they must have been resting in the dankness of their holes. The camel flies were dormant. Even the birds flew somewhere beyond our horizon.

Momentarily, a black streak emerged in the distance. I hoped another caravan would come from it and march our way. In a minute or so the streak vanished. Probably it was some image stretching out in a mirage. The Bedouins no longer talked; their faces registered fatigue, yet they walked with a strong and determined pace. Monotony was beginning to dim this romantic scene for me. I was tired. The desert seemed to be nothing more than a dull and dangerous pathway from one grazing land to another.

That afternoon we made camp in a *wadi,* or valley. With renewed energy, the Bedouins erected their tents and started the cooking fires. Now there was talk and laughter; the hard day's march was over. I rested in the sheik's side of the main tent and listened to the men who kidded each other as we passed the water bag. After the evening prayers were over, we feasted on lamb and rice.

During the night we drank coffee and listened to the sheik's stories. I was amused and a little miffed when Mohammed broke the pleasant mood of the evening. He brought out a late model short-wave radio and set it up by the sheik. With little patience the old man moved the dials from one wave length to another; all he found was static. Mohammed was pleased. He was now allowed to operate the dials of a device which was still alien to his father. Blaring Arabic music soon filled our tent.

In the morning, before we could break camp, several of the men stood on a knoll near our tents. The rising wind rippled their robes and headdresses. A spring storm was developing.

Dark clouds drifted over the sun; gusts of wind made our tents appear to breathe in and out. Sand and dirt from the direction of Saudi Arabia stung my face. Voices mingled with the braying donkeys and the groaning camels. Rain began to fall. Many of the Bedouins pounded at the stakes that held the guy wires firmly into the ground, then scampered inside.

Within the tent I could see the animals huddled outside on our leeward side. Their eyes were closed. I helped two of the men hold the tent pole before I sat down with the others. The roar of the storm grew louder as rain pelted our tent. All of us huddled within the protective covers of our headdresses and robes. Stoically, we waited for the storm to pass.

One section of our tent was blown open, and a large white object fell inside. It was the baby camel seeking refuge. Mohammed and I held him down while several others tied the tent section together. The men around me were smiling; our pet was safe.

During the afternoon when the storm had eased a little, the sheik sat beside me. Carefully he unwrapped a small framed photograph of a young man in Arab Legion costume.

Above the drone of the wind, he said, *"Malok."* "King."

"Hussein," I said.

Nodding in agreement, the sheik and I began a conversation about the young King of Jordan, who was about my age. In a mixture of sign language, Arabic and English, we discussed King Hussein. I gathered the impression that the King was respected by most of the Bedouins. He had recently married and was helping the people of Jordan protect themselves from the invading soldiers of Israel. At this time, the Israelis occupied part of the holy city of Jerusalem. With mounting anger, the sheik lashed out against the new state of Israel; he pulled his dagger from his belt and gestured with it. When the storm subsided, his anger disappeared, and he sheathed his weapon.

My thoughts turned to this brave new ruler of the Hashemite Kingdom of Jordan, whom I had once tried to meet. Through one of his Arab Legionnaires, I had learned that the King was in residence in his palace. My past record in meeting kings and maharajas had been very

232

good, and so I fantasized over being his guest. With the overconfidence of youth, I dressed in my only suit and hired a limousine to drive me up the hillside to the royal palace in Amman.

Brazenly, I explained my urgent need to meet the King and interview him. The stately gentleman in the King's office listened with amusement to my tales of meeting kings as well as common people around the world. When he chuckled at my overeager presentation, I knew all was lost.

"Unfortunately, the King is in a meeting of state. Only on rare occasions, does he grant interviews with journalists. The journalists must have impeccable credentials from their government. And then, only then, does he grant interviews."

"Oh, I see," I murmured with a deflated feeling. "I'm not really an official journalist."

"Perhaps you could buy a photograph of him in one of the shops in town. Literature is also available there about His Majesty."

"That sounds interesting."

After shaking hands warmly with the perceptive official, I left the palace grounds in my rented limousine and returned to my second-class hotel in downtown Amman.

I remember buying a photograph later, similar to one the sheik was now showing me. Both the sheik and I shared much respect for this young monarch.

After wrapping up the photograph of the King, the sheik gave me some goat cheese. The wind was too high to light a fire, cook or have coffee. During the evening the man who played the *rababa* tried to compete with the storm, but soon gave up. The men accepted the cold, harsh conditions with equanimity and frequent outbursts of laughter. The weather was Allah's will.

Early the next morning, the cold storm swept past our *wadi*, valley. We were greeted by a dramatic sunrise from the Arabian desert. Our mood grew optimistic. The children pranced around as though they were leaving school for their summer vacation. Much to our amusement the baby camel gamboled along with them.

With the sheik and a few others, I inspected the storm damage. Only one tent had a slight tear. While allowing the tents to dry, the Bedouins continued their routine activities. The young men and boys herded the goats and sheep; the women repaired the tent, and later the men drank coffee around the fire.

One routine day merged into another as our caravan advanced. Time was of little consequence; we were at the mercy of Allah. Perhaps we would have no more storms and would soon reach an oasis.

Several afternoons later, I saw a body of water on the horizon.

"Mohate, mohate." "Ocean, ocean," the sheik said, obviously experiencing the same illusion.

Even though I knew it was illusory, to humor him, I nodded and gazed at the mirage.

Merrily, he called to his wife to tell her about the foreigner who thought the mirage was an ocean. She giggled. Then he flapped his hand at me as if to erase this foolish thought.

By late afternoon we climbed into the worn hills on the western side of the desert. Our routine was interrupted when the sheik yelled. Swiftly, one of his sons held the baby camel in place; the sheik picked a gray tick from the pet's neck. Angrily, he flung it on the ground. The pet seemed to receive more attention than the other animals. Now that the sheik was satisfied, we continued our long climb upward. Finally, we reached the edge of a bluff, which overlooked an enormous valley.

Below us, numerous black tents curled around palm trees and a solitary stone house. Dark-robed Bedouins meandered through a noisy congregation of goats, donkeys and horses. The air quivered with the laughter of children. A camel bellowed. At last, we had reached our oasis in the valley of the Bedouins.

Wisps of dust curled up into the amber light as four camels ambled toward the well. Their ample necks bent down to sip water from a long trough. A boy drove one camel with a long rope attached to it. This rope pulled a leather bucket up from the bottom of the stone well. When the bucket reached the top, several boys poured the water into the trough.

In front of one sagging tent, a woman stood beneath her camel as she milked it. Nearby a group of men crowded around several Arabian horses. Golden streams of smoke floated up from the cooking fires. In the distance, sheep grazed. I felt as though I had been on rough seas for months, and my aircraft carrier was finally entering port.

Humming a joyous tune, the sheik led us down to the oasis. After unloading the camels and supervising the erection of the tents, he strode over to the other men who greeted him with cheek kisses. The boredom of the desert had left him, and he talked happily.

In front of the stone house, a sedentary Bedouin collected money for the use of his grounds and well. The sheik, along with several other men, greeted him. After haggling over the price for some time, the sheik grudgingly placed coins in the well owner's hands. With his camel stick held high, the sheik signaled the men of his tribe to take the horses and camels to water.

Since the horses were the most fragile of the beasts, they were allowed to drink first. Later the donkeys drank their fill. However, there was no urgency to lead the camels to the water; this was fortunate, because they seemed to be in a cantankerous mood. Even though they stood in front of the trough, they would not bend their heads down. The sheik talked to the pouting-lipped beasts as though he were coaxing children to take medicine. Sighing, the baby camel finally began to drink. When the baby camel was led away, the other camels reluctantly dipped their mouths into the water.

We led the camels down the valley when they were full. After hobbling them, we returned to our tents. It seemed that we had been invited by a wealthy sheik from another tribe for an evening feast. Eagerly, our sheik led us to the host's tent, which was much larger than all of our three tents combined.

Much to my surprise, I was the honored guest. A white-bearded elder gestured for the sheik and me to sit near him. After exchanging greetings and going through the coffee drinking ceremony, with which I was very familiar, the elder beckoned the women to enter the tent with platters of lamb and rice.

To please me, the elder had one of his servants bring me a tray with British silverware and white china. I was served lamb chops, green peas, steamed rice and pudding. Smiling to show my appreciation, I bowed to the thirty or more men assembled. Applause filled the tent. My face felt the same color as my red headdress. I was at once both pleased and embarrassed with this personal tribute. Since I was in the desert of Jordan, I would have been happy to eat the same fare as the others.

"*Alaikum al afyah,*" the elder intoned, as I slowly picked up my fork. "May you be healthy."

Later in the evening, the elder pressed his face close to mine and gave me a teasing grin.

"*Nuwar,*" he whispered. "Gypsy."

Before I could reply, several gypsy entertainers filed through the tent and filled an open space on the Oriental rugs near us. Three boys thumped away on drums as two swarthy girls in their late teens began to dance slowly. With sinuous, seductive gestures, they moved in circles, arched their backs and twirled their hands over their bare midriff costumes. Also accompanying them was a man playing the string of the *rababa.* It was barely audible above the drums.

Unlike the dancers in Hollywood movies, these girls were unglamorous and dull; they were trying too hard to be sensual. I had the impression that most of the men who were snickering and whispering were making fun of them, for their wives were far more attractive than these camp followers. Any diversion, however, was well received by the good-natured nomads.

After dancing four or five dances, the gypsies dashed out of the tent while some of the men hooted and clapped. Lifting his hands upward, the elder seemed to say that this was not much, but it was the best entertainment that he could provide.

Later in the evening, the mood became serious when one of the elders started an epic story lasting around two hours. I had the impression that it dealt with desert warfare, raiding and punishment to those who did not obey the code of the Bedouin. This code was perhaps formalized centuries before biblical times. Although I tried to listen attentively, I had to fight back sleep. Others in the audience seemed weary.

It was a relief when the story ended, and the evening's festivities were over. My back was sore from sitting so long; I needed time to be alone. Although I appreciated the Bedouins' lavish and sincere hospitality, I needed to take a long walk in the cool night. Passing the musty-smelling camels, I climbed to the top of the bluff.

Spokes of light from the campfires in the valley below blurred in my watery eyes. Although it was well past midnight, the sky was gray; moonlight filtered through the clouds. The mountainous desert encompassed me. Below, someone occasionally strolled past one of the small fires. The yonka-yonka-yonka brays of the jackasses overpowered the periodic grunts of the camels.

While resting on a rock, it occurred to me how the bleakness of the hills and desert had inspired many of the holy men in the past. The land had little to offer for personal comfort, but it provided an ideal asylum where temporal longings could be subdued and thoughts of the spirit exalted. Perhaps some of the holy men of ancient times had lived in this same area. It was in this part of the world that these men formulated the concept of one god and aided in developing three of the world's great religions: Islam, Judaism, and Christianity.

Our camels were loaded in the early morning light. When I patted the baby camel, my head tingled as though sparks were igniting all over it. Lice were attacking me! Swearing in my best naval language, I tore off my headcloth. The Bedouins laughed at my predicament. In a frenzy, I ran toward the well. Desperately, I pulled up a bucket of water and poured it over my head. After several buckets, the fiery parasites disappeared, and I no longer burned.

In unmistakable sign language, the sheik explained that some camel urine dabbed on my hair and face would keep the lice away. At first, I overlooked his suggestion. However, I later yielded to his good advice.

One of the nomads' daughters bobbed quietly on top of the lead camel until we reached a level part of the desert. She slid down the camel's neck into her big brother's arms. After tapping this camel into a kneeling position, the brother said something and escorted me to the animal's right side. With a smile, he gestured for me to sit on the ornate saddle. In a little while the camel straightened out its knobby legs, thrusting me back and forth. Abruptly, I found myself some thirteen feet above the desert floor.

With pleasure, I rocked along on the soft-stepping camel. As we circled toward the horizon, clumps of dry grass drifted slowly under us; however, I had little sensation of forward movement. For some reason the monotony of the landscape gave me the strange feeling we were traveling on a treadmill outside the realm of time. Finally, I grew so sleepy I decided to walk in order to stay awake. As I slid down the animal's neck, its teeth clacked on the sleeve of my robe. The boy jerked the guide-rope and laughed. Haughtily, the camel raised its head, stepping forward with a strip of my robe dangling from its mouth.

Only a few weeks before I had been in this general area with a few scientists from the United Nations. They had taken core samples of the soil to learn if the land could support crops, provided that there was enough water. It seemed that the government and others wanted to domesticate the Bedouins and also expand the tillable land for the farmers. Jordan was moving forward in many areas. Yet, somehow, I had the romantic wish that the nomads should never change. I admired their courage and free spirit. Bureaucracy seemed to be their enemy.

By late afternoon we saw tan figures expanding upward and shriveling down in a mirage. These red-topped peaks melted into a shimmering wave. In a minute, I realized it was the *Badia*, the Jordanian Desert Patrol, a unit designed to keep peace in the desert. The Bedouins peered at them. Since my headdress differed from those of my companions, I pulled it off and tried to hide behind the camels.

If these troopers were to see me, they might hold me for questioning.

Although Brahim had assured me that I would need no official papers to travel with his tribe, I wanted to avoid any difficulty. Now the patrol emerged from the blinding light of the mirage on their camels like ancient gods riding sea serpents. Drowsily, they filed across the skyline and turned away from us, disappearing back into the mirage. I put on my headdress with a feeling of relief.

In the predawn light of the following morning, we continued our march. I was trailing along at the end of the column, riding one of the donkeys. My long legs barely cleared the ground. Near the front of the caravan, the sheik and his wife were arguing. Trying to ignore them, I dropped back as far as possible. Their voices clashed. Striking her firmly across her back, he motioned for her to leave him. Expressing no pain, she continued as though the endless journey had made her insensitive to such abuse.

As we entered the hills that afternoon, we heard a sound much like someone tearing a sheet of paper. It grew louder before merging into a humming motor. We scanned the clouds, but saw nothing. As the motor droned closer, we glimpsed a Jordanian Air Force plane flying in our direction. Roaring uncomfortably close to us, it circled and flew into the desert. The camels and horses almost stampeded. Everyone ran to comfort them. Bucking, my donkey easily threw me. Later, when our animals calmed down a little, we descended into a large valley, trying to disregard this crass intrusion from the twentieth century.

In front of us we saw a taxi with a tent-like structure attached to its open doors. A horn blared. In a few seconds a man sprang out of the automobile. I was happy to see my friend, Brahim, the driver who had introduced me to his Bedouin family.

After I bowed and clasped hands with the Bedouin men to thank them for their hospitality, Brahim and I rolled up his temporary tent and drove back toward Amman.

"Did you have to wait on us very long?" I asked.

"Oh, dear me, no, no—only a fortnight," he said seriously.

"That's impossible," I said.

He laughed and said, "Well, perhaps—only a night."

Brahim drove me back to Amman in his customarily fast manner. I had grown accustomed to the slow, eternally-paced movements of the desert Bedouins; his speed was unsettling.

Before dropping me off at my small hotel in downtown Amman, Brahim was amused when I offered him a stack of Jordanian dinars from my hidden money vest. Reluctantly, he took only a few bills and smiled.

"This is for petrol, only petrol. My sheik and I expect no payment—you were our guest," he said proudly.

"Well, thanks. Remember, you said you might try to find some way of getting me into Israel."

"This I did. But it is quite impossible, impossible! No amount of money could do this. The soldiers from Israel or from Jordan would put you in jail and throw away the key," he said scowling. "Dear me, they would shoot you."

"I still have my heart set on working in a kibbutz over there."

"This I know," he said angrily. "You Americans always want the best of both worlds. You must work on a farm here."

In my small hotel room, which I shared with two other guests, I sipped *arak* to calm my upset stomach. Although Brahim and I left on fairly good terms, I was still embarrassed over my brashness.

Gradually, I became sleepy on my comfortable bed while musing over my trip with nomads: the kindness of the sheik and Brahim, the playfulness of the baby camel, the gypsy girls, the sincere hospitality and the endless, barren landscape.

I drifted into sleep, dreaming about my future journey to the golden land of Homer, Plato and Aristotle.

~ 28 ~

Night Fishing In The Aegean

After traveling by bus and train from Jordan to Greece, I searched for the ideal village where I could live and learn more about fishing.

The Greek fishing village seemed to be asleep except for a waterfront *taverna*. After draining my copper cup of resinous wine, I gazed outside. A long row of *caiques*, fishing boats, nuzzled a pier that stretched out into the black Aegean Sea. Suddenly, a gust of wind rocked the boats and filled the tavern with the odor of tar and fish.

In one corner, two drunken sailors argued. Their disagreement rose to shouts, but they failed to rouse the pudgy *taverna* keeper, who dozed near his huge barrels of wine like an incarnation of Dionysus, the god of wine.

"Too much noise, yes?" the fishing boat skipper asked.

"The sailors are going wild," I replied.

Cursing louder, the seamen wobbled to their feet and started fighting. They tipped a table over. As one sailor recovered from a blow, he stepped on the tail of a cat, sending it shrieking behind the wine barrels. Without budging from his chair, the *taverna* keeper blinked, shook his head and frowned.

"Is enough," the brawny skipper grumbled, rushing over to separate the men.

In disbelief they looked at the skipper and slowly lowered their arms. The sailors grew indignant. Finally, to prevent another skirmish, the exasperated *taverna* keeper lumbered over and pleaded with the sailors. Soon, they wove around the empty tables into the sobering night air.

The skipper and I laughed when we heard their voices soar into a friendly drinking song while they stumbled down the pier. We returned to our table and ordered a dish of ripe olives and more wine.

"Now we speak no more of sailors—we speak of fishing," the skipper said. "Do you still want to work on my boat?"

"Right, I'm ready to go tomorrow," I said.

"Is agreement you bring cheese and wine for my crew?" he asked and licked his black mustache.

"Agreement," I said and grinned.

"Yasu," we muttered together. "To your health."

He then straightened his brown turtleneck sweater and walked down the pier. Timidly, a frightened cat peered from behind the barrels. I chortled at the lively events of a long evening. After paying the *taverna* keeper, I strolled beyond the dark warehouses to my small inn on top of a high bluff.

The waterfront of Rafina resounded with activity the next morning. Hammering sounds emanated from the beach where carpenters worked on the framework of a ship that resembled a whale's skeleton. Heavy trucks braked down the hill to the warehouses. Sea gulls squabbled over bits of fish. Periodically, fishing boats revved up their motors before puttering around the pier into the Aegean Sea.

At the far side of the beach, several fishermen sat on an enormous brown net while they mended it. Old men lingered at small tables outside a coffeehouse to enjoy the warming sun; I walked past them and entered the *taverna.*

After buying cheese and two wine jugs in hamper-woven jackets, I joined the skipper on the pier next to his thirty-five-foot long fishing boat.

While the skipper and his three-men crew uncoiled the lines from the bollards on the pier, I sat beside a withered old man in the stern of the boat. Anxiously, he fingered a rosary of amber beads; he barely acknowledged my greetings.

Our white *caique* trembled as the engine started. Soon it swished through the clouded waters along the coast toward the island of Euboea, which bulged upward into the endless blue sky. As we rocked through the foamy swells, the skipper barked an order. Hermes, the teenage mate, jumped to his feet, yanked his khaki skullcap down and scrambled up the rope ladder of the mainmast. After untying the binders around the sail, he dropped to the roof of the pilot cabin. The pulleys squealed when the other fishermen tugged the white sail upward.

A light breeze rippled this main sail. While one of the mates hoisted the jib sail into its place over the bow, a pine-scented cool wind rushed over us. Our sails puffed out; our *caique* lurched forward at a thrilling speed. The skipper turned off the motor. When we dipped into each sea trough, the water exploded and sprayed coolly over us. I pulled down my skullcap, which reeked of fish, and glanced back at the shrinking waterfront.

"By the way, where are we going?" I asked.

"You are impossibly carefree," the skipper said. "This I like—we perhaps this day sail to Tenos."

"That's an island to the south?"

"Yes. We take this old pilgrim to visit the holy shrine. Now, if you still want to do work, Hermes will show you how."

"Good enough," I said as Hermes gave me a sponge, a mop and a bucket.

We washed the portholes in the green pilot cabin, scrubbed off many parts of the *caique* and lolled on the deck near the pilgrim. The skipper yelled something. Hermes shrugged, cursed to himself and took a dead octopus from a bucket. After flinging the gray body on the deck, he whacked it with a wooden pestle to soften it for cooking.

Euboea's mountains receded on our portside while the island of Andros seemed to swim toward us like a massive turtle from Greek mythology. We furled in the sails and drifted toward the coast of Andros.

To keep our boat from drifting farther, the skipper turned on the engine. We then waited for a motorboat to draw closer. When the boat was secured alongside, the skipper displayed several baskets of cloth to a merchant from a remote village. In a few minutes, the skipper bargained violently with this man, almost striking him with his flurry of histrionic gestures.

At last, the skipper and the merchant agreed on a mutually-satisfying price. Both men adopted a smug air as though each had made the better bargain. We lowered the baskets of cloth into the motorboat, waved farewell to the merchant and continued southward.

The skipper was glowing. He swaggered around the deck, counting and re-counting his money. Fishing was good; yet, the skipper seemed very eager to supplement his income.

Some time later we tacked across the bewitching blue waters surrounding the island of Tenos. Although several miles away, the low mountains, terraced with fields of wheat and olive orchards, looked unusually close in the clear, magnifying atmosphere. Whitewashed houses rested here and there like randomly cast dice.

The wind shifted, and we sailed down the coast. Near the southern tip of the island we swerved toward a city of houses that climbed from the waterfront halfway up a mountain. Beyond the harbor stood a long file of commercial buildings. We lowered our sails. Hermes started the engine. Squinting into the blinding light, the skipper maneuvered past a rowboat and pointed our bow toward the wharf.

When we backed into our berth, the foul odor of motor exhaust hovered over us. I felt very sorry for the old pilgrim. His hands were twisted with arthritis. After he gathered up his suitcase and other bundles, I helped him across the gangplank onto the wharf. His waiting relatives immediately engulfed him. The women were sobbing; the men's faces were charged with emotion. Perhaps his condition would be alleviated by prayer before the miraculous icon in the Church of Panaghia Evanghelistria.

The fishermen and I strolled down the wharf and took seats in a crowded *taverna*. From somewhere in the rear came the languorous notes of a mandolin. The service was unusually fast. Greedily, we ate plates of cold white beans and lettuce soaked in olive oil; and wine calmed our stomachs. Before hurrying back to the *caique*, our skipper talked with several other fishermen at an adjoining table.

"Some men at the *taverna* sail behind us. Is good we fish together," the skipper said.

"You mean we fish tonight?" I asked.

He smiled and flung out his hands. "Is tonight. If Saint Nicholas—the saint of mariners—bless us with good weather, I show you enough fish to fill your Yankee Stadium."

The dull sunset faded. Tenos grew black in its own shadow and seemed to float off into the Aegean as we sailed away. One by one, pin-pricks of light extended from the city and harbor.

Dark clouds divided. Now the moonlight outlined six boats, swaying on the waves behind us. A bell rang. The clank of metal and cries of excited voices re-echoed from one small boat to another. Our motor idled. Effortlessly, the other dark fishing boats swished closer.

Soon, the boats separated to our rear. Three lined up on our port side, while three drifted to our starboard. The skipper was in command. His excitement grew into arrogance. With his arms akimbo, he stood on the bow like an admiral surveying a flotilla of ships. He bellowed some command to the other boats.

Hoarse voices replied. Suddenly, the boats flared up in a brilliant white light as though they were exploding. The sea appeared as radiant as it did at noon. After my eyes adjusted to the unexpected brightness, I saw acetylene lights dangling on the stern of each craft. The skipper growled at Hermes. In a fumbling manner, the young mate adjusted our light, and it soon burst into a hot sun.

"Is damn beautiful, eh?" the skipper asked.

"Damn beautiful...," I muttered, overwhelmed with the spectacle.

"You have nothing in the United States Navy like this?"

"No, nothing."

"All the boats have many lines out. On each line is five million hooks—no, maybe five hundred hooks. You wait, the fish think the light is beautiful too," he said and proudly slapped my arm.

Our *caique* pulsed along easily through the coolness of the spring night. The island of Delos, home of the ancient shrine of Apollo, bobbed along in front of us like a buoy. Two of our mates peered back at the trolling lines with boredom. The rest of us sipped black coffee and waited. Dark figures in one boat heaved in a net of fish that shimmered like quicksilver as they passed through the light.

"Vira, vira," the skipper yelled. "Haul 'em in." After pulling in a few of our lines and slinging the fish into the icy hold, we sat quietly on the deck.

Much later, the skipper rang a bell. A jangle of bells then floated over the water as a reply. Gradually, the boats circled much closer to us. With an abrupt thud, the first boat skimmed alongside and tied onto our bulwark. For a moment, our powerful light bleached the other fishermen, giving them the illusion of ancient marble statues brought to life.

The skipper leaned over and jested with them. A flurry of conversation and laughter rose above the sloshing and slapping of water against the boats. Our *caique* was to receive all the fish from the other boats. Several days later, the profits from this catch would be divided.

The mates rigged a boom over our side to pull up the fish. In a minute the skipper fastened a line onto their full net and pulled a cable through the boom, locking it on the power winch. Squeaking, the winch hoisted the fish up to our deck; then it let them twirl down into the hold like a net full of silver coins.

Hermes stomped on the tail of a tossing fish, which dropped from the net. Frantically, he scooped it up and threw it into the hold. With long poles we carefully mixed the fish with chunks of ice.

The second boat added a cascade of red mullet to our heap. The others brought thrashing sea bass. In an hour, Hermes smiled with satisfaction; his shyness left him temporarily as he raised his hands and cried out in glee. Everyone was happy. After sliding the cover over the hold, we swabbed down the deck.

Turning back to Tenos, the other boats snuffed out their lights as they blended with the milky skies of dawn. Hermes smothered our light. Overhead, our sails stretched with the wind and shoved us toward the gray island called Siros. Sea gulls dipped out of the clouds and followed our wake. One gull fluttered over our deck; both the skipper and Hermes frightened it away. I was surprised to learn the romantic gulls were considered a nuisance.

"Kali tyhi." "You bring us luck," the skipper said, handing me a cup of wine and a hunk of cheese. "Is beautiful catch of fish."

"Great. Where are we going now?" I asked.

"Piraeus—the port of Athens. Now, you sleep a little, eh? Is good."

While our boat passed between two barren-looking islands, I fell asleep in the bow. Some time later, in a muddled dream, I tried to open my eyes. A wet object squirmed against my face. Yawning, I squinted up at a dark, many-legged creature. Was some sea monster attacking me? I rolled down the deck to escape, while voices crashed together in laughter. In a few seconds I glanced up at the rigging where Hermes stood. His chubby face expanded with laughter as he swung an octopus on the end of a long rope. The skipper rang a bell. Awkwardly, I stood up, wiped my face and laughed with the others.

After unloading our fish onto a truck at the enormous port of Piraeus, we ate in a *taverna*. Most of us returned to the *caique*. I took a nap before our boat churned toward the open sea.

We rolled in the wake of an outbound luxury liner for a while before pointing our bow toward the southern island of Melos. Along the way one of the mates told with imaginative gestures, of his philanderings with a prostitute that afternoon. Each time he described his encounter, the laughter mounted. Finally, he embellished his account so much that everyone shrugged and turned away.

The white sails of the boats around us seemed to burn in the sunset's afterglow. They slowly changed into a charcoal hue that blended with the sky. Pinpoint lights from other boats now appeared on the horizon. A long net hissed as we fed it into the sea. We then kindled our light.

Twice, we heaved in the net, but caught very few fish. The drowsy skipper lifted his arms, muttered an oath to Saint Nicholas and swore at his crew and the sea. Angrily, he ordered the net pulled in for the night. He set the automatic pilot on a southerly course and posted Hermes and me as lookouts. "I sleep my wine away," he said, before swigging another cup of *retsina* and bundling up in his blanket.

His fretful snoring seemed almost as loud as the purring of our engine. The *caique* surged ahead into a calm sea; the air grew warmer. A current of phosphorescent water glided past our bow. Minutes later we were encircled by a pale silver flow speckled with green spots. I was astonished at its intensity.

On our portside, a school of flying fish whizzed out of the water, scattering bright mercurial drops behind. With their dragonfly wings they skittered in and out of the sea as they progressed. One fish whirred past my face. Hermes and I chortled in astonishment, while the fish skimmed toward the dark horizon.

Approaching a few lighted fishing boats, we awoke the skipper. He belched, gulped down some coffee and studied the weather. Soon, he ordered our nets cast overboard. We turned in a slow circle while our Cyclopean eye of light hypnotized the fish into our nets. Before dawn our nets were back on deck; a fair catch of fish quivered in the hold.

Dawn light outlined the horizon in gray. Now, the crew seemed exhausted. I had a headache and was in no mood to swab the deck. Hermes had disappeared to take a nap. The skipper was sullen and refused to talk. A cool breeze from the island of Crete was more annoying than refreshing.

When we skimmed into the the oval harbor of Melos, the volcanic mountains gave the illusion that we were inside the spread pincers of a giant crab. We crossed the blue water and tied up near several whitewashed shops. In a little while the skipper found a merchant interested in our catch of fish. Refreshed and alert, the skipper bargained with him for almost an hour. After selling the fish and refueling, we dozed under a canvas cover rigged over the afterdeck.

Before sunset, we slipped out of the harbor and headed to the north. Darkness quickly blotted the red from the sky and shrouded us. The skipper seemed uneasy. Grumbling thunder echoed in the north, but we saw no lightning.

The breeze vanished and our sails grew limp. Peering through his German field glasses, the skipper cussed and hurried into the pilot cabin to study the charts. He argued sharply with the helmsman. Again, he scanned the horizon. While the crew furled in the sails, the skipper ordered the helmsman to set a new course.

From the north came a stinging wind, filled with a sour odor. A wave sprayed my boots. Hermes helped me tug a long net across the deck into one of the forward holds. Now the sea churned up white water; cold rain pummeled the deck.

"*Agios Nicholas voithia mas,*" cried the skipper. "Saint Nicholas protect us." He crossed himself and looked toward the heavens. In an awkward crouch, Hermes and another mate rushed toward the safety of a partially-covered hold. While our boat pitched into a trough, I reeled, huddled inside the coffin-like pilot cabin with the helmsman and skipper. We slammed and bolted the hatch. The roar increased. We bumped together as the fragile *caique* bounced out of the water like a dolphin. I was well aware we could capsize.

The sea grew darker.

A streak of golden fire plunged into the water near us. It seemed as though Hephaestus, the god of metallurgy, had overturned his molten vat from a height of a thousand feet.

Silence... silence... silence....

Then a gigantic thunderclap exploded around us. My mind and body froze; I gasped for air. The skipper tugged at the hatch as though he wanted to escape. Although numb, I would not let him slide the hatch bolts open. His anger at me brought him back to his senses.

The red glow from the compass light somehow gave me the feeling that I no longer existed. My ears whined. Abruptly, the *caique* careened to the portside, shaking me out of a trance. One wave after another rocked us; our heavy masts sang in the wind like gigantic tuning forks. The helmsman fell back from the wheel as it spun insanely. The three of us quickly secured it. We heard the propeller churning outside the water. Now, the engine whined in a speeding revolution, spluttered and clogged.

We were adrift.

A wave lifted us higher than ever and then pulled us down, stern-first, deep into a trough. Thunder broke again, numbing our senses. An hour or more ebbed by with painful slowness. Gradually, we began a constant rocking movement as the *meltemia*, northern storm, faded.

"Is damn well finished," the skipper whispered.

"Damn well," I murmured before blowing salt water from my nose.

We opened the hatch, stepped on the rolling deck and glanced up at the star-pierced sky. I rubbed my stinging eyes and, suddenly feeling my weariness, I yawned. After crossing himself, the skipper drained a cup of fortifying wine and poured some for the rest of us. Then he tinkered with a pump near the flooded engine.

Hermes and I tossed seaweed overboard and then untangled several rope shrouds which supported the masts. Both of us were groggy and flopped down on the deck, away from the others. We rested until the skipper's voice boomed over us. Hermes slowly untied the binders on one sail before the crew and I hoisted it into a steady breeze.

Fatigue drained all my interest in the myth-haunted Aegean Islands that rose up into the morning sky. A few *caiques* loomed on the horizon like trembling white butterflies. Hermes and I cut the net from several broken glass floats and tossed the pieces overboard. Gurgling and snorting, the engine cleared its pipes and started to throb with an unsteady rhythm. We cheered. At last, the skipper turned the bowsprit toward Tenos.

"Did we lose very much last night?" I asked.

"Lose?" the skipper barked. "We lose many small things—but we lose the big power of the motor. Maybe it will take two, three days in Tenos to fix."

"Then you'll fish some more?"

He smiled and held out his arms. "Always we fish—always."

"You said you might see your wife and children soon?"

"If we sell plenty more fish, is soon. If not, it is to be another month."

Hermes scurried up the rigging that afternoon to investigate a faint splash in the distance. From the deck, I could barely see a spatter of white. As the splashing drew near, Hermes cried, *"Delphinia, delphinia."*

About twenty dolphins raced in our direction, emerging and submerging in the bright water. With enormous power they skimmed by our *caique*. They appeared to be smiling as though they were amused at our lack of speed. One of them leaped up and sprayed water across our bow. Sailing closer to mountainous Tenos, we watched the frisky dolphins undulate out to the open sea, spasmodically lifting their white undersides in and out of the water.

"Next to me, you and the crew, *delphinia* is best fisherman in all of Greece," the skipper said, and laughed.

The next day I left the fishermen on Tenos and boarded a steamer bound for the Greek mainland. Crowded next to me on the lower deck were a number of excited farmers. A woman coaxed her two goats and five children aside to let me squirm up to the rail. As the steamer's whistle blasted, I waved to the fishermen. Hermes and the skipper yelled to me but I could not understand them. In a few nights they would be fishing again. I hoped that on their next trip Saint Nicholas would give them fuller nets and calmer seas.

~ 29 ~

Herding In Attica

The idyllic notion of living the life of a shepherd in a small Greek village had always appealed to me. Not only did I want to absorb the ambience of this ancient way of life, but also to sip retsina, a resinous wine, and read paperbacks about historic Greece.

For several days I crowded into different buses in Athens and visited many inland villages. I was searching for the ideal shepherd: one who would let me work with him. No village satisfied me, however, because the land seemed too barren. To fit my somewhat romantic preconception, I wanted to find a shepherd in a more alluring locale. Gradually my thoughts recentered on the village of Rafina where I first met the skipper. It seemed much more suitable than many other villages in Attica, so I traveled back to the small inn there.

Early one morning, I strolled past a few whitewashed houses topped with red tile roofs and climbed up toward the pines. A cool breeze, spiced with iodine, hissed past me and rocked the boats in the harbor below. I paused to gaze at the mountainous island of Euboea on the foggy horizon. Several *caiques* plied coastal waters. In quick succession they unfolded their white sails to the sun. I pulled down my woolen cap and walked through a grove of contorted pines where a flock of sheep grazed.

Barking, a rusty-colored dog charged me. I held him off for a while with my short shepherd's crook. A slender old man, circled by a flock of brown and white sheep, turned and called off his dog. After sidling through his flock, I spoke to the man and handed him my letter of introduction, written by a friend from the village coffeehouse. He held it close to his flaring gray mustache; his face wrinkled in bewilderment. Then he chuckled hoarsely.

"Yes, yes," he said. *"Nai, nai."* After muttering something, he motioned for me to herd the sheep from the rear. *"Ela maji mas,"* he added. "Of course, you can go."

With a somnolent air, the sheep ambled upward. The shepherd did very little to guide them, since they walked confidently as though they had long memorized their pathway. On climbing into a vast meadow sprinkled with red poppies, I saw a lamb prancing away from its mother.

Without barking, the dog scuttled after it. A growl made the lamb halt and race back to the flock. A few sheep lifted their black faces to peer, with stuporous eyes, at the commotion before they continued feeding.

The elongated shadows of the pines shrank closer to their own trunks when the shepherd and I sat down for lunch. His flock lay in the grass around us. From a red knit bag he took a lump of *feta*, goat cheese, and a hard loaf of brown bread. We ate slowly and washed the food down with a bottle of resinous wine. In a little while he pulled off his shoes and massaged his feet. He then slumped against the tree for a nap. A faint scent of rosemary blew over us, but it failed to mitigate the odor of his socks and of his shoes coated with sheep dung.

I gazed through the pines down at the Aegean; only one *caique* sailed along the rocky coast. Here, away from the noisy village, everything seemed unusually serene. Eventually, I nodded into sleep while looking over the Attic landscape that had probably changed very little from the time Socrates taught in nearby Athens.

A soft whistle confused. Again and again I heard the whistle; however, I could not locate its source. I walked down to the flock and saw the shepherd whistling toward the oleander shrubs. Within a minute a wayward lamb trotted into view, followed by the snarling dog. The old man yawned. Then he signaled with his staff for me to take my position at the rear of the flock.

Throughout the afternoon we guided the flock up and down the green hills. Their hooves padded through the grass, scraped along the ancient trails and clitter-clattered over the rocky outcrops. We passed a woman leading a donkey loaded with firewood. Frequently we swerved around concrete bunkers left by the Germans during Hitler's occupation of Greece. Sluggish farmers plowed behind their horses. A cool wind huffed several *caiques* into the harbor as we drove the flock to the shepherd's farm.

Herding the sheep into the pens behind the whitewashed cottage, the shepherd introduced his wife to me. She wiped her hands on her dark blue dress as she listened to the shepherd explain my presence. Her curiosity satisfied, she helped us bolt the door on each shed. Then she hurried into the house with the dog. I followed the old man around his freshly tilled garden and admired his silver-leaved olive trees and grape orchard.

Flanking the door to his house were two whitewashed gasoline cans filled with yellow jonquils. Inside, a fire in the oven provided most of the light when we closed the door. Sighing in relief, the shepherd sat down on a hard-backed chair, flung off his shoes and again rubbed his feet.

A candle in a red glass container illuminated a picture of The Virgin that sat in the far corner of the room. Its light barely reached the comfortable bed and wooden chest on the other side. From the blue rafters hung wreaths of garlic bulbs, adding a tart scent to the wood smoke. Clicking his tongue, the old shepherd pointed to a table. I walked over to examine two framed photographs of young men in military uniforms.

"*Ol Germanoi ta eskotosan,*" the old man said and crossed himself. "The Germans killed." I nodded sympathetically and assumed the soldiers were his sons. An embarrassing silence followed.

To focus our thoughts away from the war, he spoke to his wife in the kitchen. In a moment, she served us coffee. She also showed me a color photograph of an American family; it seemed her daughter had married and moved to the United States.

"City of New Yorki," she said with pride. After communicating fairly well with them through gestures, pencil sketches, and mispronounced Greek, I wished them a good night and returned to the inn for supper.

Each morning I appeared at their house around sunrise. Before we started toward the hills, the shepherd's wife always served me chunks of bread in a glass of hot milk and gave me a motherly pat on my chest.

One day was as tranquil as the next. At times the shepherd wanted to be alone in his accustomed manner; therefore, I kept at a respectful distance. Occasionally, I read passages from a paperbound volume of the *Odyssey* and enjoyed the luxury of daydreaming about ancient Greece.

The old man met me outside his house one morning; he was smiling. Tipsily, he swung a wine cup. I was puzzled, since he never drank before lunch.

"*Amerikanos, Amerikanos, ela etho,*" he said with pride. "American,

American, come here." I followed him back to a narrow stall where he motioned for me to wait. After rushing back to his house, he returned with an extra cup. With the self-assurance of a museum director unveiling a rare antique, he opened the gate to the stall. Suckling at its mother's udder was a rickety-legged lamb that was born during the night. While peering up at us with vacant eyes, the mother snorted.

"Bravo, bravo," I said, as we raised our cups. From his coat he pulled out an extra bottle. After drinking several more toasts to the lamb, we staggered away with the flock of sheep. Glancing back, I saw his wife standing indignantly in the doorway. She slammed the door. In an unconcerned manner, the shepherd clicked his tongue. I wondered if herding while "under the influence" was an offense in Attica!

A rumbling noise awakened me at the inn several mornings later. While I shuffled toward the window of my room, rain sprayed my face. In a moment the rain rippled over the hills with the sound of applause. Overhead, a black flotilla of clouds sailed in from the churning Aegean.

After closing the window, I stared at my bed where I had spent most of the last three days with a mild recurrence of malaria. Today I was feeling depressed and needed to be with the shepherd; however, on stormy days he kept his flock at home. Finally, I decided to spend the day in the comfort of the village coffeehouse.

Although early, the coffeehouse was crowded. From each table voices rose in the mellifluous Greek language as if in competition with the drone of the storm. Fortunately, I found a vacant table near a window. After ordering coffee and a *narghile*, Turkish water pipe, I relaxed and reread letters from my parents and brother.

Next to me, a farmer ran his thumb along a damp-smelling newspaper while mumbling the words printed there. Glasses of cool water sparkled on each table under the light of a single bulb. Lulling heat came from the mouth of an iron stove that resembled a black jack-o'lantern.

Some time later a group of men finished their card game and started arguing. I puffed out a white fog of smoke and listened to the men rattle away the time while fingering their amber rosaries. It seemed that these Greeks found comfort in marking time in this manner. The ambitious Greeks moved to the large cities or immigrated to other countries. Here, the farmers, shepherds and fishermen idled away their time whenever possible. Ambition also left me; I felt as though I could stay in this pleasant ambience forever.

Around noon a retired man who had once lived in America joined me.

"Ah," he said, "you're learning what it means to be Greek."

"Right, it's very relaxing," I said.

The waiter served him a glass of *ouzo*, an alcoholic beverage with the flavor of paregoric, and chalked a line by the man's name on a blackboard.

"How's that?" he asked. "We Greeks have our own credit system—not the same like Cincinnati, but is good."

*

A couple of nights later, the Rafina villagers gathered at their Byzantine-style church for the Good Friday services. I stood outside with several others near the open door. Rich farm odors mingled with incense and salt air. Chanting mournfully, the bearded priest gestured for his congregation to move aside for the *Epitaphios* or bier of Christ. The congregation grew silent. Near the altar four men lifted the ornate bier housing an icon of the Savior, on their shoulders and marched behind the priest toward us. As they continued, each person lit his neighbor's candle until there was a long ripple of light.

When a sea breeze hummed over us, petals from daisies and red poppies scattered off the bier like confetti. The wind extinguished my candle. A lady by my side rekindled it with her candle, while the congregation followed the bier into the dirt streets. She repeatedly blotted her tears with a worn shawl as though she were witnessing the actual crucifixion in Jerusalem. Several men in the procession glanced at her with no embarrassment.

I felt an uplifting inner peace. Somehow this religious ceremony released some deep, ineffable feelings within me. After all, I shared the same religious roots with the Greek Orthodox Church. The other religions in the world impressed me and stirred my emotions, but now I was returning to one of the faiths of the western world.

Playful boys tossed firecrackers behind us, but they seemed to annoy no one. At a funereal pace we moved into a back street. Our candlelight flickered mystically on the white houses and spiraling cypress trees as we passed. A feeble old lady stood in the doorway of one house; she crossed herself and bowed. The flickering candlelight gave her the air of a living saint, grieving for the sins of the world. Finally, the procession curved down another street toward the church.

When the service ended, I found my shepherd friend and his wife in the congregation. They knew I planned on leaving on the morning bus to Athens. Our parting was more emotional than I had anticipated; however, I was growing accustomed to the Greeks' open display of feelings. Although the three of us were fairly well dressed, we still could not disguise our ovine aroma.

"*Sas hereto,*" the shepherd said. "I salute you."

"*Sto kalo,*" I said and swallowed hard. "Go to the good."

~ 30 ~

The Communist Beast

Belgrade, Yugoslavia, was under Tito's Communist rule in the 1950s. The atmosphere was oppressive. Secret police were everywhere. Many citizens were eager to leave the country and go to a place where they could find a new life of freedom and peace.

Freshly cut grass tinged the night air in Belgrade's Kalemegdan Park. I hid in the shadows with a lovely Slavic girl. We were silent and a little nervous.

For over an hour we waited. On the hillside before us hundreds of Yugoslavian people strolled along wooded paths or lolled on the grass with the air of vacationers. Hidden loudspeakers filled the warm air with the strains of the *Wine, Women and Song* waltz; yet we were definitely not in a romantic mood.

In the dim light near the ramparts of an ancient Turkish fort stood several off-duty soldiers. Instinctively, we stepped deeper into the shadows as they turned and walked toward us. One soldier crooned with the music; the others kidded him and laughed. Red Communist stars adorned their caps. Somehow, their khaki uniforms and leather chest straps seemed cheaper than those of the soldiers in Greece. Tonight, these Yugoslavs did not seem as threatening as they had when marching in downtown Belgrade the day before.

Nada, my friend, and I froze. A little man in a drab suit walked down the path behind the soldiers. He was scowling.

"Is the beast," Nada whispered.

"It's the same secret policeman," I murmured, as she put her arms around my waist. "He followed us all afternoon."

When we were fairly sure he had left the park, we stepped closer to the footpath. Moments later we turned and quickly withdrew into the shadows, stopping abruptly. Much to our relief, it was our friend, Jovanaka.

"Forgive my being late," she said. "I now see the beast leave the park entrance."

"Good, maybe we won't see him again tonight," I said in relief.

"Ever since we meet you in the museum he has been following us," Nada said. "The police will never permit us to be close friends with foreigners. Now, until later, we speak no more English."

We climbed up the steep hill and thumped across a drawbridge leading to the stairs of the ancient citadel. After reaching a stone wall, we rested. We peered down the park to make certain the secret policeman had not returned. After catching our breaths, the girls and I walked out to the edge of a wide rampart.

Below us the lights of the city beamed through the spring foliage and suffused the clouds with red. Turning, we watched a small boat drift down the river. Here and there a red neon star of Communism glowed from the tops of buildings. After glancing around for the beast again, we hurried into an open-air restaurant and sat down at a corner table.

After draining tiny glasses of *shlivovitza*, a plum brandy, we relaxed a little. The aroma of spices and searing meat filled the air. Here the people seemed better dressed and more affluent than those in the park. No doubt many of the patrons were the elite of the Communist Party. Finally, our two waiters ambled over and served us *raznjici*, savory bits of pork roasted on skewers.

"If you are spoken to by some *gentes*, people, tell them you are Russian," Jovanaka said.

"You know I don't speak Russian," I said. *"Nemoguce."* "Impossible."

"Nemoguce?" Jovanaka said and we laughed. "You are not speaking our Serbo-Croatian either. *Nemoguce*—such pronouncing. Is better you speak soft, but never, never speak English too loud or with 'mucho gusto' as they say in Madrid."

"You lived there?"

"Si, but we speak of this later."

In a far corner, a gypsy ensemble finished tuning its instruments and nodded to the diners. While three violinists drew bows across their strings, an old man hammered away on the wires of his *cembalo*, evoking sounds like a rippling player piano. The long introduction burst into a frenzied crescendo. Applause greeted the gypsies. With much feeling, the bass viola player led the other musicians in a doleful Hungarian melody that perhaps recalled memories of sad events. As they continued, everyone seemed to bask in this mood of self-pity.

From the direction of the Danube River came a breeze that swayed the long green skirt of the woman vocalist. Eventually, the music chugged forward with the tempo of a locomotive gaining speed. The violins wailed exuberantly. With a feral glint in her eyes, the vocalist twirled and shivered her tambourine over her head. Angrily, the *cembalo* twanged. At last the violins churned to a whining stop.

"Ah, I think you like gypsy music," Nada said, as we applauded.

"It's wonderful. You know I plan on traveling with them in Spain."

"I am glad it is Spain and not here," Jovanaka whispered. "Here they are not having much freedom. And gypsies must have freedom."

"Is the same for everyone," Nada said softly.

Our wine sank lower in the bottle as the evening progressed. I was enthralled by the fiery music, but the girls failed to share my enthusiasm. They were preoccupied. During the evening, both of them glanced around for the secret policeman assigned to us. To our delight, we did not see him. We finished our Turkish coffee and went into the wooded area of the park.

Only a few people strolled along the trails. Fortunately the blaring loudspeakers were silent, and I could enjoy the afterglow of the gypsy music. We left the park and turned down a broad, tree-bordered street. From a neighboring avenue came the sound of a truck changing gears, followed by the clop-clops of a horse. Lights still beamed in a few shop windows. We paused in front of one filled with communist propaganda books, flimsy shoes and summer dresses. Both girls looked wistfully at the shoes.

"When we finish university and take jobs, it will take us one month's salary to buy this one pair of shoes," Nada said.

"Is true," Jovanaka added. "This is one of the reasons we want to leave the country. We must—so we can have a life with beauty and happiness."

A man passed through the light on the far corner before walking in our direction. Jovanaka moaned and clutched my arm, and the three of us hurried away from him. Glancing back, I noticed that he had stopped.

"Are you sure that's another secret policeman?" I asked.

"Da, da," Nada said with irritation. "Yes, yes." "But I think he has not noticed us yet. You must return to your boat. We return to our flats."

"You remember where we are meeting tomorrow?" Jovanaka asked.

"Yes, see you at nine."

"Laku noc," they murmured. "Good night." Then they rushed down a side street.

Annoyed, yet still enjoying the intrigue of the cloak-and-dagger atmosphere, I hurried down another street. Several times I halted, but no one followed me. At last I crossed the gangplank to my small houseboat hotel and stepped below deck to a bunkroom. A photograph of Lenin was on the far wall. My six Yugoslav roommates were asleep and snoring. After a while, I settled into my bunk, and all my thoughts drifted out of my mind with the same ease that the Sava River swished under our houseboat.

In the morning I pretended to read a Belgrade newspaper while sitting on a park bench. Most of the other benches were filled with aged men and women. Periodically, I glanced up for the girls, who were later than usual. Perhaps the police had detained them. A rose vendor passed by me and finally sold a bloom to an old lady. Sometime later I saw Jovanaka stride down the sidewalk. Her face was drawn. On passing me, she whispered, "Follow slowly." With a casual air, I folded my newspaper before strolling out of the park behind her. When we reached a crowded intersection, I joined her.

"Where's Nada?" I whispered.

"We have thought it best if only one of us comes today," she said. "By this manner we may fool the police."

"Are we still going to the countryside?"

"Is true, but enough talking—just follow."

A number of people waited on a tree-shaded corner for the outbound bus. Without speaking, Jovanaka and I mingled with the crowd.

All eyes focused on an old farmer who stepped down from a battered horse cart. As his driver whipped the horse on, the farmer put his baskets down several yards away from the curb. His *opankes*, shoes, curled up at the toes. After straightening his fur cap, he clasped his hands behind his back and glowered like a hawk at a uniformed policeman.

In a minute the policeman asked the farmer to move his baskets out of the street. Shouting, the farmer refused. Jovanaka sighed apprehensively. In an unexpected show of tolerance, the policeman shoved the baskets to the curb. But the farmer did not move. An argument began; it continued until the bus arrived. Then the policeman waved his hand toward the old man as if to dismiss the matter.

"These peasants—very proud," Jovanaka whispered. "He could be sent to prison. The state—it is having many troubles with the peasants."

Our packed bus hummed toward the outskirts of Belgrade. Frequently, we passed crews of men and women constructing new apartment buildings; their work was designed to alleviate the housing shortage. We left Belgrade on a black road that unrolled itself up and over the green hills.

We stopped briefly near a small cooperative village of white stucco houses with red tile roofs. These solidly built houses seemed as though they could last for centuries. Jovanaka pointed to a tractor on a far hillside. Near the village several women with red bandannas were hoeing an onion field. To conserve their shoes, they worked barefooted. I was surprised to see them laughing as though they were models for a government poster glorifying the happy Communist farmer.

Again, our bus raced forward. Vineyards and rust-colored fields receded behind us as we drew closer to the hill of Avala. Jovanaka and I left the bus at the foot of this lushly wooded hill and climbed to the summit. The Unknown Soldier's Tomb, a black marble mausoleum, rested there. Eight enormous statues of peasant women flanked the door to the casket and supported the roof on their heads in much the same manner as the caryatids did at the Erechtheum in Athens. However, these brawny women seemed better qualified and more comfortable holding up the roof than did the delicate Grecian females. Fresh wreaths placed by a Russian delegation circled the casket inside.

After paying our silent respects, we meandered downward to a restaurant and sat below a photograph of Marshal Tito. Jovanaka ordered sweet rolls and coffee. Since all the other tables were empty, we could talk freely.

"You know," I said, "these rolls are even better than the ones we had that first day."

"Is true," she said. "I remember it—after you introduced yourself to me at the museum. We were soon taking coffee at the little sidewalk cafe."

"Right. And then we took a bus out to the homes of the rich Communists."

"Yes, they live on such a beautiful hill with such fine houses—servants—motorcars. Once the leaders of old Yugoslavia lived there. Remember, I showed you Nada's old house?"

"It was a mansion."

"But as you are knowing, the high party members forced them to leave. Oh, but for the rest of the people..." she said, holding back tears.

"What do you mean?"

"The rest of the people, they are still crowded in their little flats. For

us food, clothing—everything—is dear. Even the peasants find it difficult; true, they now live a little better, but what is better without freedom?"

"I guess it was a lot different before the war?"

"Is true; much different. My father had a diplomatic post in Madrid.
That is where I learned speaking Spanish and other languages. We had
a beautiful life," she added as she put her head in her hands. "But then
come the Communist war-lords; my father is put in prison, and there he
dies. No, no, the beasts, all of them—the little ones, the big ones—they
had him killed. There was no trial—everything covered up."

After a long silence, I cleared my throat and asked her about Nada's
father.

"He held a good position in the old government, but now he is a sick
man and lives in a poor village close by the Greek frontier."

"Oh, I'm very..."

"But what can be done to erase all this?" she said, rocking her pretty
head from one side to the other in Slavic resignation.

That night Jovanaka and I met Nada at an outdoor restaurant in downtown Belgrade. We dined to the spirited music of another gypsy ensemble and then strolled down the back streets toward their apartment. All
evening the girls had seemed unusually apprehensive. On reaching a
small park, they asked me to walk straight ahead while they scurried
down a narrow street.

In this way we hoped to puzzle the secret policeman if he were following us. Finally, I located their gray stucco apartment building. After
surveying the dark street for the policeman, I rushed into the entrance-
way and climbed five flights of stairs to their small apartment. The
moldy-smelling hallway was quiet. I saw no one. As I gave a secret
knock, I chuckled to myself over the uniqueness of the situation. Somehow I felt like an actor in a third-rate spy thriller, but the excitement was
wearing off.

Jovanaka opened the door very cautiously and pulled me inside by my
coat sleeve.

"Is good you are here," she said, then sighed. "Earlier we were thinking we saw the beast. Is the hall empty?"

"No one there—I'm sure," I said and laughed.

"Is not funny," Nada snapped. Then her head drooped. "Please forgive my temper. It is my nerves. Please take some wine."

I sat between the girls on a couch that smelled like the musty-scented
upholstery of a train seat. Near the window stood a handsome antique

bookcase, a vestige of their former status in life. A small lamp on the dining table beamed on a French travel poster of the Statue of Liberty, a landmark of their dreams. I uncorked the wine bottle and let Jovanaka pour. While we drank a few glasses of the white wine, the girls shifted uneasily and giggled at many of my statements which were not intended to be humorous.

Jovanaka filled my glass for the fourth time and said, "Is that we have something to say to you."

"What is it?" I asked.

Both girls remained silent for a while. Nada stroked my arm and quickly drew her hand back in embarrassment.

"What do you have in mind?"

Nada drained her glass and spoke in a voice constricted with emotion, "Is this... would you please marry one of us?"

"Marry!" I spluttered.

"Is true," Jovanaka said. "Marry."

"Well, uh..."

"It is that we want to leave our country for a better life somewhere else," Nada said. "And the only way it is to be done is to marry a foreigner."

"But I don't know you all too well," I said while staring at the white curtains swaying in the window.

"Yes, yes," Nada said. "But you can marry one of us by proxy. After this, your new wife will go to America, divorce you and see you no more. Is a promise."

"Oh, I see, but I'd like to think about it."

"Of course," Jovanaka said. "Which one of us you decide on, you must write. At the beginning make the letters warm. Very soon you must make them romantic, so the censor can see the romance blooming."

"I see. Maybe I can write from Italy."

"Bless you," Nada said as she refilled my glass. "But remember you must choose only one."

Both girls snuggled closer to me while I sipped more wine and gazed out the window in bewilderment. A horse drawing a cart clopped along in the street below. I struggled to rearrange my thoughts; the wine had already blurred reality. I was seriously playing with thoughts of engagement.

Confused and contradictory thoughts filled my head as I walked back to the houseboat. Marry? I had no intention of marrying for many years. I was fond of them both, but I loved neither one of them. Yet it would be exciting to have a pretty Yugoslav bride. But, I had no means of supporting a wife. My parents would be shocked! Nevertheless, I felt I should try to help one of them escape their country. What if the bride I chose decided not to divorce me by proxy in New York? I would be in a lot of trouble. Could the girls who were trying to entrap me in some way be government agents? No, no, they seemed too kind and sincere.

The following night the girls escorted me down many back streets to the central railroad station, where the Italian-bound train waited. While we walked under a banner with the Communist star on it, Nada's eyes widened. "It is the beast—I see him," she said tremulously. "Your coach is the third one there. Do not look back at us. And please, please do not forget your promise."

"I'll try," I said.

"We are leaving you and will vanish within the crowd," Jovanaka called out.

I hurried aboard the train and peered out of my window for the girls but could not locate them. As the train rocked forward, I saw the secret policeman wandering through the crowd. With a relieved feeling, I leaned back in my seat. Soon the lights of Belgrade dimmed, and the train roared into the Serbian countryside. The next day I would be away from the oppressive police state atmosphere.

While the train chugged faster, the gypsy music came back to me, and I relaxed even more in my second-class coach. Each girl needed help; it was a toss up between them. I was fond of them both, but which one should I choose?

After thinking seriously about them for a long time, I decided that now was the time to make a decision. From my suitcase under my seat, I pulled out a piece of writing paper. I had made my decision and was greatly relieved. Slowly, I wrote:

> *My dearest Jovanaka,*
> *I have missed you more than you will ever*
> *know. Our time spent together in Belgrade was*
> *very precious to me. You will always be...*

~ 31 ~

Sanctuary of Silence

After searching through many countries in Europe, I
finally found a Trappist monastery where the monks
allowed me to live, work and worship with them.

Dark and imposing, the ancient Trappist Monastery of Achel,
located in the northern part of Belgium, near the river Mose,
towered above me. A chapel spire topped by a cross stood out against
the moonlit clouds. Flanking the entrance, a curving brick wall gave the
monastery an eerie resemblance to a medieval castle.

After I rang a bell at the gatehouse, an elderly monk leaned out of the
window, muttered something in Dutch, and finally opened the enormous
iron gate for me. In the dim light he read my letter of introduction
written by a priest whom I had met in the Belgian town of Avennes.
Nodding approvingly, he ambled off to the main part of the abbey.

In a few minutes, the guest master, dressed in a white robe with a
black hood over his head, greeted me.

"I am apologizing that I was not here for you," he said in a soft voice.
"You understand we did not expect you until the morning."

"My apologies. I caught an early train," I said.

"You must now be going to your room in the guest house."

As he escorted me across the courtyard, I heard the old monk close
the gate with a chilling clang. I had the uneasy feeling of being sealed
from the outside world forever. The guest master escorted me to a small
room which contained a simple bed and table. Next to the window
overlooking the moonlit flower garden was a crucifix.

"At present time is nine in the evening," the guest master said. "The
Compline, the final worship of the day, is finished; the monks are
sleeping."

"This early?" I asked.

"Indeed, yes, we are rising tomorrow at three; I am knocking for you soon after."

Bowing slightly, he left me shuffling through the literature I had collected about this ancient order. The Cistercians of Strict Observance, also known as the Trappist Order, was some four hundred years old. It had monasteries around the world. Through prayer and a life of self-sacrifice, the monks hoped to bring the world closer to divine salvation.

Originally, I learned of this order when Dr. Tom Dooley lent a copy of Thomas Merton's *The Seven Story Mountain* to his "fallen Protestant friend" when we were in Japan. Merton, a Trappist monk from the Gethsemane Abbey in Kentucky, lived a worldly life in Europe and in New York while attending Columbia University. Eventually, his inner calling to be a priest, and later a monk, led him to the abbey in Kentucky, where he took his initial vows of poverty, chastity and obedience. His book inspired me to visit a Trappist monastery while on my journey around the world.

At three the next morning the guest master knocked on my door. I had been so tired the night before that I had fallen asleep with my clothes and shoes on. He looked at me, his disheveled visitor, chuckled and said, "Is not to be upset; all of us in the monastery sleep with our robes on."

"Oh," I yawned, and smiled.

"Indeed, yes, we *do,* each night, take off our shoes," he said with a gleam in his eye.

Later the rich voices of the usually silent monks filled the chapel with an ancient Gregorian chant. With their hoods removed, some forty monks sang from time-worn hymnals. Although most of them were in their middle years, several were of varying ages from late teens to early eighties.

The ornate stained glass windows were dark; it would be hours before daybreak ignited their dormant colors. Two unshaded light bulbs illuminated the monks and their partially-shaved heads. These lights were the only anachronistic accents to this otherwise medieval scene. Incense wafted up to the balcony where I knelt. A few of the young monks sang with strained faces as though their intensity would attract more attention from God; the older monks seemed to have found their peace. Somehow, even though I was drowsy, I was overcome by this stirring music and the joy of this predawn service.

By the time the lengthy chorale prayers of the Vigils and the Lauds ended, the stained glass windows began to glow. Prisms of multicolored light soon checkered the monks' faces and robes. The brothers knelt for prayer, then quietly filed out to begin their daily studies or work on the vast community farm.

After giving me a work apron and a pair of surprisingly comfortable wooden Dutch shoes, the guest master led me through the farm complex.

"I'm startled to find all your farm buildings so modern," I said.

"Indeed, most of you from the outside world say this. We have tractors, trucks—everything you find on a Dutch or Belgian farm."

"Do the products from the farm help support the monastery?" I asked.

"The cheese, milk—all farming goods and contributions from outside supporters are keeping us on a firm foundation."

Before we strode out into a vast field, we passed a bearded old lay brother who was shelling green beans; his eyes seemed to glisten with an inner satisfaction. He was so absorbed in his thoughts that he did not even glance at us.

"How long has he been a member of your order?" I asked.

"Since eighteen years."

"Eighteen!" I said in disbelief.

"Silence—we are needing no more of this talking. The custom is soft talking to me only. Remember, we Trappists have taken the vows of silence."

"You do have confession, don't you?" I whispered.

"Indeed, yes, that is one talking exception."

In simple Trappist sign language, the guest master introduced me to a group of novices, many of whom were about my age. They stopped hoeing a potato field and greeted me with self-conscious smiles.

"You must be laboring by the side of Matthew. He must continue learning by having responsibility—you are his added responsibility. You must not be speaking to him. However, you can be referring this novice to me in the name of Frater Matthew in Latin or Broeder Matthew in Dutch or..."

"Could I refer to him as Brother Matthew?"

"Yes, in English, this is satisfactory."

Without speaking, this young lay brother, who was not designated to become a priest, gave me a hoe, smiled and motioned for me to follow him. He was a tall, heavyset novice whose eyes revealed a strange intensity. Soon we joined the others in hoeing the potato field. Nodding with authority, the guest master tucked his hands in the folds of his long sleeves and departed with his head bowed.

We loaded baskets of potatoes in the back of a wheelbarrow held by another novice, who then rolled them toward a barn. At first, hoeing potatoes in the large field was pleasant. However, as the sun floated higher in the sky, I became tired and somewhat restless. Maintaining the Trappists' silence was difficult.

"What time do we go back to the abbey?" I asked Brother Matthew.

The sound of my voice stunned him; he dropped his hoe and gazed uneasily at me.

"One moment...," he said before slapping his hand over his mouth. Both of us were guilty of speaking. He was not yet accustomed to the rules of his new order, and I was an impulsive guest.

He frowned and whispered, "Two hours more."

Silently we joined the others, who had ignored us and continued hoeing. I was sorry that I had provoked him into speaking, a sin which he would have to discuss with his priest at the next confession.

Compared to the others, who seemed to be at ease with their work, Brother Matthew was very uncomfortable. While most of the novices sliced the earth in steady motions, he hoed feverishly as though he were in a self-imposed race. Perspiration rolled down his ruddy face. All too often, he stopped to catch his breath, take off his straw hat and wipe his shaved head.

As we continued our work, without speaking, all sounds were amplified. The sharp, crunching noises of the hoes and the scraping thuds of our wooden shoes merged with periodic shrieks of the swallows. Occasionally, the tattoos of monks hammering on a barn roof echoed across the farm. When a tractor started up, it seemed unusually loud; it coughed, sputtered and eventually settled down to a softer, throbbing beat.

My work was interrupted when I felt a tap on my shoulder. A middle-aged novice, who had come to this vocation late in life, smiled and motioned for me to follow the others back to the abbey. The sun had ascended to its apex; it was time for the midday meal. I returned to the small dining room in the guest house while the novices and other monks assembled in their refectory. After an elderly lay brother served me a meal of green beans, boiled potatoes and a crust of brown bread, he bowed and left me alone. I was ravenous. Within a minute or two, I devoured all the food and was sipping on a mug of lukewarm coffee. This sparse meal left me very hungry and lightheaded.

Since I was a guest, I was allowed the freedom to go to the library in the afternoon, while the novices returned to the fields. I joined the priests, who were reading tempting antique books in Dutch, Latin, Hebrew and English. One priest cleared space at his large table and offered me several books in English on different world religions. He had selected these for me at the request of the guest father.

Initially, I was surprised that the Trappists had such a vast number of books on different religions, but as I learned more about their intellectual curiosity, I realized that many of them felt a mystical kinship with other holy men. While skimming through these books, I reflected on my time spent at the Koyasan Buddhist monastery in Japan. Although the priests there were scholarly, they seemed to place more emphasis on group meditation and relaxed discussions, often punctuated by laughter. Also, on Mount Koyasan I was allowed to chat freely with the novices while working.

In sharp contrast, there were no peals of laughter in the Trappist monastery. However, the mood of silence that pervaded this sanctuary seemed more conducive to the harmonious understanding of religious mysteries. Both the Buddhists and Trappists emphasized physical work, but the younger monks, in both monasteries, did most of the chores that were physically demanding. I enjoyed the hard work in both locations, yet the ritual in the Trappist Monastery of Achel appealed more to my western background. In particular, the rousing Gregorian chants lifted my spirits into a higher dimension. Often the chants of the Buddhists appealed only to my appreciation of the exotic. Perhaps it would take more than a lifetime to realize many of the finer spiritual nuances existing in these Christian and Buddhist orders.

In my eagerness to learn more about Trappist and other religious orders, I went on a reading binge. For several afternoons in the library and for many nights in my room, I read stacks of books. Although these religions shared many similarities, I found their differences bewildering. Often I could not pass beyond the words to explore the underlying meanings of some difficult texts.

One afternoon a few days later, as I was reading in the library, someone stood by my side. It was a minute or so before I noticed that it was the guest father. He smiled as he closed my book.

"Enough reading," he whispered. "Is the afternoon hour in which you must be out in the woods—alone with Him."

"Should I do anything in particular?"

"You must relax and be smelling the woods and the wild flowers and listening to the wind. Be still and you will come to know our Lord."

Slowly, I walked through the late afternoon sun and finally rested on a knoll where I could see the monastery. Hooded priests and lay brothers were strolling around the abbey or sitting quietly under the many shade trees. There seemed to be tranquility everywhere. However, as I gazed down on the barnyard, I saw Brother Matthew.

Pacing back and forth in his muddy Dutch shoes, he appeared to be wrestling with some inner conflict. Prayerfully, his hands were clasped as he held his head down. Could he be in anguish over his trivial sin of talking to a guest, or was something deeper bothering him? Perhaps he was questioning his decision to join the Trappist vocation.

Although I knew very little about Brother Matthew, I tried to empathize with him. I had learned from the guest father that he came from a deeply religious family in a Belgian town. A year before he had graduated from high school, and without leaving his country or working in the real world, he had taken his initial vows at the monastery. Now he was only nineteen. Somehow I felt that this was an unusually young age to make a lifetime commitment. The thought that I might have done the same thing at his age was frightening.

Before visiting the monastery, I had traveled to West Berlin to visit American friends who worked as translators for the United States government. Their lifestyle was luxuriant compared to the penurious way in which I had been living. Their leisure-time passions were wine, women and off-keyed song. It was with enthusiasm that I had joined their way of life in that festive city. Unlike the novice, my young friends or I could enter a monastery with the feeling that we had seen something of the world. I remembered reading that Thomas Merton, the American Trappist, had also indulged in such unrestrained pleasures. Maybe all of us had seen too much, and my novice friend had not yet seen enough.

I caught myself daydreaming offensive thoughts: I was ashamed over my debauchery in Berlin. To refocus on the Trappists, I strolled over to the cemetery near the chapel. In uniform rows stood the metal crosses of the Trappists. It was the desire of each monk to lead a life devoted to God and to be buried beside his brothers. After the Requiem Mass, the body of the Trappist was borne by his fellow monks to an open grave and reverently lowered into it without a coffin.

After finding a bench near the cemetery, I sat down and was joined by the guest father. Both of us remained silent for a long time while we enjoyed the protection of the monastery and the peacefulness of the golden afternoon.

"Were you relaxing and listening to the wind?" the father eventually asked.

"Yes—I believe that I'm beginning to advance beyond words—words in books. My mind was interrupted with too many worldly thoughts; I did try to relax and open myself to nature, or, uh, rather God, but even partial understanding seems, well, far beyond my grasp," I said with hesitation.

"It is a lifetime pursuit. Some of us travel beyond the bonds of the temporal and rise to a higher awareness of God; many of us do not."

"A Buddhist monk told me somewhat the same thing."

"Indeed, yes, but the Buddhists believe it will take them many lifetimes or reincarnations to do so," the father said and smiled with compassion.

"One of the worldly things that bothers me most is atomic war."

"This—it is both a worldly and religious concern. We Trappists spend much of our time in prayer asking God to prevent this destruction of the world."

"Were the German armies here in World War II?"

"Indeed, yes, we have experienced war; battles were fought near here. This—it has added to our enduring appetite for peace."

As the afternoon approached evening, the chapel bell tolled; the monks left their meditation in the woods and the abbey grounds and merged into a long procession under the shadows of the cloisters. It was time for the chorale prayer of Vespers. After taking a seat in the balcony, I was uplifted by the melodious voices blending with the organ. Soothing incense filled the air.

Bright sunlight beamed through the stained glass windows, blinding me with a spray of colors. While squinting through rays of yellow and red light, I reminisced about a few of my religious experiences during the past few years. In a swirling rush of color and sound, I could almost see and hear the Hindu Untouchables praying at the funeral pyre, the Buddhist monks meditating as the sun glowed in their bamboo garden, the Indian sadu contemplating his gods around the night fire, and the Moslem Bedouins worshiping at sunset.

Somehow the voices of the Trappists had a comforting closeness to the deep chanting Buddhists. I was intoxicated by this Catholic music and left with a renewed sense of calmness. Gradually, the organ and voices merged into a crescendo; then the chapel fell into profound Trappist silence.

After overcoming the initial restlessness that I experienced in the Buddhist monastery in Japan, I had grown more relaxed and comfortable with each succeeding religion that I had encountered. I was even fascinated by the animistic reverence that the Kubus and Untouchables had for their own spirits. Each religion had exposed new viewpoints which I found both exciting and enriching.

After Vespers ended, I returned to the small dining room in the guest house. At last, I had adjusted to the sparse fare and was thankful for whatever was served. A calm feeling remained, and I fantasized about becoming a Trappist, or some other monk, and pursuing the contemplative life. Deliberately, I avoided opening the books on the table as I gazed with wonder at the darkening garden outside.

While the monks were sleeping in their individual cells on hard straw mats, I tried to rest on my bed. I was, however, too stimulated to sleep. Throughout the night I sat up gazing at the light from the gatehouse and at the clouds scudding past the trees. I was eager for the morning prayers of the Vigils to begin.

With renewed enthusiasm, I followed the Vigils and other rituals of The Trappist Abbey of Achel. Making hay in the fields with the novices and studying with the priests added to my appreciation of the Cistercian way of life. Every night I stayed up later than the monks, to read, pray and meditate. It was during these late hours that I suffered most from hunger and fatigue. The temptation to eat an unsanctioned snack became unbearable.

During my long trip I developed the habit of taking food with me wherever I traveled. My visit to this monastery was no exception. Inside my bag were rich nuggets of Belgian chocolate. They were hidden in the event I could not subsist on monastic fare. Late one night, in a moment of weakness, I unwrapped the chocolate. After I devoured many pieces, my stomach felt queasy as though I were seasick. My system could not digest this rich treat; it was now more accustomed to simple Trappist food. In a flood of nausea and guilt, I stayed awake all night, gazing out of the window at the dark garden. My admiration for the monks' self-control and devotion grew stronger than ever.

*

On the morning I left Achel, a light rain swept over the grounds of the monastery. After putting on my wooden work shoes, I made a final stroll around the many buildings. The rain was refreshing in the summer heat, releasing fresh scents from the earth. Most of the novices and lay brothers were sloughing through the muddy fields as they dug potatoes and weeded long rows of vegetables. The novices continued to work with much intensity while the older lay brothers worked slowly and peacefully.

As I walked by one of the cowsheds, I saw Brother Matthew in the doorway, shoveling manure into a large wagon. After glancing around to see if anyone was watching, he motioned for me to take a shovel and help him. He faced the unpleasant job of cleaning the entire area. We were careful not to speak as we had previously done by accident. However, we had developed a rapport using facial expressions and a few of the Trappist hand signs I knew.

We worked feverishly to complete the distasteful job before the noon meal. After our stinking mound had filled the wagon, we were interrupted by the guest father.

"For you, I have been searching," he said.

"Oh, I wanted to help my friend."

"This was his responsibility—his alone," he whispered with ill-disguised anger.

"I apologize. It seemed he needed help."

"Indeed, this Brother Matthew has been in need of help and has been confused for many, many months. The abbott is sending him home this afternoon to consider if this is his true vocation."

"Will he be allowed to return?"

"Only if his attitude improves. We will all pray for him."

"I will too."

"Well and done. It seems that you both will be on the same afternoon train."

After taking off my mud-covered wooden shoes and work apron, I changed into my suit and met the guest father and Matthew at the gate house. A monk slowly pushed open the heavy door, revealing the outside world. After saying our good-byes, we left the guest father and walked toward the train stop. Behind us the gate closed with a pleasing metallic ring.

Originally, I was apprehensive when I entered the monastery and heard the giant gate close, sealing me inside. Gradually, I realized my fears were unfounded. My experience there had spiritually enriched me, and when the gate again opened, I stepped back into the outside world with a new awareness of my religious nature.

Soon the drizzle turned into a downpour. We could see only vague outlines around us. As Matthew and I continued toward the train stop, our long strides turned into a jog; I slipped and bumped into him. Yelping, he stumbled and fell. When I stopped and looked back, I saw him sprawled in a pool of water. Slowly he lifted his shaved head, smiled faintly and, rising, bent forward.

As I helped him up, I thought he had fallen again; however, he was on his knees praying for guidance. His religious frock had been stored in the monastery. He looked very uncomfortable and incongruous in his sportswear. My initial amusement merged into sympathy for a sincere yet awkward novice who had seemed continually bewildered.

While we sat together on the crowded train, he kept his head down and appeared much too ashamed to speak. His ignominious leave of absence from the monastery, followed by an awkward exit, left him in a stupor. Miles later, he began mumbling to himself as he perhaps realized he was free to talk. Although I tried to cheer him up, he did not respond and continued staring, inconsolably, at the floor.

We passed trim farmhouses surrounded by level fields and crossed shining black roads clogged now and then with long lines of traffic. Several windmills drifted past us as their blades sliced through the gray storm clouds.

Matthew's parents and his four younger brothers were waiting anxiously under their umbrellas as the train screeched to a stop in his town. Before leaving the coach, he gave me something wrapped in a handkerchief. We did not speak but nodded good-bye.

As the train jolted forward toward Brussels, I opened his gift, a small wood and silver crucifix. After reflecting on its significance, I thought of the devoted monks at the Monastery of Achel; it was almost time for them to gather for the chorale prayers of Vespers.

~ Epilogue ~

Putting Into My Home Port

Y awning, I opened my eyes and peered out of the dark train window at the dots of light passing in the rural Pennsylvania countryside. A dry taste lingered in my mouth; I was uncomfortable from having sat up all night. The coach swayed and creaked as it rounded a curve at a road crossing. "Ding, ding, ding, ding;" sounds of the signal bells grew louder and then quickly receded behind the train, which had left Grand Central Station the afternoon before.

Several hours later a blue-gray light outlined the rolling hills of Virginia. Red and yellow leaves that had recently changed from their summer colors jutted above the ground fog. Leaning back in my seat, I dozed until the powerful diesel engine pulled its load up a sharp incline. Eventually, we descended into the hills and valleys leading toward the Appalachian countryside of East Tennessee.

Before noon, the train stopped at the Bristol city station near the Virginia-Tennessee state line. I stepped down on the boarding platform and greeted several relatives who had missed Sunday church to meet me and Uncle Jess. A dapper, white-haired man in his early seventies, Uncle Jess had returned with me from New York on the same train after having taken in a few baseball games. Smiling, he emerged from the first-class sleeper, full of zest and the scent of sour mash on his breath.

"Yes sir boy, Fleming, I want you to meet some of your Bristol kin, the Stanleys."

After Uncle Jess described for our relatives the prearranged meeting at a New York hotel and our jaunts to several baseball games, he paused in astonishment.

"Damnation, the train's leaving you behind, boy."

"Don't worry," Mrs. Stanley said; "it always goes down the track a ways. Usually, it drops a coach off and comes right back."

The others nodded in agreement as they smiled over my concern. After chatting some twenty minutes, we finally realized the train had, indeed, departed.

"Mercy, this is the first time it's done that," Mrs. Stanley said. "What a shame. You seemed to have made good time around the world, and here you are way behind schedule in Bristol. Tell you what we'll do. Let's pick up the twins at Sunday School and go home for Sunday dinner."

"I hope there's another train this afternoon. I'm eager..."

"Yes, yes, another one stops by in a few hours."

We picked up the twin girls at a downtown church and drove out of Bristol into the lush farmland. Soon we passed through the entrance of a white fence and drove up the hill to a graceful, two-story frame house with columns.

Before we gathered in the dining room, crowded with antique furniture, Uncle Jess called me aside and whispered something. In a few minutes we were outside the house in the shadows of the horse barn. Without hesitation, he pulled a half-empty bottle of Jack Daniel's from a paper sack and held it above his head.

"To you, the New York Yanks, the U.S. Navy and armed forces everywhere," he said, before he guzzled down most of the forbidden liquor.

I drank the remainder of the bottle and chuckled with him over cheating on our Bible Belt customs—in much the same surreptitious fashion that my Moslem friends in Sumatra drank alcohol.

Uncle Jess and I wheezed, caught our breaths, tossed mints into our mouths and soon returned to the dining room. With hands joined and heads bowed, he said a grace that almost turned into a sermon on the disgrace of not keeping the Sabbath. Generous helpings of fried country ham, mashed potatoes, collard greens and buttermilk biscuits were passed. I pretended to enjoy the southern food, but it was hard to readjust to its almost-forgotten taste. Somehow I could foresee a long period of reconciliation to my former type of food and way of life.

After dinner we gathered in the living room. The lovely sixteen-year-old girls took their seats at the upright piano and played a medley of hymns including "Amazing Grace" and "Love Lifted Me." In a few minutes, they ended their performance with "Autumn Leaves" and "Lady of Spain."

Everyone smiled as the stage was set for me to tell them a little about my world trip. After I rushed through the highlights of my adventures in Japan, Malaya and Java, Uncle Jess interrupted me.

"Did they have any quiz programs in Java?"

"No, sir," I said, somewhat surprised by his question, "they don't have TV yet."

"What, no '$64,000 Question'?"

These queries opened up a heated discussion about this highly popular quiz program. I was stunned at their recall of each contestant and his or her category and was somewhat peeved at their lack of interest in my trip.

In a mischievous mood, the girls interrupted the conversation with their version of "Hound Dog," a song made famous by the new sensation, Elvis Presley. At first, their mother was upset over this boistrous tune, but she soon joined us in an outburst of laughter and applause.

After my relatives saw me off on the afternoon train, I settled back in a coach seat to enjoy the Tennessee scenery. Autumn trees punctuated the dull brown of harvested tobacco fields and gave pastel colors to the distant mountains. Trim white farmhouses and unpainted barns swept past as the train rocked along. A group of abandoned cars, gleaming like some monstrous crop in a field, came into view. In a cedar-studded meadow, I saw a handsome log home topped by a grotesque television antenna. When I had left my native state for the service, there was no television; now it seemed to be a permanent part of our environment.

A dignified old lady, whose deeply wrinkled face testified to many years of farm living, sat across from me. After smoothing out her white shawl, she put down her religious tract, wiped her circular glasses and looked at me with inquisitive, yet kind eyes.

"You're getting off at Jefferson City, too, son?" she asked.

"No, ma'am, I'm putting into my home port, Knoxville—haven't been there in around four years."

"Land sakes, where in the world have you been?"

"Almost the whole world," I said and chuckled. "Not really, but I saw a lot of it. I was in the Navy for a while, then I started traveling from Japan back to the States...."

"I'm not one to get personal, but what did you do such a thing for?"

"I wanted to learn a little more about different people."

"Well, now, that's real nice. But, tell me, were those folks real friendly?"

"Oh, yes, in most cases. After you meet them and show respect for them, they show respect for you."

"I reckon folks is just folks everywhere."

"In basic ways, yes, but in each country they act and think differently.

You know, it's those differences that make the world interesting."

"Oh, that's nice. Let me put this to you," she whispered as she leaned close to me, "do you understand foreigners now?"

"No, ma'am, but I learned a lot about them. I'll probably digest only a part of what I experienced. I'm still unclear about some cultures, and well... things like an out-of-body experience I had in India."

"Land sakes, what's a body want to leave a body for, exceptin' to die?"

"I'm really not sure."

"Now, I don't know a thing about that. But, you need to keep your body in your body and put some meat on your bones. You look right sickly now. All that strange food and water have taken their toll."

"Yes, ma'am, I think you're right."

"Rest and good home cooking is the tonic you need."

After I carried her valise off the train at the Jefferson City Depot, I marveled at how much she reminded me of my grandmother who had passed away when I was in my early teens. It was in this same area that she rode horseback to Mossy Creek Academy before most of our family settled in Knoxville. After strolling around the station house, I admired the old potbellied stove in the waiting room. In a few weeks it would be glowing to stave off the cold weather.

*

As the train raced toward Knoxville, channel fever, the seaman's thrill on entering a favorite port, engulfed me. I was too restless to sit. Nervously, I wandered from coach to coach. My stomach was queasy. Sour juices surged into my throat. The heavy Sunday meal had hit me hard.

Racing for the nearest men's room, I tripped and almost fell before seeing an "occupied" sign on the door. In the next coach I found a vacancy in the restroom and shoved the door open, breathed deeply in a vain attempt to keep my food down, vomited, doused my face with cold water and stepped into the roaring passageway between coaches.

It seemed ironic that I was "seasick" on the last part of my journey. Cold sweat covered me as I tried to regain my composure. Somehow I wanted to keep traveling to other countries; my wanderlust remained strong, but my health had faded, and I was in debt for the last part of my trip. I was looking forward to seeing my friends and my family—my mother, father, brother and Aunt Willie Bea. However, an uninspiring nine-to-five job in real estate was waiting for me. No longer could I capriciously travel when and where I pleased. My grand adventure was racing toward an end.

My thoughts turned to my friends and "adopted families" that I had lived and worked with around the world: Masako, the *ama* girl, and her family were probably through with the diving season and ready for a hard winter; the Buddhist monks were perhaps trying to keep warm as they meditated on top of Mount Koyasan; the Malayan soldiers were very likely patrolling the humid jungles; the *Chokorda* in Bali was no doubt looking forward to reigning over the next festival; Hasan, my guide to the jungle Kubus, was possibly back in the safety of his bureaucratic office. Maybe Harsha, the young Untouchable, was leading his bullock to pasture in the hills south of Bombay....

As the train thundered forward, scenes of the local countryside flashed by: rolling hills, subdivisions of comfortable houses, highways crowded with expensive American cars, billboards advertising Coca-Cola and Tennessee football, open fields, woodlands, church steeples, used car lots and apartment buildings.

A glimpse of the Great Smoky Mountain foothills thrilled me. I was reminded of my climb up Mount Fuji where I had dreamed about my world trip. Unfortunately, I had lost touch with Dr. Tom Dooley and my other climbing companions.

In a few minutes I hurried back to my seat. Soon I would be among my family and friends in the idyllic, middle-class neighborhood where I had grown up and come of age. The conductor opened the door from the rear coach and let it close with a bang. "Knoxville, Knoxville, Knoxville," he yelled as he passed by. A porter scurried toward the Pullman cars. We rolled into the dark shadows of brick warehouses flanking the switching yard and squealed past the White Lily Flour mill, coated by years of white dust.

Suddenly the train emerged into the bright afternoon sun at the Southern Railway Station, flushing pigeons into the sky above the crowd waiting on the platform. Squinting into the sunlight, I tried to control my excitement as I located the half-forgotten faces of my neighbors, friends and family. Finally, I had completed my long journey home.

~ Afterword ~

S everal people and places have changed considerably since the
author made this world trip.

*

Dr. Thomas Dooley, the author's friend and Mount Fuji climbing
companion, became a world-famous medical missionary in southeast
Asia. Dooley did admirable work in the jungles of Laos and later
founded MEDICO, a series of remote hospitals around the world. His
public battle to control disease in others met with success; however, his
private battle against his cancer was lost. Courageous Dr. Dooley died
in 1961.

*

In 1957 Malaya was granted independence from Britain. Six years
later the Federation of Malaya and the former British Colonies of
Singapore, Sarawak and North Borneo united to become Malaysia.
Fortunately, the Chinese Communist terrorists were subdued before this
independence was granted.

*

Borobudur, the gigantic Buddhist temple in Java, has been
refurbished by both local and international agencies and is now a big
attraction for tourists and pilgrims.

*

Many development programs in India continue to raise the lifestyle of
thousands of Indians. Agriculture, public health and education have
continued to make great strides forward.

*

Unfortunately, the Maharaja of Jaipur, whom the author met, was killed in a plane crash. His heirs have turned his palace into an international hotel.

*

Kenya became independent from Britain in 1963, following the Mau Mau terrorist uprising. A year later, Kenya became a republic within the Commonwealth of Nations. Jomo Kenyatta, who was sympathetic with Mau Mau terrorism, served as this country's first president until his death in 1978. Kenya now seems to be making significant progress.

*

Uganda gained its independence from Britain in 1962. Milton Obote served as its first prime minister. Later, Uganda became a member of the United Nations and the Commonwealth of Nations.

*

Major General Idi Amin Dada later won power by a military coup. Under his leadership, Uganda, the country of "peace and promise," fell into a reign of terror. Idi Amin invaded the adjoining country of Tanzania and was later deposed by Tanzania's army. Uganda has yet to fulfill its promising destiny.

*

Many wild animals in both Kenya and Uganda have been decimated by poachers. Elephants, rhinoceroses and other animals are now considered endangered species. Unless local governments and international groups act with more determination, these animals will become extinct.

*

Belgium granted independence to the Congo in 1960. Patrice E. Lumumba became the first president. Rebellion among the many tribal factions soon followed. In 1971 the Democratic Republic of the Congo changed its name to the Republic of Zaire. This new country is a one-party republic, ruled by the *Mouvement Populaire de la Revolution.* Its progress is impeded by internal strife.

*

The mountain gorilla has been recognized as an endangered species and is under the protection of Zaire, Rwanda, and Uganda. After the determined work of Dian Fossey, who studied the gorillas for many years, their importance became known worldwide. In 1989 a motion picture, *Gorillas in the Mist,* starring Sigourney Weaver, helped to publicize the plight of these great apes.

*

Finally, after exchanging letters with the lovely Yugoslav girl, Jovanaka, the correspondence stopped abruptly. The author received no further letters from her; all of the letters that he mailed to this police state were returned with the imprint, ADDRESS UNKNOWN.

*

W. Fleming Reeder is married to an American and is a writer-director of documentary and scientific motion pictures, here and abroad. Now he is based in his home port, Knoxville, Tennessee.

To order additional copies of . . .

The Long Journey Home
by W. Fleming Reeder

**Send $23.95
for each book ordered
(includes taxes and handling)
Send to**

WARSHIP PRESS, INC.
Suite 155, 9307-A Kingston Pike
Knoxville, TN 37922